Lecture Notes in Computer Science 8204

Commenced Publication in 1973
Founding and Former Series Editors:
Gerhard Goos, Juris Hartmanis, and Jan van Leeuwen

Editorial Board

Benedikt Gierlichs   Sylvain Guilley
Debdeep Mukhopadhyay (Eds.)

Security, Privacy, and Applied Cryptography Engineering

Third International Conference, SPACE 2013
Kharagpur, India, October 19-23, 2013
Proceedings

 Springer

Volume Editors

Benedikt Gierlichs
KU Leuven, ESAT/COSIC
Kasteelpark Arenberg 10, 3001 Heverlee, Belgium
E-mail: benedikt.gierlichs@esat.kuleuven.be

Sylvain Guilley
Institut MINES-TELECOM, TELECOM-ParisTech
CNRS LTCI (UMR 5141)
COMELEC Department, Crypto Group (SEN)
46 rue Barrault, 75013 Paris, France
E-mail: sylvain.guilley@telecom-paristech.fr

Debdeep Mukhopadhyay
Indian Institute of Technology
Department of Computer Science and Engineering
Kharagpur 721302, India
E-mail: debdeep@cse.iitkgp.ernet.in

ISSN 0302-9743   e-ISSN 1611-3349
ISBN 978-3-642-41223-3   e-ISBN 978-3-642-41224-0
DOI 10.1007/978-3-642-41224-0
Springer Heidelberg New York Dordrecht London

Library of Congress Control Number: 2013948608

CR Subject Classification (1998): E.3, C.2, K.6.5, D.4.6, J.1

LNCS Sublibrary: SL 4 – Security and Cryptology

Typesetting: Camera-ready by author, data conversion by Scientific Publishing Services, Chennai, India

Printed on acid-free paper

Springer is part of Springer Science+Business Media (www.springer.com)

Benedikt Gierlichs   Sylvain Guilley
Debdeep Mukhopadhyay (Eds.)

Security, Privacy, and Applied Cryptography Engineering

Third International Conference, SPACE 2013
Kharagpur, India, October 19-23, 2013
Proceedings

 Springer

Volume Editors

Benedikt Gierlichs
KU Leuven, ESAT/COSIC
Kasteelpark Arenberg 10, 3001 Heverlee, Belgium
E-mail: benedikt.gierlichs@esat.kuleuven.be

Sylvain Guilley
Institut MINES-TELECOM, TELECOM-ParisTech
CNRS LTCI (UMR 5141)
COMELEC Department, Crypto Group (SEN)
46 rue Barrault, 75013 Paris, France
E-mail: sylvain.guilley@telecom-paristech.fr

Debdeep Mukhopadhyay
Indian Institute of Technology
Department of Computer Science and Engineering
Kharagpur 721302, India
E-mail: debdeep@cse.iitkgp.ernet.in

ISSN 0302-9743   e-ISSN 1611-3349
ISBN 978-3-642-41223-3   e-ISBN 978-3-642-41224-0
DOI 10.1007/978-3-642-41224-0
Springer Heidelberg New York Dordrecht London

Library of Congress Control Number: 2013948608

CR Subject Classification (1998): E.3, C.2, K.6.5, D.4.6, J.1

LNCS Sublibrary: SL 4 – Security and Cryptology

Typesetting: Camera-ready by author, data conversion by Scientific Publishing Services, Chennai, India

Printed on acid-free paper

Springer is part of Springer Science+Business Media (www.springer.com)

Preface

We are glad to present the proceedings of the third International Conference on Security, Privacy, and Applied Cryptography Engineering, SPACE 2013 held during October 19–23, 2013 at the Indian Institute of Technology Kharagpur, West Bengal, India. The conference focuses on all aspects of applied cryptology attempting to make cryptographic engineering provide solutions for security and privacy. This is indeed a very challenging field, requiring the assembly of expertise from diverse domains.

In response to the call for papers, we received 39 submissions, out of which 8 submissions were accepted for presentation at the conference after a detailed review process. The submissions were evaluated on the basis of their significance, novelty, and technical quality. Most submissions were reviewed by three members of the Program Committee. The Program Committee was aided by 37 sub-reviewers. Reviewing was double-blind, meaning that the Program Committee was not able to see the names and affiliations of the authors, and the authors were not told which committee members reviewed their papers. The Program Committee meeting was held electronically, with intensive discussions over a period of almost seven days.

The program also included 9 invited talks and tutorials on several aspects of applied cryptology, delivered by prominent researchers in their respective fields: Elena Trichina, Simha Sethumadhavan, Patrick Schaumont, Michail (Mihalis) Maniatakos, Claude Carlet, Sanjay Burman, Anish Mathuria, Veezhinathan Kamakoti, and Srivaths Ravi.

SPACE 2013 was the third conference in the SPACE series. The two previous conferences provided the necessary platform, and the support of a strong Program Committee, which was very helpful in launching the third event. In this context we would like to express our gratitude to the previous years' Program Chairs, Michael Tunstall, Marc Joye, Andrey Bodganov, and Somitra Sanadhya for laying strong foundations.

SPACE 2013 was held in cooperation with the International Association for Cryptologic Research (IACR). We are extremely thankful to the IACR for awarding this status. It helped considerably to make the conference a success. We would like to extend our gratitude to Bimal Roy for his support through the aegis of the Cryptology Research Society of India (CRSI) to back the conference. We are also thankful to the Defence Institute of Advanced Technology (DIAT) for being in association with the conference.

The conference was sponsored by the Defence Research and Development Organisation (DRDO), the Ministry of Communication and Information Technology, and the Cryptology Research Society of India (CRSI). We would like to thank these organizations for their support, which has helped us to reduce registration fees and make the conference a success.

There is a long list of people who volunteered their time and energy to put together the conference and who deserve acknowledgment. Thanks to all the members of the Program Committee and the external reviewers for all their hard work in the evaluation of the submitted papers. Our hearty thanks to easy-chair for allowing us to use the conference management system, which was largely instrumental in the timely and smooth operation needed for hosting such an international event. We also thank Springer for agreeing to publish the proceedings as a volume in the Lecture Notes in Computer Science series. We are further very grateful to all the people who gave their assistance and ensured a smooth organization process: the Local Organizing Committee of the Indian Institute of the Technology. Special thanks to our General Chairs Dipanwita Roy Chowdhury and Anish Mathuria for being prime motivators. Also sincere gratitude to our Honorary General Chairs Bart Preneel and Indranil Sengupta for their advice and strong support of the event. We would also like to thank Abhijit Das, Rajesh Pillai, and Arun Mishra for their active involvement with SPACE 2013. We would like to thank Ramesh Karri for taking on the extremely important role of Publicity Chair. Sanjay Burman, Veezhinathan Kamakoti, Pramod Saxena, and Chandrasekhar Pandurangan have been backbones for this conference and their support and advice has been instrumental for the smooth running of the event. No words can express our sincere gratitude to Rajat Subhra Chakraborty, not only for his support in assembling a nice tutorial and workshop program, but also for his crucial help in managing local affairs. We thank Durga Prasad for maintaining the website for SPACE 2013.

Last, but certainly not least, our sincere thanks go to all the authors who submitted papers to SPACE 2013, and to all the attendees. We sincerely hope you find the program stimulating and inspiring.

October 2013

Benedikt Gierlichs
Sylvain Guilley
Debdeep Mukhopadhyay

Message from the General Chairs

We are pleased to extend a warm welcome to all participants of the Third International Conference on Security, Privacy, and Applied Cryptography Engineering. SPACE provides a major forum for researchers from academia, industry, and government to present and discuss ideas on challenging problems in the ever expanding field of security and cryptography. The third conference in this series is being held at IIT Kharagpur, India during October 19–23, 2013. The first meeting was named InfoSecHiComNet and held in Haldia, India in 2011. Its proceedings were published by Springer as LNCS 7011. The second event was renamed to SPACE and held in Chennai, India in 2012. Its proceedings were published by Springer as LNCS 7644. All instances of this conference series have been organized in cooperation with the International Association for Cryptologic Research (IACR).

The Program Chairs, Benedikt Gierlichs, Sylvain Guilley, and Debdeep Mukhopadhyay, deserve a special mention for their efforts in selecting an outstanding Program Committee and conducting a rigorous review process. Our sincere thanks go to the Program Committee members for their time and efforts in reviewing the submissions and selecting high-quality papers. The main technical program is accompanied by several tutorials, invited talks, and specialized workshops.

We are extremely grateful to DRDO, India and all the other sponsors for their financial support. The conference would not have been possible without their support. Last but not least our special thanks to the local host for making the smooth operation of the conference possible.

We hope you benefit from excellent technical and social interactions during the conference. Thank you for your participation, and have a wonderful time at the conference.

October 2013

Anish Mathuria
Dipanwita Roychowdhury

Organization

Program Chairs

Benedikt Gierlichs   KU Leuven, Belgium
Sylvain Guilley   Institut MINES-TELECOM,
     TELECOM-ParisTech; CNRS LTCI
     (UMR 5141), France
Debdeep Mukhopadhyay   IIT Kharagpur, India

Program Committee

Rafael Accorsi   University of Freiburg, Germany
Toru Akishita   University of Tokyo, Japan
Elena Andreeva   KU Leuven, Belgium
Josep Balasch   KU Leuven, Belgium
Bruhadeshwar Bezawada   International Institute of Information
     Technology, India
Shivam Bhasin   TELECOM ParisTech, France
Swarup Bhunia   Case Western Reserve University, USA
Andrey Bogdanov   Technical University of Denmark, Denmark
Rajat Subhra Chakraborty   IIT Kharagpur, India
Abhijit Das   IIT Kharagpur, India
Kris Gaj   George Mason University, USA
Dieter Gollmann   Hamburg University of Technology, Germany
Tim Güneysu   Ruhr-University Bochum, Germany
Aniket Kate   Saarland University, Germany
Ilya Kizhvatov   Riscure, The Netherlands
Gregor Leander   Ruhr-University Bochum, Germany
Kerstin Lemke-Rust   University of Applied Sciences
     Bonn-Rhein-Sieg, Germany
Giovanni Livraga   Università degli Studi di Milano, Italy
Keith Martin   Royal Holloway, University of London, UK
David Naccache   Ecole normale supérieure, France
Chandrasekaran
     Pandu-Rangan   IIT Madras, India
Arpita Patra   University of Bristol, UK
Joachim Posegga   University of Passau, Germany
Bart Preneel   KU Leuven, Belgium
Francesco Regazzoni   ALaRI, Switzerland and TU Delft,
     The Netherlands
Vincent Rijmen   KU Leuven, Belgium

Matt Robshaw   Impinj, USA
Bimal Roy   Indian Statistical Institute, India
Kazuo Sakiyama   The University of Electro Communications,
                                     Japan
Somitra Sanadhya   Indraprastha Institute of Information
                                     Technology, India
Sumanta Sarkar   Indian Statistical Institute, India
Jörn-Marc Schmidt   Graz University of Technology, Austria
Berk Sunar   Worcester Polytechnic Institute, USA
Carmela Troncoso   Gradiant, Spain
Michael Tunstall   University of Bristol, UK
Gilles Van Assche   STMicroelectronics, Belgium
Bo-Yin Yang   Academia Sinica, Taiwan
Yongbin Zhou   Chinese Academy of Sciences, China

Additional Reviewers

Basak, Abhishek   Palmieri, Paolo
Belgacem, Boutheyna   Pandit, Tapas
Bhattacherjee, Sanjay   Poeppelmann, Thomas
Bilzhause, Arne   Qian, Wenchao
Choudhury, Ashish   Reparaz, Oscar
Datta, Nilanjan   Rial, Alfredo
Delclef, Joris   Rothstein, Eric
Eisenbarth, Thomas   S., Sree Vivek
Fuchsbauer, Georg   Sasaki, Yu
Hermans, Jens   Scholl, Peter
Heuser, Annelie   Schwabe, Peter
Hofheinz, Dennis   Sen Gupta, Sourav
Karwe, Markus   Shibutani, Kyoji
Kawai, Yutaka   Ullmann, Markus
Khovratovich, Dmitry   Wang, Xinmu
Li, Yang   Xu, Jing
Majumdar, Bodhisatwa   Zhang, Bin
Moradi, Amir

Thoughts on the Security Problem
(Invited Talk)

Sanjay Burman

Centre for Artificial Intelligence and Robotics,
C V Raman Nagar, Bangalore-560093, India
sanjayburman@gmail.com

Abstract. The spectacular failure of the system developers to deliver on the security requirements, with the simultaneous need to achieve security goals in an interconnected world that depends on information systems is astounding. Security vulnerabilities in the mainstream systems continue to be rampant. Commodity platforms for computing and for networking continue to leverage Moore's law to deliver on performance with increasing number of features or functionality. However, these systems deliver little or no security assurance. The *success* of the security industry in marketing such *no-assurance* products is primarily due to the cognitive limitation of humans in the context of security. The sheer lack of market incentive for delivering secure systems has led the system developers to ignore the significant body of knowledge already available for design of secure systems. This talk aims to explore the reasons for this state of (in)security, the gaps from theory to practice to deployment of *engineered secure systems*.

Table of Contents

Signatures

Three Design Dimensions
of Secure Embedded Systems

Patrick Schaumont and Aydin Aysu

Secure Embedded Systems
Center for Embedded Systems for Critical Applications
Bradley Department of ECE
Virginia Tech, Blacksburg, VA 24061, USA
{schaum,aydinay}@vt.edu

Abstract. This contribution explores the design dimensions, the primary quality factors of a design, of secure embedded systems design. Design dimensions define the design space, and they enable a designer to distinguish a high-quality design from a low-quality design. Besides well-known dimensions such as performance and flexibility, secure embedded systems design introduces a new one: risk, or the potential for loss. Risk is on equal footing with flexibility and performance. The design challenges for risk cannot be met by optimizing for performance or flexibility alone. Hence, secure-embedded system design requires a trade-off between flexibility, performance, and risk. We illustrate this trade-off for each pair of factors through several driver applications, including parallel cryptography, integration of physical unclonable functions and side-channel countermeasures.

Keywords: Design Methods, Hardware/Software Codesign, Montgomery Multiplication, PUFs, Countermeasure.

1 Introduction

Embedded Systems are characterized by specialized architectures, optimized towards a specific application or application domain. Hardware/software codesign is a methodology to produce such specialized architectures. Traditionally, hardware/software codesign seeks a balance between flexibility and performance, under constraints such as power and cost [14]. Software is used when application flexibility is required; hardware (parallelism) is used when performance is needed. The decomposition of an application into hardware and software components is not unique, and there is a trade-off between the flexibility and the performance for each possible solution.

This makes embedded system architecture design an exciting research subject. An embedded system designer faces many options in deciding the proper target architecture. Indeed, starting from a single application (Figure 1a), a designer can opt for a wide range of architecture targets: ASIC, SoC, ASIP, RISC,

B. Gierlichs, S. Guilley, and D. Mukhopadhyay (Eds.): SPACE 2013, LNCS 8204, pp. 1–20, 2013.

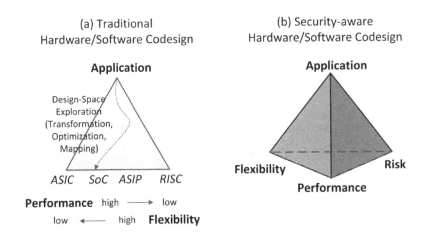

Fig. 1. Traditional Hardware/Software Codesign versus Security-aware Hardware/Software Codesign. (a) The original pyramid [48] reflects the trade-off between flexibility and performance when mapping an application to a target architecture. (b) This paper investigates how risk influences this trade-off, using several examples.

just to name a few [48]. The selection criteria leading to the proper architecture are complex, but flexibility and performance are undeniably of primary importance.

Flexibility refers to the ability to (re)define runtime behavior; it encompasses everything from RISC software, DSP software, FPGA bitstreams, to dedicated peripheral parameter settings. Performance refers to the ability of meeting real-time constraints or energy constraints. It is well known that specialized architectures (with reduced flexibility) have a better performance than flexible, general-purpose architectures (see eg. [37], Chapter 5).

The purpose of this contribution is to explore the impact of security on the classic trade-off between performance and flexibility. Several authors have argued that security creates a separate dimension in the design space [28,12,40], but they did not clearly label the dimension.

More work is needed to quantify the security dimension, and it is a notoriously complex task. Anderson argues that security engineering is what you do at the crossroads of policy, incentive, mechanism and assurance [2]. The *policy* is the set of rules that tell what is secure, *incentives* are the forces that defend or threaten the policy, *mechanisms* are the technologies that support or enforce the policy, and *assurance* is the confidence that mechanisms won't fail. Embedded systems engineering tends to focus on the mechanisms, since that is where cryptography and cryptographic engineering resides. For this contribution, it's important to see that decisions such as cryptographic keylength or protocols have a broader context (policy, incentives, and assurance).

We will map security as a single extra dimension to the embedded design space. We propose to use *risk* as the dimension in embedded systems design that reflects security. Risk is the potential of loss. For example, sending unencrypted credit card numbers by email carries a greater risk than sending the same in encrypted form. In terms of Anderson's factors, risk is roughly the opposite of assurance (assuming that the policy and incentives are known). Risk is a combination of these factors. Achieving a desired level of risk will require resources, time, and energy. Hence, risk can be factored in the design space, next to flexibility and performance.

In this contribution, we discuss risk in the context of embedded system design, and we discuss the trade-offs it brings with flexibility and performance. We discuss how the traditional embedded systems pyramid (Figure 1a) transforms into a three-dimensional pyramid (Figure 1b). We suggest that there is a trade-off between risk, flexibility, and performance, just as there is a trade-off between flexibility and performance. We will illustrate these trade-offs through three case studies, based upon literature as well as on our own ongoing work.

The paper is structured as follows. In the next section, we discuss the System-on-Chip concept, which will be used as a generic embedded systems architecture template (i.e. the target of embedded systems design). Then, we discuss three types of trade-off. We first show a classic case of performance versus flexibility, using the Montgomery multiplication as the driving application. Next, we discuss the trade-off between flexibility and risk, using several recent proposals for Physical Unclonable Functions. Finally, we present the trade-off between performance and risk, using countermeasures against side-channel attacks as the driving application. We then conclude the paper while looking forward to some of the open issues in design methods for secure embedded system design.

2 The SoC, a Universal Architecture for Embedded Systems

In this section, we briefly introduce several key concepts in embedded systems design. We use the System-on-Chip (SoC) as a universal template for embedded systems. The SoC is arguably the best example of a successful trade-off between flexibility and performance. It dominates the majority of modern embedded systems, from microcontrollers for motor control, to cable-modem set-top box chips, to high-end mobile computing chips.

2.1 Characteristics of the SoC Architecture

In an SoC, a general-purpose RISC processor orchestrates and collaborates with specialized modules. The specialized modules are often dedicated hardware designs, but they may be programmable elements (DSP for signal processing, GPU for graphics, ..) in their own right. A flexible communication network, based on on-chip bus or specialized point-to-point connections, supports data- and

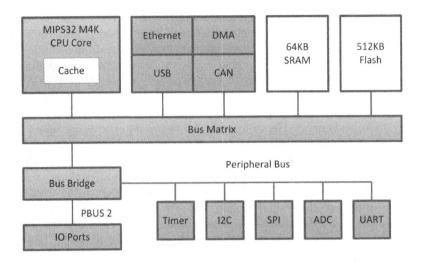

Fig. 2. Example of a typical SoC: The PIC32MX795F512L Microcontroller. Two bus systems - a high-speed bus matrix and a slower peripheral bus - integrate a heterogeneous set of modules, each with a different specialization and a different level of flexibility. A MIPS32 core acts as system controller, organizing the activities of high-speed and low-speed peripherals. This system employs distributed and heterogeneous communication, computation, and storage, and a hierarchy of control.

command-transfer between modules of the SoC. In addition, an elaborate storage hierarchy ensures that each module has an appropriate amount of local storage, and it ensures parallel operation of the modules.

For example, the PIC32MX795 is a modern high-end microcontroller that can serve applications from automotive to industrial computing. It is constructed around a 32-bit MIPS32 microcontroller and a high-speed bus matrix. The bus matrix also hosts 512KB flash memory, 64KB RAM, a set of high-speed peripherals with direct-memory access (Ethernet, USB, CAN), and a bus bridge towards a lower-speed bus. A bus matrix is an interconnection mechanism between multiple bus masters and bus slaves, such that multiple bus transfers can proceed concurrently [43]. The slower peripheral bus integrates a large number of peripheral modules with low bus-communication needs, including timers, timing measurement, pulse-width modulators, pin-change detectors, A/D converter, real-time clock, UART, SPI, I2C, among others. Each peripheral includes a limited amount of local storage for parameter settings and local operands. The peripherals are memory-mapped into the MIPS address space, which implies that processor-peripheral communication is implemented through bus transfers between the processor and the local storage of the peripheral. An SoC (like the PIC32MX795) combines four architectural ideas: (a) Distributed and specialized computation, (b) distributed and specialized storage, (c) distributed and specialized communication, and (d) a hierarchy of control. Distribution and specialization are key to real-time performance and to energy efficiency; flexible system control is key to flexibility. It is remarkable how consistenly the SoC idea has been applied to so many different markets, and so many different chips.

2.2   Security Risk and the SoC

The SoC is strongly defined by a trade-off between flexibility and performance: flexible yet specialized modules collaborate in order to achieve an overall objective. The SoC is also well-suited at dealing with security risks; the following example illustrates this point.

First, recall that risk is the potential for loss: the product of the probability of a successful attack, times the cost of the resulting loss [3]. Let's assume that a security policy requires us to store a secret key, and that we consider the risk of an adversary stealing this key. In each of the following cases, the cost of the resulting loss (loosing the key) is the same; but the probability of a successful attack is not. Hence, the risk for each case is different.

- **High Risk**: We store the key at a shared memory space, at a supposedly 'secret' location (Example: Brocious [5]).
- **Medium Risk**: We store the key in shared memory space, and control access to it using the privilege runlevel of the processor and its memory-management unit. This requires that the (operating system) software properly enforces privileges (Example: Linux).
- **Low Risk**: We store the key in an isolated memory space, i.e. a memory segment with hardware-enforced access control. This protects the key from software attackers, but still may allow hardware tampering (Example: ARM Trustzone [49]).
- **Very Low Risk**: We store the key in an isolated, tamper-proof memory space. Tamper-resistance can be achieved eg by physical shielding of key storage, or by encrypting the key before storage. While this prevents one from probing the key, the SoC may still be susceptible to implementation attacks on its operation (Example: AEGIS [44]).
- **Even Lower Risk**: We store the key in an isolated, tamper-proof memory space and process it using only side-channel resistant and fault-tolerant processing units, either by special design of processor software, or by using a specialized hardware peripheral for encryption/decryption (Example: Regazzoni *et al.* [38]).

While none of the above configurations is absolutely secure, they have decreasing levels of risk, meaning that an adversary will need an increasing level of sophistication to succeed. Secure solutions will degrade performance and flexibility (as compared to insecure solutions). Indeed, access controls and physical countermeasures will result in runtime overhead, and in additional hardware/memory overhead.

This last aspect - the trade-off between risk, flexibility, and performance - is the main subject of our contribution. In the following sections, we will describe three different examples, each highlighting one particular trade-off. The examples are taken from the field of cryptographic engineering.

3   Flexibility vs. Performance: Montgomery Multiplication Example

Our first example illustrates the trade-off between flexibility and performance. Even though this trade-off is not specific to embedded security, cryptographic engineering provides excellent case studies. We will use the Montgomery Multiplication (MM), an efficient implementation of a modular multiplication. This operation is extensively used in modern public-key cryptographic primitives, including RSA, discrete-logarithm based cryptography, Diffie-Helman key exchange. Such operations require modular exponentiations using large, random (non-standard) moduli. These exponentiations can be decomposed as a series of MM. It is fair to say that the modular multiplication and its related operations account for over 90% of the computation cycles in modern public-key operations.

The Montgomery Multiplication builds on the Montgomery Reduction (MR), which allows a modulo-operation with a complex prime m to be replaced with a modulo-operation with a power of 2. As a result, a modulo operation that would require division or an iterative algorithm, can be implemented by means of a truncation. The Montgomery Multiplication is defined as $MM = A.B.r^{-1}$ mod m, with operands A, B, and modulo m. r is a parameter such that $r = 2^k$ and $2^{k-1} < m < 2^k$. For a detailed description of the Montgomery Multiplication, we refer the reader to several excellent references [34,26].

The MM is an interesting research subject for embedded systems because of the long word-lengths commonly encountered in public-key algorithms, which are much longer than the typical SoC machine word-length. Hence, the implementation of MM requires one to map long-word-length operations into shorter machine-size operations. Koc *et al.* presented seminal work in strategies to decompose the Montgomery Multiplication onto processor architectures [25]. Their solutions are specified as architecture-agnostic sequential algorithms in C.

From Koc's work in the early 90's, there have been developments in three areas. All of these developments aim at improving performance on specific architectures.

- A first group of authors proposes algorithmic transformations to partition the MM into coarse-grain subtasks that are easy to execute in parallel. Kaihara *et. al.* proposed the Bipartite Modular Multiplication [24], a formulation of the MM which computes $A.B.r^{-1}$ mod m in two parts, by rewriting $B = B_H.r + B_L$. The resulting multiplication is $(A.B_H)$ mod $m + (A.B_L.r^{-1})$ mod m. This transformation thus results in a regular modular multiplication and a Montgomery multiplication, each with half the complexity compared of the original one. Sakiyama *et. al.* further refined Kaihara's technique by decomposing the multiplication systematically using Karatsuba's expansion. This results in the Tripartite Modular Multiplication technique [42]. More recently, Giorgi *et al.* investigated the performance of k-partite Modular Multiplications (i.e. using recursive Karatsuba decomposition) on multi-core processors [19].

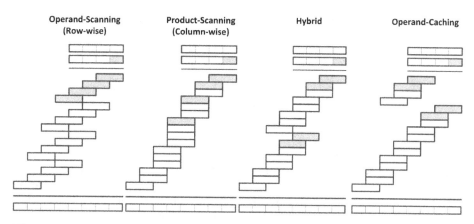

Fig. 3. Four approaches at multi-precision multiplication. Partial products are computed sequentially, top-to-bottom. The shaded products indicate the multiplications with the least significant word of the lower operand. The hybrid and operand-caching methods optimize the number of memory accesses under register constraints [21,23].

The design decisions made by these authors illustrate the flexibility versus performance trade-off. For example, Kaihara and Sakiyama consider hardware implementations, and therefore they aim to shorten the multiplier operands and to minimize the number of multiplications. Giorgi, on the other hand, targets a shared-memory multiprocessor, and is interested in improving symmetry and in reducing the number of synchronization operations between subtasks running on different processors.

- A second group of authors have worked on optimizations for Koc's algorithms on micro-controllers (Figure 3). Gura *et al.* realized that different implementations of the Montgomery Multiplication require a different amount of registers, memory-load and memory-store operations [21]. Their analysis, performed on the regular multiplication, compares the column-wise (aka Comba or product-scanning) implementation with the row-wise (aka operand-scanning) implementation. They propose an intermediate solution called hybrid multiplication, which combines the advantages of column-wise and row-wise approaches. Later, Hutter *et al.* further optimized the hybrid multiplication strategy with an operand caching technique that further reduces memory accesses [23]. The optimization techniques of Gura and Hutter are essentially performance-optimizations; apart from introducing a weak architecture dependency, they leave the level of flexibility unchanged.
- A third group of authors aimed at a direct mapping of Koc's multiprecision algorithms on parallel processors. Fan presents a VLIW (very-large-instruction word) version of the operand scanning algorithm [13]. He achieves high data parallelism, but the specialized nature of the design (both in datapath as well as in control) clearly limits the flexibility. Chen studies the same

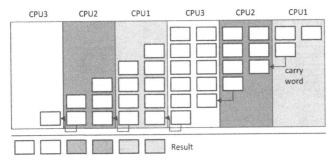

Fig. 4. Multi-core schedule of the Montgomery Multiplication following Chen [8]. Each white box computes a partial product and a partial Montgomery reduction. Three CPU cores in a ring network each process one-third of the partial products for the overall Montgomery Multiplication. The carry information is passed forward to the next processor in the ring. When the multiplication completes, each processor has one-third of the result.

algorithms in the context of a loosely-coupled multiprocessor architecture [8]. Chen shows that it is possible to obtain uniform balancing among multiple cores, and that it is possible to achieve near-linear speedup with the number of cores (Figure 4). However, as the communication latency increases, unfulfilled data-dependencies eventually appear, and some of the cores stall on intermediate results.

We summarize this example as follows. The original modular-multiplication proposed by Montgomery was reformulated by Koc with multi-precision arithmetic [25], such that it could run on software processors (most flexible). Later, additional optimizations have been proposed, virtually always to improve performance (throughput). These optimizations aim for a broad variety of architectures: custom hardware [24,42], microcontrollers [21,23], dedicated VLIW machine [13], symmetric multi-processor machines [19], and loosely-coupled multi-processors [8]. The resulting algorithms are less general: they are created with a specific architecture in mind. By removing this generality, the resulting designs are also less flexible.

4   Flexibility vs. Risk: PUF Example

This section briefly reviews the PUF concept, and then describes three related PUF constructions. Each design has a different flexibility/risk trade-off.

4.1   Physical Unconable Functions

No two electronic components are identical. Due to unavoidable imperfections in the fabrication process, tiny variations can occur in the dimensions and composition of electronic devices. These variations affect their electrical performance.

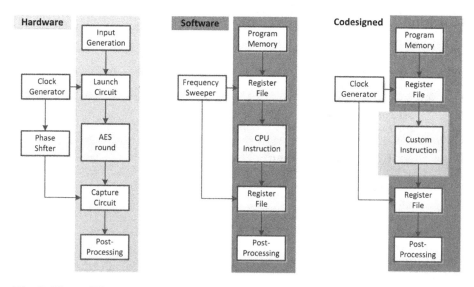

Fig. 5. Three different implementations for a Delay PUF. (a) HELP is a full-hardware design that uses the complex delay paths of an AES round [1]; (b) Instructions from a regular processor can be used as a delay PUF, resulting in a software-driven PUF [31]; (c) A carefully-designed custom-instruction extension achieves the same effect, but avoids the need for a sweeping clock.

Physical Unclonable Functions are constructions that harvest these variations, and convert them into a device-unique digital fingerprints.

PUFs have been intensively studied over the past decade, and many different constructions have been proposed. The reader may refer to Maes *et al.* for an excellent overview of PUFs [30]. In this case-study, we will analyze Delay PUF, constructions that exploit the variability of propagation delay through combinational logic implemented as a data-path. We will investigate three different constructions presented by Aarestad *et al.* [1], Maiti *et al.* [31], and the authors. Each of them exploits the same type of process variation, but uses a different architecture to harvest it. We refer to the design by Aarestad, Maiti and the authors as the hardware Delay PUF, the software Delay PUF, and the co-designed Delay PUF, respectively.

4.2   A Delay PUF in Hardware

Figure 5a shows the simplified high-level block diagram of the Hardware Embedded Delay (HELP) PUF [1]. The HELP architecture is a full-hardware PUF design based on delay measurement of complex combinational paths in an Advance Encryption Standard (AES) round operation. The objective is to generate a cryptographic key for the AES module. In order to get a stable, random key, only an extremely conservative small subset of these paths is used.

Algorithm 1. Software Delay PUF operation

1: **procedure** PUF($min, max, response$)
2:      $failcount \leftarrow 0$
3:      $a \leftarrow 0xFFFFFFFF$
4:      $b \leftarrow 0x00000001$
5:      **for** $freq \leftarrow min, max$ **do**
6:          $set\_timing(freq)$
7:          **for** $i \leftarrow 1, 100$ **do**
8:              $c \leftarrow add(a, b)$
9:              **if** $c \neq 0x00000000$ **then**
10:                  $failcount \leftarrow failcount + 1$
11:              **end if**
12:          **end for**
13:          $response(freq) \leftarrow failcount$
14:      **end for**
15:      **return** $response$
16: **end procedure**

In the HELP PUF, the Input Generation block loads a random value into the Launch Circuit, an array of scan-chained flip-flops. The value propagates through the AES round and arrives at the Capture Circuit, which is an array of scan-chained flip-flops as well. The Capture Circuit uses a phase-modulated clock (generated by the phase-shifter) to obtain a time-to-digital conversion. After capture, the resulting bitstrings are post-processed to improve reliability, and to compensate for temperature effects.

4.3 A Delay PUF in Software

Figure 5b shows the simplified high-level block diagram of a software-based Delay PUF. This PUF measures the timing delay of complex instructions in a CPU. The Launch/Capture circuit is implemented with the outputs/inputs of the register file of the processor. To accurately determine the timing delay of a given instruction, the frequency of the processor is swept, either using an external clock generator or else using internal clock PLLs.

Algorithm 1 shows the pseudocode for the delay calculation. The target instruction in this case is the *add* operation, and the test loop will gradually increase the processor frequency until a fault occurs. The target instruction requires careful selection: it should be the slowest instruction of the test loop. The result of the test loop is the number of times the test instruction fails at a given frequency. Maiti shows how the resulting set of <*freq,failcount*> tuples can be converted into a device-unique bitstring [31].

4.4 A Co-designed Delay PUF

Figure 5c shows the block diagram of a hardware/software co-designed PUF. Instead of the native instructions of the processor, this architecture uses a custom

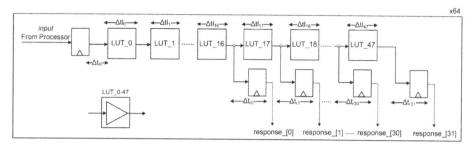

Fig. 6. High-level block diagram of the custom instruction

instruction (hardware) integrated into the processor. The custom-instruction is a time-to-digital converter, which enables this design to operate with a fixed clock. In contrast, the software PUF still requires a sweeping clock. In terms of flexibility, the co-designed PUF holds the middle ground between the previous two. It is less flexible than the software PUF because it requires a dedicated custom-instruction in the processor. However, it is more flexible than the hardware PUF because post-processing is entirely handled in software.

Figure 6 details the architecture of the custom instruction. The custom instruction performs time-to-digital conversion with a buffered delay line [22]. When the custom instruction executes, the processor injects a logic-1 into the delay line, and captures how far it ripples at the 32-bit output. This architecture is then replicated 64 times, resulting in a 64-bit in, 32-bit out structure. A suitable software post-processing is then used to map custom-instruction execution to the response. For example, we used temporal majority voting to filter out the low frequency noise. We further use differential techniques that encode the responses in pairs. Differential encoding reduces the effects of correlation and bias such as temperature [6].

4.5 PUF Performance

Two well-known metrics for performance evaluation of PUFs are Uniqueness and Reliability, which reflects the inter-chip Hamming Distance and intra-chip Hamming Distances on responses respectively. The expected values for Uniqueness and Reliability are 50% and 100% respectively; refer to [30] for further details. Table 1 shows the results for the Hardware Delay PUF [1], Software Delay PUF [31], and our co-designed PUF. This last PUF was evaluated on 15 Cyclone IV FPGA's.

4.6 Risk Analysis for PUF

Risk analysis for PUF requires an assumption of the actions of the adversary. In the following, we evaluate four different scenario's which may or may not involve an adversary. Each of them illustrates a different risk.

Table 1. Quality of the PUF responses

	Hardware PUF	Software PUF	Co-designed PUF	Co-designed PUF with Output Hash
Uniqueness	50.0019%	37.54%	38.2%	49.2
Reliability	99.99%	97.91%	99.92%	96.7%

False Reject/False Accept. False reject causes a valid response to appear as invalid. The higher the reliability value, the lower the risk of false reject. False accept causes an invalid response to appear as valid. The closer the uniqueness value to 50 %, the lower the risk of false accept.

The reliability and the uniqueness results of PUFs are given in Table 1. The results reveal a trade-off between flexibility and false accept/false reject probability. The hardware Delay PUF offers almost an ideal quality. It has the lowest flexibility, but it also has the lowest chance of false accept/false reject. The software Delay PUF has the highest flexibility as everything is retrofitted into the processor, but it also has the highest false accept and false reject probability. The co-designed solution offers a middle ground, it has a medium-level of false verification, and a medium-level of flexibility because of the custom instruction required for the operation of PUF.

For this class of risk, developing dedicated hardware for PUF operation has the advantage of higher reliability. Hardware redundancy, having a lot of possible candidates (as in the paths of AES implementation) and choosing only the most reliable ones, improves reliability. The post-processing mechanisms implemented in hardware further helps to increase reliability. All these mechanisms thus offer a lower risk at the cost of flexibility.

Challenge/Response Harvesting. Challenge/response harvesting is the process where an adversary eavesdrop on PUF challenges and responses. Worst-case, in possession of the device, the adversary could perform this exhaustively. With knowledge of the challenge/response behavior of the PUF, the adversary can implement replay attacks and hence impersonate the device. This process requires the adversary to gain the control of the PUF. The software and co-designed PUFs both use a software routine to control the PUF and therefore may be susceptible to malware. Moreover, the software-based PUF uses variable-frequency generator, which could be tampered with.

A trivial solution to protect the system against challenge/response harvesting is to have a large number of CRPs so that it is infeasible to store them all. In this case, the hardware-PUF (as discussed) may be at an advantage because of the higher number of paths in the AES round which could be utilized to generate a large set of CRPs. The software-PUF, on the other hand, is limited to the existing instruction set of a processor. Finally, the entropy of the custom instruction used in co-design PUF is not as rich as hardware-based PUF. However, the number of time to digital converter blocks used in the co-design implementation could be increased to increase the number of CRPs.

Model Building. Model building attacks are used for mimicking the behavior of the PUF [41]. The adversary tries to construct a model of a PUF based on available CRPs and/or knowledge of the PUF design. Regression models and evolutionary algorithms are used to this end. Model building attacks are practically easier than challenge/response harvesting because they only require a small subset of CRPs. Alternatively, the adversary could also probe the device and use the side-channel leakage of the PUF [33].

If the adversary can only eavesdrop on CRPs, then model building attacks can be thwarted by hashing the output (controlled PUF [16]). Software-based and co-designed PUFs could do this in software; but the hardware-based PUF requires the implementation of a Hash function in hardware.

Physical Cloning. Physical Cloning is manipulating a device during or after fabrication to make a copy that acts as a preexisting one. The cloned device should replicate the response of the original device for the same challenge. Helfmeier *et al* shows a technique for cloning of an SRAM PUF by capturing the photonic emissions during SRAM switching, and using a focused ion beam technique to replicate the observation on another SRAM [10]. Oren *et al.* show another method based on remanence decay [50]. Physical cloning is a very new class of risk for PUFs. To understand their trade-off factors, additional research is needed on their feasibility.

5   Performance vs. Risk: SCA Countermeasures Example

The third example investigates the trade-off between performance and risk. We will use side-channel analysis (SCA) countermeasures as the driving application. The objective of side-channel analysis, in cryptographic engineering, is to extract secret key material out of a cryptographic implementation. SCA has been intensively studied for the past decade, and we refer to several excellent overviews and seminal work, such as by Mangard *et al.* [32] or Kocher *et al.* [29].

We assume an adversary who uses differential power analysis (DPA). This adversary observes multiple encryption/decryption operations, and collects side-channel leakage at each operation. The collected traces are then mapped into a secret key estimate by means of statistical analysis.

The quality of an SCA countermeasure can be expressed in terms of the number of traces that the adversary needs to collect. Assume that the adversary can break an unprotected reference implementation with N_1 traces. After applying an SCA countermeasure, the same attack requires N_2 traces. Hence, the SCA countermeasure improves the side-channel resistance with a factor N_2/N_1. This quality metric works, but it comes with a few pitfalls. First, it assumes that the

Table 2. Performance/Risk Trade-off for some SCA Countermeasures. Because of the great variation in SCA and implementation technologies, care must be taken in comparing the results of one author with another (ie. the table should be interpreted across rows, not across columns).

Author	Technique	Technology	SCA Improvement (ratio)	Area Cost (ratio)	Performance Cost (ratio)
Tiri [47]	WDDL Hiding	AES ASIC	120x	x3.1 (GE)	x3.9 (f_{clock})
Bhasin [4]	WDDL Hiding	AES FPGA	10.9x	x2 (RAM+LUT)	x1.3 (f_{clock})
Chen [9]	WDDL Hiding	AES SW	25x	x3.3 (KB)	x6.5 (time)
Suzuki [45]	RSL Masking	AES ASIC		x2.1 (GE)	x1.8 (f_{clock})
Moradi [35]	Threshold (d=1)	AES ASIC		x4.5 (GE)	x1.2 (time)
Rivian [39]	Masking (d=1)	AES SW			x36 (time)
Genelle [17]	Masking (d=1)	AES SW			x12 (time)

GE = Gate Equivalent = Area of a NAND2 gate.
(d=1) refers to a countermeasure against order-1 attacks.

SCA technique is known, and fixed. An adversary is not bound to this. Second, the factor N_2/N_1 only applies to a single SCA technique. It does not guarantee that there may be another SCA technique that would render the countermeasure useless. Metrics such as Mutual Information (Gierlichs *et al.* [18]) and Student's t-distribution (Goodwill *et al.* [20]) have been proposed as a more generic measure of SCA leakage.

Risk is inversely proportional to the improvement in side-channel resistance. To evaluate the trade-off between performance and risk, we will determine, for various countermeasures, the overhead on performance versus the proportional increase in SCA measurements they force upon the attacker.

We consider three different approaches to SCA countermeasure design. *Hiding* suppresses the generation of side-channel leakage. *Masking* renders side-channel leakage useless towards SCA by randomizing the execution (the operations and/or their arguments). *Re-keying* reduces the lifetime of the secret key, and hence establishes an upperbound to the number of traces that the adversary can collect. The first two techniques, hiding and masking, can be applied on software as well as on hardware implementations, and they have been applied to different forms of side-channel leakage (timing, power, EM). The following gives a few examples of each - without attempting to be comprehensive; Table 2 shows a summary.

Hiding. The *hiding* technique prevents side-channel leakage from appearing, by suppressing power/timing variations, or by generating unrelated power/timing variations (noise). Tiri pioneered a logic-level technique (Wave Dynamic Differential Logic) in ASIC which achieves a 120-fold average improvement at the cost of three times the area and four times the power dissipation [47]. WDDL is a differential logic style with the property that *every* logic gate shows a single active transition per evaluation (clock cycle), regardless of the logic activity. Hence, WDDL suppresses power variations by consistently consuming the maximum power. This property, together with the differential circuit stytle, is the reason why WDDL is much larger and power-hungry than classic CMOS logic.

WDDL has been scrutinized for second order effects, including asymmetry in arrival times and loading of differential signal pairs. This has lead to the development of improved circuit styles, at the expense of additional power and area. For example, Popp *et al.* show how iMDPL address asymmetry concerns, but at the expense of an additional factor of 3 in area [36]. Since the future generation of chips has a growing inherent variability, one may think that differential logic styles are a bad idea altogether. This view seems too pessimistic. Measured results in literature consistently show SCA resistance improvements of one to two orders of magnitude [47,4,9].

Several authors evaluated how to port WDDL to other technologies. Basin *et al.* present an implementation on FPGA [4], and Chen *et al.* present an implementation in software (using custom instructions) [9]. These authors have shown, for their respective technology, how to support the symmetry required for a differential logic implementation. The hardware design of Bhasin presents an SCA improvement of 11 times at an area increase of 2 times. The software design of Chen shows an SCA improvement of 25 times at a performance cost of 6.5 times.

Hiding can also be achieved by degrading the quality of the side-channel signal, for example by injecting random noise or by inserting random delays during execution. This last technique works well in software. Coron presented a random delay insertion technique [11]. An implementation of AES on an AVR microcontroller achieves very high SCA resistance at an overhead of 953 cycles per AES round.

Masking. The *masking* technique aims to randomize the algorithm, so that its execution does not yield useful side-channel leakage [7]. This is achieved by injecting random values (masks) during execution and removing them afterwards. Examples of reversible masking operations include bitwise XOR (Boolean masking), modular addition (additive masking) and multiplication (multiplicative masking). The design of masked algorithms, or the transformation of unmasked algorithms into masked ones, is a design challenge by itself; we refer to Magnard *et. al* for a discussion [32]. The challenge of masking is to demonstrate that the masking is adequate, ie. that the side-channel leakage of the implementation becomes fully independent of the secret key. Even though it is possible to formulate this requirement formally (so-called *perfect masking*), there is no systematic design method that shows how to achieve it, which leads to a great variety of approaches to masking.

Suzuki *et al.* presented a chip in Random Switching Logic (RSL), which uses mask bits to switch a circuit between complementary states [45]. Provided that the mask bits are switched frequently, and that they each control a very small portion of the circuit, the resulting power traces will be effectively randomized and protected against SCA. RSL is a technique for hardware implementations, and costs about a factor of two in area and in performance. However, as Suzuki's chip demonstrates, each algorithm requires a careful, manual transformation into an RSL version of it. Nikova et al. describes a correct-by-construction technique based on *threshold* implementations. Such circuits perform computations on secret shares (such as masked values and random masks), and avoid accidental mixing of different shares which may cause side-channel leakage. Moradi *et al.* present a compact threshold implementation of AES on an ASIC [35]. The countermeasure comes with an area overhead of 4.5 times, and a performance overhead of 1.2 times.

Masking has also been investigated for software implementations. Rivain *et al.* and Genelle *et al.* each present fully masked AES implementations which are secure against an order-d adversary. Such an adversary is able to combine d independent observations of a trace in an effort to estimate the secret mask. The performance overhead for a masked software implementation is significant, even for a first-order SCA: 36 times and 12 times, respectively.

Rekeying. Both hiding and masking countermeasures have a clear trade-off between risk and performance. An obvious technique for risk mitigation is to prevent a secret key from being used more than N times. In the limit, one can prevent DPA altogether by using every secret key only once, making it effectively impossible to sample more than a single trace of side-channel leakage from the implementation. This is an interesting take on the SCA problem: rather than worry about the side-channel leakage of an implementation, one worries about the utility of side-channel leakage for an adversary.

An implementation of this idea is *rekeying*. Every time a key K_i is used, a new key K_{i+1} is generated out of it. We briefly mention three such recent proposals. Kocher describes a rekeying technique that uses a hash algorithm: the next key is generated by hashing the previous one [27]. Gammel shows a similar implementation suitable for use in smart card [15]. In that case, the next key in the chain is generated by encrypting the previous one using AES. Finally, Taha *et al.* recently argued that the overhead of a hash operation or an encryption operation for every key may be too big for lightweight implementations; he proposes to use a non-linear feedback shift register instead [46]. Rekeying, just as hiding and masking, comes with a performance versus risk trade-off.

6   Conclusions

In this paper, we argued for a quantifiable metric for security in embedded systems design. Using examples from various domains, we shave shown how an embedded systems designer makes design decisions along three dimensions: flexibility, performance, and risk. There are trade-offs to be made between any pair of these. A significant open challenge is the creation of methodologies and tools that navigate the design space created by these dimensions. This includes tasks such as design space exploration (how much risk reduction for how much performance loss?), transformations and optimizations (how to make this design 2 times less risky?), mapping and refinement (how to map this into hardware without increasing risk?). Much work remains to be done. For example, only in the past few years, the first (compiler) tools have appeared that can systematically apply countermeasures. The balance of risk with performance and flexibility in embedded design is all open, and there's still room for a few PhD's.

References

1. Aarestad, J., Ortiz, P., Acharyya, D., Plusquellic, J.: HELP: A Hardware-Embedded Delay PUF. IEEE Design Test 30(2), 17–25 (2013)
2. Anderson, R.J.: Security Engineering - A Guide to Building Dependable Distributed Systems, 2nd edn. Wiley (2008)
3. Aroms, E.: NIST Special Publication 800-39 Managing Information Security Risk. Create Space, Paramount, CA (2012)
4. Bhasin, S., Guilley, S., Souissi, Y., Graba, T., Danger, J.L.: Efficient Dual-Rail Implementations in FPGA Using Block RAMs. In: ReConFig, pp. 261–267 (2011), http://doi.ieeecomputersociety.org/10.1109/ReConFig.2011.32
5. Brocious, C.: My Arduino can beat up your hotel room lock. Black Hat 2012 (July 2012), http://demoseen.com/bhpaper.html
6. Chakraborty, R., Lamech, C., Acharyya, D., Plusquellic, J.: A Transmission Gate Physical Unclonable Function and on-chip Voltage-to-digital Conversion Technique. In: DAC, p. 59 (2013), http://doi.acm.org/10.1145/2463209.2488806
7. Chari, S., Jutla, C.S., Rao, J.R., Rohatgi, P.: Towards Sound Approaches to Counteract Power-Analysis Attacks. In: Wiener, M. (ed.) CRYPTO 1999. LNCS, vol. 1666, pp. 398–412. Springer, Heidelberg (1999), http://dx.doi.org/10.1007/3-540-48405-1_26
8. Chen, Z., Schaumont, P.: A Parallel Implementation of Montgomery Multiplication on Multicore Systems: Algorithm, Analysis, and Prototype. IEEE Trans. Computers 60(12), 1692–1703 (2011), http://doi.ieeecomputersociety.org/10.1109/TC.2010.256
9. Chen, Z., Sinha, A., Schaumont, P.: Using Virtual Secure Circuit to Protect Embedded Software from Side-Channel Attacks. IEEE Trans. Computers 62(1), 124–136 (2013), http://doi.ieeecomputersociety.org/10.1109/TC.2011.225
10. Helfmeier, C., Boit, C., Nedospasov, D., Seifert, J.P.: Cloning Physically Unclonable Functions. In: IEEE Int. Symposium on Hardware-Oriented Security and Trust, HOST (2013)
11. Coron, J.-S., Kizhvatov, I.: Analysis and Improvement of the Random Delay Countermeasure of CHES 2009. In: Mangard, S., Standaert, F.-X. (eds.) CHES 2010. LNCS, vol. 6225, pp. 95–109. Springer, Heidelberg (2010), http://dx.doi.org/10.1007/978-3-642-15031-9_7
12. Fan, J., Reparaz, O., Rozic, V., Verbauwhede, I.: Low-energy Encryption for Medical Devices: Security Adds an Extra Design Dimension. In: DAC 2013 (2013), http://doi.acm.org/10.1145/2463209.2488752
13. Fan, J., Sakiyama, K., Verbauwhede, I.: Elliptic Curve Cryptography on Embedded Multicore Systems. Design Autom. for Emb. Sys. 12(3), 231–242 (2008), http://dx.doi.org/10.1007/s10617-008-9021-3

14. Gajski, D.D., Abdi, S., Gerstlauer, A., Schirner, G.: Embedded System Design: Modeling, Synthesis and Verification, 1st edn. Springer Publishing Company, Incorporated (2009)

15. Gammel, B., Fischer, W., Mangard, S.: Generating a Session Key for Authentication and Secure Data Transfer. US Patent Application US 2010/0316217 (December 2010)

16. Gassend, B., van Dijk, M., Clarke, D.E., Torlak, E., Devadas, S., Tuyls, P.: Controlled Physical Random Functions and Applications. ACM Trans. Inf. Syst. Secur. 10(4) (2008), http://doi.acm.org/10.1145/1284680.1284683

17. Genelle, L., Prouff, E., Quisquater, M.: Thwarting Higher-Order Side Channel Analysis with Additive and Multiplicative Maskings. In: Preneel, B., Takagi, T. (eds.) CHES 2011. LNCS, vol. 6917, pp. 240–255. Springer, Heidelberg (2011), http://dx.doi.org/10.1007/978-3-642-23951-9_16

18. Gierlichs, B., Batina, L., Tuyls, P., Preneel, B.: Mutual Information Analysis. In: Oswald, E., Rohatgi, P. (eds.) CHES 2008. LNCS, vol. 5154, pp. 426–442. Springer, Heidelberg (2008), http://dx.doi.org/10.1007/978-3-540-85053-3_27

19. Giorgi, P., Imbert, L., Izard, T.: Parallel Modular Multiplication on Multi-core Processors. In: IEEE Symposium on Computer Arithmetic, pp. 135–142 (2013), http://doi.ieeecomputersociety.org/10.1109/ARITH.2013.20

20. Goodwill, G., Jun, B., Jaffe, J., Rohatgi, P.: A Testing Methodology for Side-channel Resistance Validation. In: NIAT (2011)

21. Gura, N., Patel, A., Wander, A., Eberle, H., Shantz, S.C.: Comparing elliptic curve cryptography and RSA on 8-bit CPUs. In: Joye, M., Quisquater, J.-J. (eds.) CHES 2004. LNCS, vol. 3156, pp. 119–132. Springer, Heidelberg (2004), http://dx.doi.org/10.1007/978-3-540-28632-5_9

22. Henzler, S.: Time-to-digital converter basics. In: Time-to-Digital Converters. Springer Series in Advanced Microelectronics, vol. 29, pp. 5–18. Springer, Netherlands (2010), http://dx.doi.org/10.1007/978-90-481-8628-0_2

23. Hutter, M., Wenger, E.: Fast Multi-precision Multiplication for Public-Key Cryptography on Embedded Microprocessors. In: Preneel, B., Takagi, T. (eds.) CHES 2011. LNCS, vol. 6917, pp. 459–474. Springer, Heidelberg (2011), http://dx.doi.org/10.1007/978-3-642-23951-9_30

24. Kaihara, M.E., Takagi, N.: Bipartite Modular Multiplication Method. IEEE Trans. Computers 57(2), 157–164 (2008), http://doi.ieeecomputersociety.org/10.1109/TC.2007.70793

25. Koç, C.K., Acar, T., Kaliski, B.: Analyzing and Comparing Montgomery Multiplication Algorithms. IEEE Micro 16(3), 26–33 (1996)

26. Koç, C.K., Walter, C.D.: Montgomery Arithmetic. In: Encyclopedia of Cryptography and Security (2005), http://dx.doi.org/10.1007/0-387-23483-7_263

27. Kocher, P.C.: Complexity and the Challenges of Securing SoCs. In: Proceedings of the 48th Design Automation Conference, DAC 2011, pp. 328–331. ACM, New York (2011), http://doi.acm.org/10.1145/2024724.2024803

28. Kocher, P.C., Lee, R., McGraw, G., Raghunathan, A.: Security as a New Dimension in Embedded System Design. In: Proceedings of the 41st Annual Design Automation Conference, DAC 2004, pp. 753–760. ACM, New York (2004)

29. Kocher, P.C., Jaffe, J., Jun, B., Rohatgi, P.: Introduction to Differential Power Analysis. J. Cryptographic Engineering 1(1), 5–27 (2011), http://dx.doi.org/10.1007/s13389-011-0006-y

30. Maes, R., Verbauwhede, I.: Physically unclonable functions: A study on the state of the art and future research directions. In: Sadeghi, A.R., Naccache, D. (eds.) Towards Hardware-Intrinsic Security. Information Security and Cryptography, pp. 3–37. Springer, Heidelberg (2010),
http://dx.doi.org/10.1007/978-3-642-14452-3_1

31. Maiti, A., Schaumont, P.: A Novel Microprocessor-intrinsic Physical Unclonable Function. In: FPL, pp. 380–387 (2012),
http://dx.doi.org/10.1109/FPL.2012.6339208

32. Mangard, S., Oswald, E., Popp, T.: Power Analysis Attacks - Revealing the Secrets of Smart Cards. Springer (2007)

33. Merli, D., Schuster, D., Stumpf, F., Sigl, G.: Side-Channel Analysis of PUFs and Fuzzy Extractors. In: McCune, J.M., Balacheff, B., Perrig, A., Sadeghi, A.-R., Sasse, A., Beres, Y. (eds.) TRUST 2011. LNCS, vol. 6740, pp. 33–47. Springer, Heidelberg (2011), http://dx.doi.org/10.1007/978-3-642-21599-5_3

34. Montgomery, P.L.: Modular Multiplication without Trial Division. Mathematics of Computation 44(170), 519–521 (1985)

35. Moradi, A., Poschmann, A., Ling, S., Paar, C., Wang, H.: Pushing the Limits: A Very Compact and a Threshold Implementation of AES. In: Paterson, K.G. (ed.) EUROCRYPT 2011. LNCS, vol. 6632, pp. 69–88. Springer, Heidelberg (2011),
http://dx.doi.org/10.1007/978-3-642-20465-4_6

36. Popp, T., Kirschbaum, M., Zefferer, T., Mangard, S.: Evaluation of the Masked Logic Style MDPL on a Prototype Chip. In: Paillier, P., Verbauwhede, I. (eds.) CHES 2007. LNCS, vol. 4727, pp. 81–94. Springer, Heidelberg (2007),
http://dx.doi.org/10.1007/978-3-540-74735-2_6

37. Rabaey, J.: Low Power Design Essentials, 1st edn. Springer Publishing Company, Incorporated (2009)

38. Regazzoni, F., Cevrero, A., Standaert, F.-X., Badel, S., Kluter, T., Brisk, P., Leblebici, Y., Ienne, P.: A Design Flow and Evaluation Framework for DPA-Resistant Instruction Set Extensions. In: Clavier, C., Gaj, K. (eds.) CHES 2009. LNCS, vol. 5747, pp. 205–219. Springer, Heidelberg (2009),
http://dx.doi.org/10.1007/978-3-642-04138-9_15

39. Rivain, M., Prouff, E.: Provably Secure Higher-Order Masking of AES. IACR Cryptology ePrint Archive 2010, 441 (2010), http://eprint.iacr.org/2010/441

40. Rostami, M., Burleson, W., Koushanfar, F., Juels, A.: Balancing Security and Utility in Medical Devices? In: DAC 2013 (2013),
http://doi.acm.org/10.1145/2463209.2488750

41. Rührmair, U., Sehnke, F., Sölter, J., Dror, G., Devadas, S., Schmidhuber, J.: Modeling attacks on physical unclonable functions. In: Proceedings of the 17th ACM Conference on Computer and Communications Security, CCS 2010, pp. 237–249. ACM, New York (2010), http://doi.acm.org/10.1145/1866307.1866335

42. Sakiyama, K., Knezevic, M., Fan, J., Preneel, B., Verbauwhede, I.: Tripartite Modular Multiplication. Integration 44(4), 259–269 (2011),
http://dx.doi.org/10.1016/j.vlsi.2011.03.008

43. Schaumont, P.R.: A Practical Introduction to Hardware/Software Codesign, 2nd edn. Springer Publishing Company, Incorporated (2013)

44. Suh, G.E., O'Donnell, C.W., Devadas, S.: AEGIS: A single-chip secure processor. Inf. Sec. Techn. Report 10(2), 63–73 (2005),
http://dx.doi.org/10.1016/j.istr.2005.05.002

45. Suzuki, D., Saeki, M., Shimizu, K., Satoh, A., Matsumoto, T.: A Design Methodology for a DPA-Resistant Circuit with RSL Techniques. IEICE Transactions 93-A(12), 2497–2508 (2010),
    http://search.ieice.org/bin/summary.php?id=e93-a_12_2497
46. Taha, M., Schaumont, P.: A Key Management Scheme for DPA-protected Authenticated Encryption. In: DIAC 2013: Directions in Authenticated Ciphers (August 2013)
47. Tiri, K., Hwang, D., Hodjat, A., Lai, B.-C., Yang, S., Schaumont, P., Verbauwhede, I.: Prototype IC with WDDL and Differential Routing - DPA Resistance Assessment. In: Rao, J.R., Sunar, B. (eds.) CHES 2005. LNCS, vol. 3659, pp. 354–365. Springer, Heidelberg (2005), http://dx.doi.org/10.1007/11545262_26
48. Verbauwhede, I., Schaumont, P.: Skiing the Embedded Systems Mountain. ACM Trans. Embedded Comput. Syst. 4(3), 529–548 (2005),
    http://doi.acm.org/10.1145/1086519.1086523
49. Wilson, P., Frey, A., Mihm, T., Kershaw, D., Alves, T.: Implementing Embedded Security on Dual-Virtual-CPU Systems. IEEE Design Test of Computers 24(6), 582–591 (2007)
50. Oren, Y., Sadeghi, A.-R., Wachsmann, C.: On the Effectiveness of the Remanence Decay Side-Channel to Clone Memory-based PUFs. In: Bertoni, G., Coron, J.-S. (eds.) CHES 2013. LNCS, vol. 8086, pp. 107–125. Springer, Heidelberg (2013)

Investigating the Application of One Instruction Set Computing for Encrypted Data Computation

Nektarios Georgios Tsoutsos[1] and Michail Maniatakos[2]

[1] Computer Science and Engineering,
New York University Polytechnic School of Engineering,
New York City, USA
nektarios.tsoutsos@nyu.edu
[2] Electrical and Computer Engineering,
New York University Abu Dhabi,
Abu Dhabi, UAE
michail.maniatakos@nyu.edu

Abstract. The cloud computing revolution has emphasized the need to execute programs in private using third party infrastructure. In this work, we investigate the application of One Instruction Set Computing (OISC) for processing encrypted data. This novel architecture combines the simplicity and high throughput of OISC with the security of well-known homomorphic encryption schemes, allowing execution of encrypted machine code and secure computation over encrypted data.

In the presented case study, we choose `addleq` as the OISC instruction and Paillier's scheme for encryption, and we extensively discuss the architecture and security implications of encrypting the instructions and memory accesses. Preliminary results in our implemented hardware–cognizant software simulator indicate an average execution overhead of 26 times for 1024–bit security parameter, compared to unencrypted execution of the same OISC programs.

Keywords: Encrypted processor, homomorphic encryption, Paillier, cloud computing.

1 Introduction

In the modern era of computing, the ability to process encrypted data and execute encrypted programs is widely regarded as the holy grail of cloud computing [31,34]. Whether in the form of a private cloud, or in public infrastructures, the confidentiality of the data or the confidentiality of the algorithm itself are of the highest value. Contemporary cloud service providers vouch themselves for the privacy of the user data, as well as the security of the computed results. This is essentially the only foundation for the users' trust. Hence, at their current form, cloud infrastructures are in practice prohibitive for applications where privacy is mandatory and the risk of compromise is unacceptable.

The latest solution to cloud security issues is to use an encryption scheme in order to make the private data unreadable by curious entities or even the cloud

B. Gierlichs, S. Guilley, and D. Mukhopadhyay (Eds.): SPACE 2013, LNCS 8204, pp. 21–37, 2013.

providers themselves. Not all encryption schemes, however, provide the ability to manipulate encrypted data and then decrypt to something meaningful; this property is called *homomorphism* and only specific schemes support it. Until recently, all known homomorphic encryption schemes supported only specific manipulations over encrypted data, and the ability to apply arbitrary manipulations remained unsolved. A very important step towards the solution was made in the recent years with the invention of Fully Homomorphic Encryption (FHE), and more specifically the Gentry scheme [13,35,37,16]. Since then, there has been significant progress on the FHE frontier: The authors of [5] propose an approach for secret program execution, based on fully homomorphic encrypted circuits. On the theoretical front, the authors of [6] provide theoretical proof of the correctness of an encrypted processing unit.

While several large corporations, like IBM, invest in such research [7], an encrypted processor based on FHE is not yet available. Some argue that these fully homomorphic schemes are *not yet* practical for everyday use or even for arbitrary manipulation of encrypted data, due to the tremendous overhead of the scheme [33,15]. The release of HELib [18,4] is a step towards the reduction of this overhead. The alternative approach would be to emulate the desired arbitrary manipulation of encrypted data (which is essentially equivalent to encrypted computation) using ordinary *partially homomorphic* encryption schemes, which are significantly faster and practical, compared to fully homomorphic schemes.

Even though homomorphic encryption seems to be very promising, none of the existing computer architectures can leverage the power of developed homomorphic schemes. A major reason for this is that existing computer architectures (including both RISC and CISC) are in fact designed towards efficiency and speed and not towards the security of the computation. Therefore, architecture specifications need to be redefined to include the security of computation.

To address this problem, our contribution in this paper is a novel idea for an encrypted computer architecture, able to perform arbitrary computation on encrypted data, using encrypted instructions, and thus preserving the security and privacy of both the data and the algorithm. The proposed solution in this paper is based on a Turing complete flavor of a One Instruction Set Computer (OISC) [25,22]. OISC architectures are very appealing for computation of encrypted data, since the stripped design provides great flexibility to incorporate support for homomorphic encryption. Without loss of generality, in this work we focus on addleq-based OISC [27,11], which requires a basic computational unit that supports the addition operation. This requirement drives the selection of an additive homomorphic encryption scheme as our candidate method for protecting data and program instructions.

To the best of our knowledge, this is the first effort towards an encrypted computer architecture that can be used in practice and is not based on the very expensive fully homomorphic encryption schemes. We combine the simplicity and high-throughput of OISC with an effective partially homomorphic encryption scheme, as presented in Section 2. Section 3 describes the architecture of the proposed addleq computer in the encrypted domain as well as theoretical and practical design considerations. The rest of this paper is organized as follows: Section 4 presents technical details and our experimental setup, while Section 5 provides performance results of the proposed solution. Section 6 features a discussion on the security properties of the proposed solution and future directions, followed by conclusions in Section 7.

2 The OISC Architecture

One Instruction Set Computers (also called Ultimate RISC computers) are architectures that support only one instruction. A careful selection of the aforementioned instruction can provide OISC architectures the capability of Turing–complete computation [12]. OISC computers are very simple but powerful; given their clean design and high throughput at certain configurations [26], they can be proper alternatives to ordinary RISC computers. In addition, having a single instruction renders the instruction operation code unnecessary, and thus only the instruction arguments are required to define a meaningful OISC program.

There are several types of OISC computers, depending on the single instruction supported. Common Turing–complete variants include the following: *Reverse subtract and skip if borrow*, *Subtract and branch unless positive*, *Plus one and branch if equal* and *Add and branch unless positive*. While these variants are seemingly different in terms of the operations performed by the single instruction, they share a common pattern: a simple mathematical operation (addition or subtraction) between instruction arguments, followed by a binary decision based on a condition. This straightforward format, as well as the existence of a single addition or subtraction, makes these OISC variants an excellent match to homomorphic encryption schemes, which are capable of preserving these mathematical operations in the encrypted domain.

In order to demonstrate how the OISC architecture can be modified to support encrypted data and encrypted instructions (using homomorphic encryption), and in order to investigate potential design or security issues, we focus on the `addleq` variant. `Addleq`'s single instruction has three arguments (namely A, B and C) and is defined as follows:

1. add the contents of two memory locations defined by arguments A and B,
2. put the results of the addition in the memory location defined by B, and
3. if the result of the addition is not positive, then jump to the instruction that starts at the memory location determined by argument C of the current instruction.

More formally, `addleq` performs the following:

$$\text{Mem[B]} = \text{Mem[B]} + \text{Mem[A]};$$
$$\text{if Mem[B]} \leq 0 \text{ then goto C}$$
$$\text{else goto next instruction}$$

From the description above, there are three important observations about `addleq`:

(a) `addleq` uses indirect addressing (i.e. instruction arguments are the memory addresses of the memory contents to be added, and the arguments are not actually added themselves),

(b) each instruction requires comparison with zero and

(c) arguments A, B and C should be grouped together.

2.1 Benefits of Using OISC

A major challenge towards an efficient architecture that processes encrypted data is the privacy of the algorithm and the instructions. Depending on the key, the encryption of the same instruction would be different each time. This means that any implementation of an encrypted computer (either in hardware or in software) would always require the decryption key in order to decrypt the instruction operation code (opcode) in order to decide what is the next operation (for example, to determine if the next instruction is a `read`, `write`, `add` etc). Providing the decryption key, however, defies the purpose of requiring encrypted computation.

The major contribution of this paper is the use of an OISC architecture to solve this problem; the benefit of this approach is that any implementation of the encrypted computer would not be required to decrypt the opcode of the next instruction: *All instructions are the same* and only the instruction arguments would be different (and still encrypted). Essentially, this proposed solution overcomes the problem of how to discriminate different instructions, while having the entire program in encrypted format. An attacker that may try to guess the algorithm (i.e. the instruction stream) being executed in the ultimate RISC computer, would gain no information, since all instructions are the same and the instruction arguments are already encrypted.

One may envision this architecture, as a standard Harvard architecture, where the instruction memory only contains the instruction arguments in encrypted format (no opcodes are required, since we only have a single instruction code), and a data memory that also contains encrypted data. This idea, however, also works if the architecture uses a unified memory where instruction arguments and data coexist and the code is self-modifying (i.e. instruction arguments and data are treated indistinguishably and instructions are allowed to modify other instruction arguments as well as data). Before analyzing the encrypted `addleq` architecture any further, however, it is necessary to provide basic background information on the homomorphic encryption scheme that is used to protect the privacy of the program data and instructions.

2.2 Homomorphic Encryption Background

Any encryption scheme that allows applying a specific function on encrypted data, so that the output of the function is an encryption of the result that comes from applying the same function directly on unencrypted data, is called *homomorphic* [23,36]. Essentially, the homomorphic property allows applying a function *after* encrypting the data, and the decryption of the result equals the output, if the function was applied on plaintext data. Some existing encryption schemes that support homomorphic properties are the following [14]: the RSA scheme [32], the El Gamal scheme [10], the Paillier scheme [30], the Goldwasser-Micali scheme [17], as well as recent schemes such as the Gentry scheme [15] and variants like the BGV scheme [4] and others [13,35,37].

From those schemes above, some of them only support a single function (either addition, or multiplication but not both) and are referred to as partially homomorphic, while only the Gentry scheme (and its variants) support both addition and multiplication and are referred to as fully homomorphic. The schemes that support a single function are either *additive* homomorphic (like Paillier and exponential El Gamal [8,24]) or *multiplicative* homomorphic (like RSA, standard El Gamal etc). Informally, this means that the applied function yields an output that is a preimage of the addition of the plaintexts (for the additive case) or a preimage of the product of the plaintexts (for the multiplicative case). More formally, homomorphism is defined as follows [23]:

$$Encrypt[m1] \diamond Encrypt[m2] = Encrypt[m1 \circ m2] \tag{1}$$

where ($\circ$) usually is addition ($+$) or multiplication ($*$) depending on the scheme.

In this paper, without loss of generality, we focus on `addleq` OISC, which uses the addition operation for the purposes of performing arbitrary computation. Addition operation in the encrypted domain is supported by partially homomorphic schemes like the Paillier and exponential El Gamal schemes, as well as fully homomorphic variants of the Gentry scheme. As mentioned earlier in this paper, because fully homomorphic schemes have tremendous overheads (several orders of magnitude [15,33]) and since the exponential El Gamal scheme suffers from high decryption overhead [8,24], we focus on the Paillier encryption scheme.

2.3   Paillier Scheme

The Paillier scheme is the first efficient additive homomorphic scheme [30]. The Paillier scheme is based on the *decisional composite residuosity assumption,* which states the following:

Given a composite number n and an integer z, it is *hard* to decide whether there exists y such that

$$z \equiv y^n \pmod{n^2} \tag{2}$$

The Paillier scheme is a public key cryptographic scheme and is defined as follows [23]:

Let p and q be two large prime numbers of equal length, randomly and independently chosen of each other, and $n = pq$ the product of these numbers (where $\log_2 n$ is the security parameter of the scheme); the knowledge of p and q would be part of the private key and n would be part of the public key. In addition, let

$$\phi(n) = (p-1)(q-1) \tag{3}$$

be Euler's Totient function for n. Then, using the Paillier scheme, the encryption of a plaintext message "m", and the decryption of ciphertext "c" are defined as follows:

$$Encrypt[m] = (n+1)^m * r^n \pmod{n^2} \tag{4}$$

for random r in the multiplicative group $\mathbb{Z}_n^*$.

$$Decrypt[c] = \frac{(c^{\phi(n)} \pmod{n^2})) - 1}{n} \phi(n)^{-1} \pmod{n} \tag{5}$$

where $\phi(n)^{-1}$ is the modular multiplicative inverse of $\phi(n)$ in $\mathbb{Z}_n^*$.

The scheme supports the following additive homomorphic properties:

$$Encrypt[m1] * Encrypt[m2] = Encrypt[m1 + m2 \pmod{n}] \tag{6}$$

which essentially means that the multiplication of the encryptions of two messages is a preimage of the encryption of the addition of these messages. Therefore, the encryption of the sum of two plaintexts equals the result of multiplying the ciphertexts.

3   Addleq in the Encrypted Domain

As already discussed in the introduction section of this paper, our goal is to define an architecture for a computer that is capable of performing computations on encrypted data, as well as executing encrypted instructions, in order to protect the privacy of the algorithm and the program itself. We investigate an architecture that exploits the simplicity of addleq OISC computer as well as the additive homomorphic properties of the Paillier encryption scheme.

3.1   Basic Components of the Design

A starting point in designing an encrypted addleq computer would be to determine all necessary components. Since addleq supports self–modifying code by design, a single *main memory* is necessary. This main memory would contain both data and instructions, and would incorporate a memory control unit responsible for addressing, as well as for reading and writing bytes. In addition, the design should have an *ALU unit*, that will be used for performing *modular multiplication* in the encrypted domain (equivalent to normal addition in the unencrypted domain). Program execution is controlled by a *control finite state machine (FSM)* responsible for execution and fetching operations, as well as the *program counter*. For storing memory data and addresses, a *temporary register* is also necessary. Since addleq needs to branch if the ALU output is not positive, a *sign identification unit* is required as well.

These basic components are presented in Fig. 1 and the addleq datapath is described in Section 3.2.

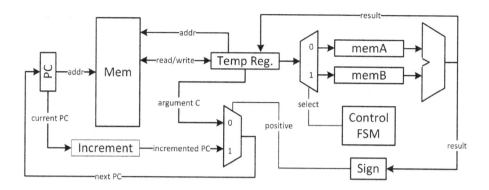

Fig. 1. Basic components and datapath of the `addleq` OISC computer

3.2 Addleq Datapath

The datapath of *addleq* is inherently simple, as seen in Fig. 1. In order to execute a single `addleq` instruction (that has three arguments), these steps are followed:

  i. Initially, the program counter address is used to read from main memory and the returned value is stored to the temporary register (fetching of argument A).
 ii. The contents of temporary register are used as the address sent to main memory for reading, and the returned value is stored back to the temporary register (fetching of *memA*, which is the ALU input referenced in memory by argument A).
iii. Through a demultiplexer controlled by the control FSM, the contents of the temporary register are stored in the *first* input register of the ALU.
 iv. The program counter value goes through the increment unit and a multiplexer, and the address of the next memory location is written back to the program counter.
  v. The program counter address is used to read from main memory and the returned value is stored to the temporary register (fetching of argument B).
 vi. The contents of the temporary register are used as the address sent to main memory for reading, and the returned value is stored again to temporary register (fetching of *memB*, which is the ALU input referenced in memory by argument B).
vii. Through a demultiplexer controlled by the control FSM, the contents of the temporary register are stored in the *second* input register of the ALU.
viii. The modular multiplication ALU uses the two register inputs and generates a result that is then sent back to the temporary register as well as to the sign identification unit.
 ix. The contents of the temporary register are sent to the main memory to be stored at the same location where *memB* was fetched from, as the program counter still points to that address (location referenced in memory by argument B).

x. The program counter value goes through the increment unit and a multiplexer, and the address of the next memory location is written back to the program counter.

xi. The program counter address is used to read from main memory and the returned value is stored to the temporary register (fetching of argument C).

xii. The sign identification unit determines if the last ALU result is positive and configures the program counter multiplexer. The program counter value goes through the increment unit and the multiplexer selects between the incremented program counter and the contents of the temporary register (essentially argument C) and the selected value is written back to the program counter.

3.3   Design Challenges

Encrypted Memory Addressing. Since instruction arguments and data are in a unified memory, then *memory addressing should also be encrypted*. Instruction arguments and program counters would obviously require to reference data locations or other arguments (for self-modifying code, as discussed in Section 2.1), and the same program should be oblivious of the encryption key (i.e. every encryption of the instruction arguments and the data should be able to reference any memory location). Since any implementation of the encrypted computer would not have access to the decryption key, the architecture should work on encrypted memory addressing. Our proposed architecture, however, also addresses this concern and allows encrypted addressing and encrypted program counters.

Matching Instruction Arguments. Porting addleq to the encrypted domain, raises another issue: Since addleq uses a single memory space for instruction arguments and data (indistinguishable to each other), it is required to match arguments A, B and C. This issue can be solved by storing inside the program memory the encryptions of each element (either instruction argument or datum) along with the encrypted address of the next encrypted element. Essentially, each element also points to the next one, by using encrypted references.

For example, without loss of generality, we assume that the program counter contains the encrypted address of a memory location that contains instruction argument A and the encrypted address of the next element (i.e. the address of instruction argument B). The addleq computer retrieves from memory the contents of the memory location pointed by argument A and then the program counter loads the encrypted address of the next element. The addleq computer then retrieves the memory contents pointed by argument B similarly. The addleq ALU multiplies the retrieved memory contents (pointed by arguments A and B) and if Paillier encryption has been used, due to additive homomorphism this corresponds to simply adding these two values in the unencrypted domain. The result is stored to the memory location pointed by argument B, and the addleq computer decides if a branch is required or not. If a branch is required, the program counter becomes equal to argument C, otherwise the program counter becomes equal to the address of the next argument.

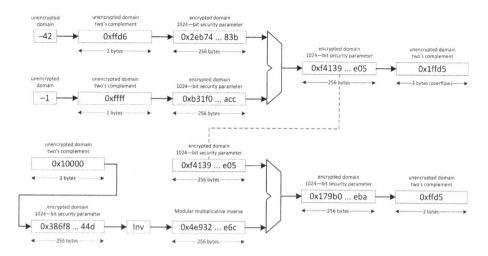

Fig. 2. Overflow correction for homomorphic addition of representations of negative numbers

Addition Overflow Detection. In this paper, for our `addleq` case study, we are investigating 16–bit memory addressing for the unencrypted programs. This implies that the size of each memory location would be 16 bits, equal to the size of a memory address. For representing negative numbers, the standard two's complement approach is used and the proposed range of supported numbers is set from -2^{15} to $(2^{15} - 1)$. One reason why the use of two's complement to represent negative numbers is mandatory, is the fact that Paillier's scheme only supports the encryption of *positive* values (for example, using two's complement for a range of 2^{16} numbers, it means that –1 is represented as $(2^{16} - 1)$).

Due to subtle homomorphic addition properties, however, adding the representations of two negative numbers in the encrypted domain, would cause a result *out of range*. For example, adding –42 with –1, which corresponds to adding $(2^{16} - 42)$ with $(2^{16} - 1)$, would result to the encryption of $(2^{17} - 43)$ instead of the encryption of $(2^{16} - 43)$ (the representation of signed number –43). This inconsistency occurs because in the encrypted domain the range of numbers is much higher (e.g. with 1024–bit security parameter size, the encrypted range is 2048 bits), compared to 2^{16} in the unencrypted domain. The issue is addressed, however, by homomorphically subtracting the encryption of 2^{16} (or equivalently, by adding the *modular multiplicative inverse* of the encryption of 2^{16}, which is always the same and can be precomputed) to get the correct result (i.e. $(2^{16} - 43)$ in the previous example). An elaboration of this example is shown in Fig. 2.

In order to detect an overflow, an *overflow lookup table* is introduced. This lookup table matches the encryption of numbers from 0 to $(2^{17} - 1)$ with one bit that indicates "over $(2^{16} - 1)$" or "not over $(2^{16} - 1)$". If the ALU result matches

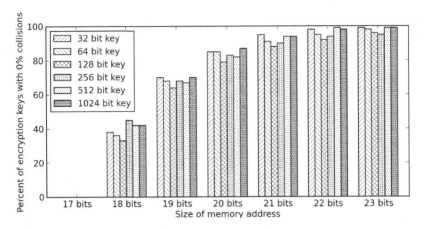

Fig. 3. Percentage of encryption keys with 0% collisions in 2^{17} encryptions for given memory addressing sizes

a value in this overflow lookup table, then a correction by "subtracting" 2^{16} is performed.

Memory Addressing Size. Given a security parameter of 1024 bits and encrypted memory addressing, the actual implementation of the proposed architecture would require memory addresses of 2048 bits, as shown by Eq. 4. Such memory, besides its prohibitive cost, is also unnecessary as in the unencrypted domain we only need 16-bit memory addressing. In this work, we propose to use a fraction of this 2048 bit address to successfully identify the requested memory address. Specifically, we seek to identify how many bits are required to discriminate memory addresses with high probability and for a high percentage of different encryption keys. As previously discussed, for 16–bit memory addressing in the unencrypted domain, a total of 2^{17} unique encryptions are addressed in the overflow lookup table, while up to 2^{16} unique encryptions are addressed in the main program memory.

Fig. 3 demonstrates the number of memory address bits required to discriminate the maximum number of unique encryptions (i.e. 2^{17}) with 0% collisions, for several encryption key sizes (i.e. security parameter sizes). Depending on the Paillier encryption security parameter size, the actual encrypted values have twice as many bits (e.g. for 256–bit security parameter, the encrypted value is 512 bits). As the diagram demonstrates, if we use memory addresses of 22 bits, we can accommodate all 2^{17} different encryptions for at least 90% of the encryption keys used (the analysis is based on a random sample of *100 keys* for each key size, and for confidence level 95% the confidence interval is ≤ 9.8). Of course, in this case there is about 10% probability that this addressing size would not be enough for a specific encryption key, and in this scenario memory re-encryption *with a different key* would be required.

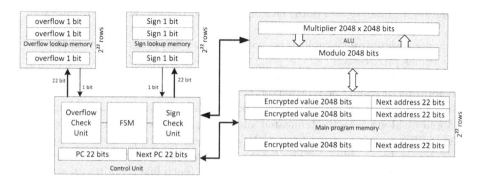

Fig. 4. High level view of additional units of the *addleq* encrypted computer to address sign identification and overflow detection in the encrypted domain (security parameter 1024–bits)

Jump Decisions in the Encrypted Domain. An additional problem, already mentioned in the previous paragraphs, is the problem of determining if the result of the ALU modular multiplication is less than or equal to zero (i.e. not positive). Since the computation is performed on encrypted data, there is no straightforward way of comparing an encrypted value with zero without decrypting it. There are proposed schemes that allow *order-preserving encryption* [1], but these schemes are not additive homomorphic and the Paillier scheme is not order-preserving either. Furthermore, if an encryption scheme allows comparing an encrypted value with zero, this would automatically allow decryption, simply by doing a *bit–by–bit binary search*. To solve this problem, in this work we propose the use of a *sign lookup table* that contains that mathematical sign for the encryptions of a range of numbers. Essentially, this table matches encrypted values with the sign of the corresponding decryptions.

The proposed sign lookup table provides matching for the encryptions of 16-bit values with the corresponding sign (0 for less or equal zero, 1 for positives). In theory, this lookup table would require memory address size equal to the encryption of each number in range from 0 to $(2^{16} - 1)$, which depending to the Paillier security parameter may be up to 2048 bits long. Instead, we propose a truncation down to 22 bits (similar to the overflow lookup table addressing truncation described earlier), since as seen in Fig. 3 this is sufficient for discriminating 2^{17} different values for the vast majority of different random encryption keys.

Fig. 4 features a high level view of the encrypted addleq architecture, including the additional sign and overflow lookup memories.

Memory Space Requirements. From the above description it becomes evident why a limitation in the possible encrypted values is required. Allowing 2^{16} possible values to be encrypted, ultimately requires two additional memories (sparsely filled) of 22 bit address size each, to support the encrypted addleq functionality. So, the addleq main memory (the one that contains encrypted instruction arguments and data) can only contain the encryptions of values up to $(2^{16} - 1)$, as well as addressing for up to $(2^{16} - 1)$ instruction arguments. This is not a significant problem, however, since addleq programs by nature use larger values progressively as the program size increases, and the vast majority of programs can easily fit in this proposed range.

In addition, it should be stressed out that the main memory of addleq needs to have adequate size to fit the encryptions of data, as well as instruction arguments A, B and C, along with the truncated address for the next element; in practice, if the Paillier security parameter is 1024 bits (so each encrypted value would be 2048 bits), and the additional bits for the truncated address of the next element are 22, this adds to 2060 bits in each memory line (each line is addressed with 22 bits). In order to execute encrypted programs, the owner of the program should encrypt (using Paillier's scheme) the main program memory (which is given by the compiler of the addleq assembly), as well as provide the two mandatory lookup tables for signs and overflows; all three memories are specific to the encryption key used each time.

4   Experimental Setup

In order to evaluate the performance of the proposed architecture, a simulator of the proposed encrypted addleq architecture has been developed. All experiments were performed using Python 2.7.4 on a virtual 64–bit Ubuntu 13.04 host running at 2.6GHz ($2 * $ i7–3720QM Intel cores) with 2GB of memory. For the implementation of Paillier's homomorphic encryption scheme, an openly available educational Python library from [21] was used.

For our experiments, four **addleq** assembly programs have been used from [27]; these programs are written directly in assembly language and after being converted to machine code, they have been homomorphically encrypted for execution in the simulator (using different security parameter sizes). Furthermore, for hardware performance figures, we assumed a hardware implementation running at 200MHz (for example, in an FPGA) and the following estimates have been used:

(a) *memory access delay* has been estimated to less than 100ns [19] for memories up to 16GB (which corresponds to 20 clock cycles at 200Mhz),

(b) *modular multiplication* has been estimated to $(h + 3)$ cycles for argument size h [9] (which corresponds to 2051 clock cycles for 2048–bit arguments using security parameter $n = 1024$ bits) based on *Montgomery* algorithm [29,2,28], and

(c) *addition* (using *Kogge-Stone* fast adder design) for 16–bit unencrypted arguments (used for comparison) is estimated to 6ns [20] (which requires 2 clock cycles at 200Mhz) .

Table 1. Simulated execution clock cycles (security parameter 1024 bits)

Benchmark	Unencrypted	Encrypted	Overhead
Program 1	$4.44 * 10^5$	$1.35 * 10^7$	30 x
Program 2	$6.28 * 10^5$	$1.67 * 10^7$	27 x
Program 3	$3.78 * 10^2$	$6.99 * 10^3$	19 x
Program 4	$4.10 * 10^4$	$1.09 * 10^6$	27 x

Table 2. Average overhead for different security parameter sizes

Security Parameter	Average Overhead
32 bits	3 x
64 bits	4 x
128 bits	5 x
256 bits	8 x
512 bits	14 x
1024 bits	26 x

5 Results

As a proof of concept, preliminary results generated using the developed simulator are presented in Tables 1 and 2. The simulator is parameterized to compare the performance of normal (unencrypted) `addleq` with the performance that our proposed encrypted `addleq` design would have had in a standard FPGA running at 200MHz, using the figures presented in Section 4. Even though memory access times are not affected by different security parameter sizes, modular multiplications have different delays, depending on the size of the arguments. Table 2 presents the average (over all four assembly programs used) encrypted execution overhead depending on the security parameter size. The results show that as the security parameter size increases, the impact of the modular multiplication operations in the encrypted OISC computer becomes higher, and the overall overhead is *26 times* for security parameter 1024 bits.

Table 1 provides information on the number of clock cycles required for encrypted program execution, compared to unencrypted execution. These results indicate that encryption requires about 2 orders of magnitude more clock cycles, primarily due to the multicycle ALU operations and memory lookup operations.

6 Discussion on Security

The proposed encrypted computer is designed to solve the problem of executing programs and manipulating data in the cloud. It is designed to address honest but curious cloud service providers that would support the proposed architecture but may try to look inside the processor. Our goal is to protect the confidentiality of the execution steps as well as the data.

The security of the system is based on the security assumptions of the Paillier scheme; the proposed architecture works with any program that is the result of addleq assembly compilation. However, since the Paillier scheme is a probabilistic scheme, it incorporates a random *helper value* "r" in the encryption of each plaintext. This helper value is necessary in order to have different encryptions each time, for the same plaintext, and essentially have semantic security in the cryptographic sense of *Indistinguishability against Chosen Plaintext attacks (IND-CPA)* [23]. OISC computers, however, cannot be probabilistic; it would not be possible to construct an OISC computer where the same plaintext has different encryptions, all at the same time: when that computer generates a result that would be used as a reference to a memory location, this reference always needs to be the same, since there would be only one actual location in memory. So, it is not possible to use Paillier homomorphic encryption in a probabilistic fashion, since intermediate values computed by addleq, to be used as memory address references, should always be the same.

In practice, this last observation means that for our proposed encrypted addleq architecture, the used Paillier's scheme implementation has to be slightly modified in order to produce the same encrypted value for the same input (i.e. become partially deterministic). In theory, this essentially makes the processor susceptible to Chosen–Plaintext Attacks (i.e. the semantic security property is partially lost), and the scheme has the same security properties as textbook RSA [3,23], which is also semantically non-secure. However, the threat of a Chosen–Plaintext Attack is not a major concern in our context of cloud computing, since the encryption of all values is performed by the program owner who knows all public key parameters (as well as private key parameters) to be able to encrypt arbitrary values; using Paillier's encryption, only the value of n (which is one half of the public key) is required by the addleq computer ALU to perform modular multiplication, and only this half needs to be revealed (in the currently used Paillier's scheme implementation, the second half of the public key is correlated with the first half, however, in general uncorrelated halves can be used as well). Thus, no third party or even the cloud provider has access to the entire public key in order to calculate encryptions of known values, and to launch a Chosen–Plaintext Attack to the processor and the encrypted memory contents.

Another concern comes from the fact the program owner provides 2 lookup tables with information about the sign of 2^{16} encrypted values as well as information if an encrypted value is larger or smaller than 2^{16}. In the strict cryptographic sense, the first lookup table reveals 1 bit of the plaintext and the second table also reveals "some" information. However, the information revealed in indeed very little, compared to the entropy of the encrypted value, and in practice the confidentiality of the information is not threatened. Of course revealing even 1 bit is less than optimal, but any Turing complete computer needs to make runtime decisions, and in this case we use the minimum amount of information to perform this mandatory task.

Finally, one concern relates to the order with which the encrypted instruction arguments are provided. If these arguments are given in sorted ordering, an attacker could guess the program counter sequence and thus launch a Chosen–Plaintext Attack. This means that if the program counter starts from (encryption of) address 0x0000 for argument A and then goes to (encryption of) address 0x0001, an attacker could potentially guess this and find the encryption of plaintext "1" and ultimately generate a *codebook* (using homomorphism, the attacker finds $1 + 1$, $1 + 1 + 1$ etc). To prevent this, the proposed architecture supports "spaghetti" memory: having that each memory location is accompanied by a reference to the next address, these addresses can be randomly chosen, without loss of generality. Essentially, the program can start from (encryption of) address zero and jump to random locations in a spaghetti code fashion; the trail is preserved since each location points to the next one, but this looks unintelligible to any third–party observer.

6.1   Future Directions

In this work we present a novel approach to solve the problem of encrypted computation for protecting the confidentiality of the program and the data. Without loss of generality of the proposed solution, we use a publicly available implementation of Paillier's scheme in Python [21]. Because this particular implementation is not recommended for "production" use (due to the quality of prime numbers generated and the randomness sources used), future work will include cryptographically safe implementations of Paillier's scheme. Our proposed architecture would work with any other implementation of the Paillier's encryption scheme, provided that the implementation is slightly modified to use deterministic encryptions (i.e. for a specific plaintext, the same helper value r is used each time, instead of a random one each time).

In addition, in this paper, for simplification of a certain subtleties of homomorphic multiplication, the same r value was used for every plaintext. The proposed architecture, however, supports having a different helper value r for each different plaintext, with minimal modifications; this option, that provides extra security, would be explored in future work.

Future directions also include exploring other OISC variants, like `subleq`; using a different variant requires only minor technical modifications, as the proposed architecture is generic. Furthermore, performance improvements using cache memories, pipelining and incorporating more than one execution units are also part this continued investigation. A hardware implementation of the proposed architecture would provide more conclusive performance figures.

7   Conclusion

In this paper we presented a novel idea for an encrypted computer architecture, capable of performing computations on encrypted data as well as executing encrypted programs written in addleq machine code. Our key contribution is a new design that combines OISC computer design with homomorphic encryption, which is an important step towards achieving privacy in cloud computing. Experimental results corroborate that the proposed architecture has the potential to be an effective solution, incurring an average overhead of 26 times compared to unencrypted OISC computation.

References

1. Agrawal, R., Kiernan, J., Srikant, R., Xu, Y.: Order preserving encryption for numeric data. In: Proceedings of the 2004 ACM SIGMOD International Conference on Management of Data, pp. 563–574. ACM (2004)
2. Blum, T., Paar, C.: Montgomery modular exponentiation on reconfigurable hardware. In: Proceedings of the 14th IEEE Symposium on Computer Arithmetic, pp. 70–77. IEEE (1999)
3. Boneh, D., Joux, A., Nguyen, P.Q.: Why textbook ElGamal and RSA encryption are insecure. In: Okamoto, T. (ed.) ASIACRYPT 2000. LNCS, vol. 1976, pp. 30–43. Springer, Heidelberg (2000)
4. Brakerski, Z., Gentry, C., Vaikuntanathan, V.: (Leveled) fully homomorphic encryption without bootstrapping. In: Proceedings of the 3rd Innovations in Theoretical Computer Science Conference, pp. 309–325. ACM (2012)
5. Brenner, M., Wiebelitz, J., von Voigt, G., Smith, M.: Secret program execution in the cloud applying homomorphic encryption. In: Proceedings of the 5th IEEE International Conference on Digital Ecosystems and Technologies Conference (DEST), pp. 114–119. IEEE (2011)
6. Breuer, P.T., Bowen, J.P.: Typed assembler for a RISC crypto-processor. In: Barthe, G., Livshits, B., Scandariato, R. (eds.) ESSoS 2012. LNCS, vol. 7159, pp. 22–29. Springer, Heidelberg (2012)
7. Cooney, M.: IBM touts encryption innovation (2009),
   http://www.computerworld.com/s/article/9134823/IBM_touts_encryption_innovation?taxonomyId=152&intsrc=kc_top&taxonomyName=compliance
8. Cramer, R., Gennaro, R., Schoenmakers, B.: A secure and optimally efficient multi-authority election scheme. European Transactions on Telecommunications 8(5), 481–490 (1997)
9. Daly, A., Marnane, W.: Efficient architectures for implementing montgomery modular multiplication and RSA modular exponentiation on reconfigurable logic. In: Proceedings of the 2002 ACM/SIGDA Tenth International Symposium on Field-Programmable Gate Arrays, pp. 40–49. ACM (2002)
10. ElGamal, T.: A public key cryptosystem and a signature scheme based on discrete logarithms. IEEE Transactions on Information Theory 31(4), 469–472 (1985)
11. Esolangs: Addleq Turing complete OISC language,
    http://esolangs.org/wiki/Addleq
12. Esolangs: One Instruction Set Computer, http://esolangs.org/wiki/OISC
13. Fan, J., Vercauteren, F.: Somewhat practical fully homomorphic encryption. IACR Cryptology ePrint Archive, 2012 144 (2012)
14. Fontaine, C., Galand, F.: A survey of homomorphic encryption for nonspecialists. EURASIP Journal on Information Security 2007 (2007)
15. Gentry, C.: A fully homomorphic encryption scheme. Ph.D. thesis, Stanford University (2009)

16. Gentry, C.: Fully homomorphic encryption using ideal lattices (2009)
17. Goldwasser, S., Micali, S.: Probabilistic encryption & how to play mental poker keeping secret all partial information. In: Proceedings of the Fourteenth Annual ACM Symposium on Theory of Computing, pp. 365–377. ACM (1982)
18. Halevi, S., Shoup, V.: Design and implementation of a homomorphic-encryption library (2012)
19. Hennessy, J.L., Patterson, D.A.: Computer architecture: a quantitative approach, pp. 72, 96–101. Elsevier (2012)
20. Hoe, D.H., Martinez, C., Vundavalli, S.J.: Design and characterization of parallel prefix adders using FPGAs. In: 2011 IEEE 43rd South eastern Symposium on System Theory (SSST), pp. 168–172. IEEE (2011)
21. Ivanov, M.: Pure Python Paillier homomorphic cryptosystem (2011), https://github.com/mikeivanov/paillier
22. Jones, D.W.: The ultimate RISC. ACM SIGARCH Computer Architecture News 16(3), 48–55 (1988)
23. Katz, J., Lindell, Y.: Introduction to modern cryptography. CRC Press (2008)
24. Lange, A.: An overview of homomorphic encryption (2011), http://www.cs.rit.edu/~arl9577/crypto/alange-presentation.pdf
25. Mavaddat, F., Parhami, B.: URISC: the ultimate reduced instruction set computer. Faculty of Mathematics. University of Waterloo (1987)
26. Mazonka, O., Kolodin, A.: A simple multi-processor computer based on subleq. arXiv preprint arXiv:1106.2593 (2011)
27. Mazonka, O.: Addleq (2009), http://mazonka.com/subleq/
28. McIvor, C., McLoone, M., McCanny, J.V.: Fast Montgomery modular multiplication and RSA cryptographic processor architectures. In: Conference Record of the Thirty-Seventh Asilomar Conference on Signals, Systems and Computers, vol. 1, pp. 379–384. IEEE (2003)
29. Montgomery, P.L.: Modular multiplication without trial division. Mathematics of Computation 44(170), 519–521 (1985)
30. Paillier, P.: Public-key cryptosystems based on composite degree residuosity classes. In: Stern, J. (ed.) EUROCRYPT 1999. LNCS, vol. 1592, pp. 223–238. Springer, Heidelberg (1999)
31. Parann-Nissany, G.: The holy grail of cloud computing – maintaining data confidentiality (2012), http://www.wallstreetandtech.com/technology-risk-management/the-holy-grail-of-cloud-computing-maint/240006774
32. Rivest, R.L., Shamir, A., Adleman, L.: A method for obtaining digital signatures and public-key cryptosystems. Communications of the ACM 21(2), 120–126 (1978)
33. Schneier, B.: Homomorphic encryption breakthrough (2009), http://www.schneier.com/blog/archives/2009/07/homomorphic_enc.html
34. Simonite, T.: Computing with secrets, but keeping them safe (2010), http://www.technologyreview.com/news/419344/computing-with-secrets-but-keeping-them-safe/
35. Stehlé, D., Steinfeld, R.: Faster fully homomorphic encryption. In: Abe, M. (ed.) ASIACRYPT 2010. LNCS, vol. 6477, pp. 377–394. Springer, Heidelberg (2010)
36. Stuntz, C.: What is homomorphic encryption, and why should I care? (2010), http://blogs.teamb.com/craigstuntz/2010/03/18/38566/
37. van Dijk, M., Gentry, C., Halevi, S., Vaikuntanathan, V.: Fully homomorphic encryption over the integers. In: Gilbert, H. (ed.) EUROCRYPT 2010. LNCS, vol. 6110, pp. 24–43. Springer, Heidelberg (2010)

Alphanumeric Shellcode Generator for ARM Architecture

Pratik Kumar, Nagendra Chowdary, and Anish Mathuria

DA-IICT, Gandhinagar
{posani_nagendra,anish_mathuria}@daiict.ac.in

Abstract. Shellcode usually refers to a piece of code that is injected into a program in order to perform some malicious actions. For any processor, the set of instructions that consist only of alphanumeric characters is generally limited is size. Therefore it is non-trivial to construct shellcode that consists of only alphanumeric bytes. There exist a number of exploit tools that automatically translate non-alphanumeric shellcode into semantically equivalent alphanumeric shellcode for x86 architecture. To the best of our knowledge, there are no such tools available for ARM architecture. We report on our progress in developing a tool for automated generation of alphanumeric shellcode for ARM architecture.

1 Introduction

Errors introduced in writing programs can often be exploited to carry out malicious attacks on computer systems. For example, the goal of code injection attacks is to force a program to execute instructions that do not even appear in the original program. Typically, code injection attacks work in the following way. In the first step, the attacker sends the malicious data as input to the program, which then stores it in memory. The data is chosen by the attacker in such a way that it represents a valid machine code that performs malicious actions when executed. The usual goal of code injection attacks is to launch a command interpreter shell. Hence data input by the attacker is often referred to as *shellcode*. In the second step, the attacker exploits a vulnerability present in the program to divert the control to his shellcode. A wide variety of vulnerabilities can be exploited for this purpose, for example stack-based buffer overflows.

Most shellcodes in their original form consist of both alphanumeric and non-alphanumeric bytes. Thus, we may block data containing non-alphanumeric bytes to defend against code injection attacks. The challenge for the attacker is that of creating shellcode that consists of only alphanumeric bytes. Rix [2] was the first to discuss how to write alphanumeric shellcodes for x86 architecture. He developed a tool which takes non-alphanumeric code as input and outputs alphanumeric shellcode. The output generated is a self-modifying program. It consists of a decoder that re-constructs the original non-alphanumeric shellcode before executing it. The main disadvantage of his technique is the expansion in the size of the alphanumeric shellcode as compared to the input shellcode.

B. Gierlichs, S. Guilley, and D. Mukhopadhyay (Eds.): SPACE 2013, LNCS 8204, pp. 38–39, 2013.

In 2004 Berend Jan Wever [1] introduced the idea of loop decoding to help reduce the output size. The shellcode is encoded in such a way that the decoding can be performed iteratively, thus decreasing the size of the shellcode.

Younan and Philippaerts [4] showed that the subset of ARM machine code programs that (when interpreted as data) consist only of alphanumeric characters (i.e. letters and digits) is a Turing complete subset. A related work [3] showed that it is feasible to write alphanumeric shellcodes for ARM. The approach followed by these earlier works, however, is not amenable to automation as it requires alphanumeric shellcode to be crafted manually. We report on our progress in developing a tool for automated generation of alphanumeric shellcode for ARM architecture.

References

1. Wever, B.J.: Alphanumeric shellcode decoder loop. Skypher (2004)
2. Rix: Writing IA32 alphanumeric shellcodes. Phrack 57 (2001)
3. Younan, Y., Philippaerts, P.: Alphanumeric RISC ARM shellcode. Phrack 66 (2009)
4. Younan, Y., Philippaerts, P., Piessens, F., Piessens, F., Joosen, W., Lachmund, S., Walter, T.: Filter-resistant code injection on ARM. Journal of Computer Virology and Hacking Techniques 7(3), 173–188 (2010)

SIMD-Based Implementations of Sieving in Integer-Factoring Algorithms

Binanda Sengupta and Abhijit Das

Department of Computer Science and Engineering
Indian Institute of Technology Kharagpur, West Bengal, PIN: 721302, India
{binanda.sengupta,abhij}@cse.iitkgp.ernet.in

Abstract. The best known integer-factoring algorithms consist of two stages: the sieving stage and the linear-algebra stage. Efficient parallel implementations of both these stages have been reported in the literature. All these implementations are based on multi-core or distributed parallelization. In this paper, we experimentally demonstrate that SIMD instructions available in many modern processors can lead to additional speedup in the computation of each core. We handle the sieving stage of the two fastest known factoring algorithms (NFSM and MPQSM), and are able to achieve 15–40% speedup over non-SIMD implementations. Although the sieving stage offers many tantalizing possibilities of data parallelism, exploiting these possibilities to get practical advantages is a challenging task. Indeed, to the best of our knowledge, no similar SIMD-based implementation of sieving seems to have been reported in the literature.

Keywords: Integer Factorization, Sieving, Number-Field Sieve Method, Multiple-Polynomial Quadratic Sieve Method, Single Instruction Multiple Data, Streaming SIMD Extensions, Advanced Vector Extensions.

1 Introduction

Factoring large integers has been of much importance in cryptography and computational number theory. Many cryptosystems like RSA derive their security from the apparent intractability of factoring large integers. Indeed, the integer factorization problem can be dubbed as the fundamental computational problem in number theory. Despite many attempts to solve this problem efficiently, researchers could not come up with any polynomial-time algorithm so far. Further studies of factoring and efficient implementation issues continue to remain an important area of research of both practical and theoretical significance.

Given a composite integer n, the integer factorization problem can be formally framed as to find out all the prime divisors $p_1, p_2, \ldots, p_l$ of n and their corresponding multiplicities $v_{p_1}, v_{p_2}, \ldots, v_{p_l}$, where

$$n = p_1^{v_{p_1}} p_2^{v_{p_2}} \cdots p_l^{v_{p_l}} = \prod_{i=1}^{l} p_i^{v_{p_i}}.$$

B. Gierlichs, S. Guilley, and D. Mukhopadhyay (Eds.): SPACE 2013, LNCS 8204, pp. 40–55, 2013.
© Springer-Verlag Berlin Heidelberg 2013

Many algorithms are proposed to solve the integer factorization problem. The older algorithms have running times exponential in the input size (the number of bits in n, that is, $\log_2 n$ or $\lg n$). The time and space complexities of the modern integer-factoring algorithms are subexponential in $\lg n$. These algorithms typically consist of two stages. In the first stage, a large number of candidates are generated. Each such candidate that factors completely over a factor base, a set of small primes, yields a relation. In the second stage, the relations obtained in the first stage are combined, by solving a set of linear equations modulo 2, to get a congruence of the form $x^2 \equiv y^2 \pmod{n}$. If $x \not\equiv \pm y \pmod{n}$, then $\gcd(x - y, n)$ is a non-trivial factor of n.

The sieving stage is introduced in the quadratic sieve method [1] in an attempt to make the relation-collection stage more efficient compared to trial division. Let p be small prime, and g an integer-valued polynomial function of a variable c such that $g(c) \equiv x \pmod{p}$ for some $x \in \mathbb{Z}$. If γ is a solution of the congruence, then all of its solutions are of the form $c = \gamma + kp$, where $k \in \mathbb{Z}$. This is how trial divisions are avoided in sieving.

SIMD (Single Instruction Multiple Data)-based architecture is a recent technology that comes with *vector* instructions and register sets. The size of these special SIMD registers is larger than (usually a multiple of) that of the general-purpose registers. Multiple data of the same type can be accommodated in an SIMD register. This is frequently called *packing*. A binary operation on two packed registers can be performed using a single vector instruction. The individual results are extracted from the output SIMD register. This extraction process is known as *unpacking*. The less the packing and unpacking overheads are, the more are the advantages that can be derived from SIMD-based parallelization.

The sieving part turns out to be the most time-consuming stage in factoring algorithms. As a result, efficient implementations of the sieving stage is of the utmost importance in the context of factoring algorithms. Sieving is, however, massively parallelizable on multi-core and even on distributed platforms. Our work is not an attempt to exploit parallelism in the multi-core or distributed level. On the contrary, we attempt to investigate how SIMD-based parallelism can provide additional speedup within each single core. In sieving, both index calculations and subtractions of log values involve data-parallel operations. SIMD intrinsics have the potential of increasing the efficiency of both these steps. Unfortunately, frequent packing and unpacking of data between regular registers (or memory locations) and SIMD registers stand in the way of this potential benefit of data parallelism. Our major challenge in this work is to reduce the packing and unpacking overheads. So far, we have been able to achieve some speedup in the index-calculation process. Achieving similar speedup in the subtraction phase still eludes us. To the best of our knowledge, no SIMD-based parallelization attempts on sieving algorithms for integer factorization are reported in the literature. The early implementations described in [2,3] use the term SIMD but are akin to multi-core parallelization in a 16K MasPar SIMD machine with 128×128 array of processing elements.

Our Contribution: In this paper, we concentrate on efficient implementations of sieving using Intel's SSE2 (Streaming SIMD Extensions) and AVX (Advanced Vector Extensions) features. We handle the sieving stages of two factoring algorithms stated below. Currently, these are the most practical factoring algorithms.

- The multiple polynomial quadratic sieve method (MPQSM) uses the same concept as the quadratic sieve method (QSM), except that the MPQSM works with a general polynomial instead of a fixed one. By varying the coefficients of this general polynomial, we generate different instances of sieving, which can run in parallel, independent of one another. We assume that on a core the polynomial remains fixed, and a sieving interval is provided to us. We use SIMD operations to sieve this interval for the given polynomial. The MPQSM is widely accepted as the second fastest factoring algorithm.
- The general number field sieve method (NFSM) is the fastest known algorithm for factoring integers, and is based upon the theory of algebraic number fields. In particular, a number ring $\mathfrak{O}$ and a homomorphism $\mathfrak{O} \to \mathbb{Z}_n$ are used. The sieving procedure is carried out in both the rings (algebraic and rational sieving). We apply SIMD parallelization to both these sieves.

The rest of the paper is organized as follows. In Section 2, we briefly discuss the background needed for the following sections. This includes a description of the sieving procedures in the MPQSM and in the NFSM, and also of Intel's SSE2 and AVX components. Section 3 illustrates our implementation details for the sieving in the MPQSM and the NFSM. In Section 4, we present our experimental results, and analyze the speedup obtained in our experiments. In the concluding Section 5, we provide some ways in which this work can be extended.

2 Background

2.1 A Summary of Known Integer-Factoring Algorithms

Modern integer-factoring algorithms typically aim to find a congruence of the form $x^2 \equiv y^2 \pmod{n}$. If $x \not\equiv \pm y \pmod{n}$, then $\gcd(x - y, n)$ is a non-trivial factor of n.

J. D. Dixon [4] proposes the simplest variant of such a factoring method. Based on the work of Lehmer and Powers [5], Morrison and Brillhart introduce another variant known as the CFRAC method [6], where relations are obtained from the continued fraction expansion of $\sqrt{n}$.

In Pomerance's quadratic sieve method (QSM) [1], the polynomial $T(c) = J + 2Hc + c^2$ (where $H = \lceil \sqrt{n} \rceil$ and $J = H^2 - n$) is evaluated for small values of c (in the range $-M \leqslant c \leqslant M$). If some $T(c)$ factors completely over the first t primes $p_1, p_2, \ldots, p_t$, we get a relation. In Dixon's method, the smoothness candidates are $O(n)$, whereas in CFRAC and QSM, these are $O(\sqrt{n})$, resulting in a larger proportion of smooth integers (than Dixon's method) in the pool of smoothness candidates. Moreover, QSM replaces trial divisions by sieving (subtractions after some preprocessing). This gives QSM a better running time than Dixon's method and CFRAC.

R. D. Silverman introduces a variant of QSM, called the multiple polynomial quadratic sieve method (MPQSM) [7]. Instead of using the fixed polynomial $T(c)$, the MPQSM uses a more general polynomial $T(c) = Wc^2 + 2Vc + U$ so that the smoothness candidates are somewhat smaller than those in the QSM.

The number field sieve method (NFSM) is originally proposed for integers of a special form [8], and is later extended to factor arbitrary integers [9]. Pollard introduces the concept of lattice sieving [10] as an efficient implementation of the sieves in the NFSM. The conventional sieving is called line sieving.

Some other methods for factoring integers include the cubic sieve method (CSM) [11] and the elliptic curve method (ECM) [12].

The linear-algebra phase in factoring algorithms can be reasonably efficiently solved using sparse system solvers like the block Lanczos method [13]. We do not deal with this phase in this paper.

2.2   SSE2 and AVX

SSE (Streaming SIMD Extensions) is an extension of the previous x86 instruction set, and SSE2, introduced in Pentium 4, enhances the SSE instruction set further. This architecture comes with some 128-bit SIMD registers (XMM). In these registers, we can accommodate multiple data of some basic types (like four 32-bit integers, four single-precision floating-point numbers, and two double-precision floating-point numbers). The basic idea to exploit this architecture is to pack these registers with multiple data, perform a single vector instruction, and finally unpack the output XMM register to obtain the desired individual results.

AVX (Advanced Vector Extensions), introduced in Intel's Sandy Bridge processor, is a recent extension to the general x86 instruction set. This architecture is designed with sixteen 256-bit SIMD registers (YMM). Now, we can accommodate eight single-precision or four double-precision floating-point numbers in one YMM register. The AVX instruction set is currently applicable for only floating-point operations.

Programming languages come with intrinsics for high-level access to SIMD instructions both for SSE2 [14] and AVX [15]. We can use these intrinsics directly in our implementations to exploit data parallelism.

2.3   MPQSM

The multiple polynomial quadratic sieve method (MPQSM) [7] is a variant of the quadratic sieve method (QSM) [1]. Instead of using a single polynomial (with fixed coefficients), the MPQSM deals with a general polynomial, and tune its coefficients to generate small smoothness candidates. This variant is parallelizable in the sense that different polynomials can be assigned to different cores. Our aim is to speed up each multi-core implementation, so we work with one of these polynomials. We have implemented the sieving part in the MPQSM using SIMD intrinsics mentioned above. Relations are collected in the MPQSM as follows.

Let us consider a polynomial

$$T(c) = Wc^2 + 2Vc + U \tag{1}$$

with $V^2 - UW = n$. We search for the smooth values of $T(c)$, where c can take integer values in the interval $[-M, M]$. W is selected as a prime close to $\frac{\sqrt{2n}}{M}$, such that n is a quadratic residue modulo W. V is the smaller square root of n modulo W, and we take $U = \frac{V^2 - n}{W}$ (which is also an integer). Multiplying Eqn (1) by W, we get $WT(c) = (Wc + V)^2 + (UW - V^2) = (Wc + V)^2 - n$, which in turn gives

$$(Wc + V)^2 \equiv WT(c) \pmod{n}. \tag{2}$$

The factor base consists of the first t primes $p_1, p_2, \ldots, p_t$, where t is chosen based on a bound B. Only those primes are needed, modulo which n is a quadratic residue. First, we calculate the values of $T(c)$ for all c in the range $-M \leqslant c \leqslant M$. Now, we try to find those values of c, for which $T(c)$ is B-smooth, that is, $T(c)$ factors completely into primes $\leqslant B$. If $T(c) = p_1^{\alpha_1} p_2^{\alpha_2} \cdots p_t^{\alpha_t}$ for some non-negative integral values of α_i, we can write Eqn (2) as

$$(Wc + V)^2 \equiv W p_1^{\alpha_1} p_2^{\alpha_2} \cdots p_t^{\alpha_t} \pmod{n}. \tag{3}$$

We include W itself in the factor base. After many such relations like Eqn (3) are collected, we combine those relations to obtain a congruence of the form $x^2 \equiv y^2 \pmod{n}$.

It is required that the number of relations obtained be larger than the number of primes present in the factor base. The advantage of the MPQSM over the QSM is that the coefficients U, V, W of the polynomial are not fixed. We can choose a different prime close to $\frac{\sqrt{2n}}{M}$ as W, modulo which n is a quadratic residue. For a given W, we get fixed values of V and U. Thus, by varying the coefficients, we can generate more relations, keeping M and B fixed.

The methods proposed earlier than QSM use trial divisions to find the B-smooth values of smoothness candidates. QSM introduces a technique called sieving to locate the smooth values using additions/subtractions instead of divisions (along with some preprocessing).

Now, we discuss sieving in the MPQSM briefly. In the MPQSM, we have different values of $T(c)$ for different c in $[-M, M]$, as shown in Eqn (1). We have to locate those c for which $T(c)$ is smooth over the factor base. We take an array A indexed by c. Initially, we store $\log |T(c)|$ in $A[c]$, truncated after three decimal places. Indeed, we can avoid floating-point operations by storing $\lfloor 1000 \log |T(c)| \rfloor$ in $A[c]$.

After this initialization, we try to find solutions of the congruence $T(c) \equiv 0 \pmod{p^h}$, where p is a small prime in the factor base, and h is a small positive exponent. Thus, we have to solve the congruence

$$Wc^2 + 2Vc + U \equiv 0 \pmod{p^h}$$

which implies

$$c \equiv \frac{-2V \pm \sqrt{4V^2 - 4UW}}{2W} \equiv \frac{-V \pm \sqrt{n}}{W} \equiv W^{-1}(-V \pm \sqrt{n}) \pmod{p^h}. \tag{4}$$

For $h = 1$, we use a root-finding algorithm to compute the square roots of n modulo p. For $h > 1$, we obtain the solutions modulo p^h by lifting the solutions modulo p^{h-1}.

Let s be a solution of $T(c) \equiv 0 \pmod{p^h}$. Then, all the solutions of $T(c) \equiv 0 \pmod{p^h}$ are $s \pm kp^h$, $k \in \mathbb{N}$. Therefore, we subtract $\lfloor 1000 \log p \rfloor$ from all the array locations $A[c]$ such that $c = s \pm kp^h$.

When all such powers of small primes in the factor base are tried out, the array locations storing $A[c] \approx 0$ correspond to the smooth values of $T(c)$. We apply trial division on these smooth values of $T(c)$. If some $T(c)$ value is not smooth, then the corresponding array entry $A[c]$ holds an integer $\geqslant \lfloor 1000 \log p_{t+1} \rfloor$.

2.4   NFSM

The relation-collection phase of the number field sieve method (NFSM) [9] and some mathematical background are described below.

NFSM involves a monic irreducible polynomial $f(x) \in \mathbb{Z}[x]$ of a small degree d and an integer $m \approx n^{1/d}$ such that $f(m) \equiv 0 \pmod{n}$, n being the integer to be factored. One possibility is to take $m = \lfloor n^{1/d} \rfloor$, and express n in base m as $n = m^d + c_{d-1}m^{d-1} + \cdots + c_0$, with the integers c_i varying in the range 0 to $m - 1$. For this choice, we take $f(x) = x^d + c_{d-1}x^{d-1} + \cdots + c_0$, provided that it is an irreducible polynomial in $\mathbb{Z}[x]$. We have $f(m) = n$, implying that $f(m) \equiv 0 \pmod{n}$, as desired.

Theorem 2.4.1: If $\theta \in \mathbb{C}$ is a root of a monic irreducible polynomial $f(x)$ of degree d with rational coefficients, then the set of all algebraic integers in $\mathbb{Q}(\theta)$, denoted by $\mathfrak{O}$, forms a subring of the field $\mathbb{Q}(\theta)$.

Theorem 2.4.2: If $\theta \in \mathbb{C}$ is a root of a monic irreducible polynomial $f(x)$ of degree d with integral coefficients, then the set of all $\mathbb{Z}$-linear combinations of the elements $1, \theta, \theta^2, \ldots, \theta^{d-1}$, denoted by $\mathbb{Z}[\theta]$, is a subring of $\mathfrak{O}$.

Theorem 2.4.3: If $\theta \in \mathbb{C}$ is a root of a monic irreducible polynomial $f(x)$ of degree d with integral coefficients and $m \in \mathbb{Z}$ is an integer such that $f(m) \equiv 0 \pmod{n}$, then there exists a ring homomorphism $\phi : \mathbb{Z}[\theta] \to \mathbb{Z}_n$ defined by $\phi(\theta) = m \pmod{n}$ (and $\phi(1) = 1 \pmod{n}$).

Now, let S be a set of pairs of integers (a, b) satisfying

$$\prod_{(a,b) \in S} (a + b\theta) = \alpha^2,$$

$$\prod_{(a,b) \in S} (a + bm) = y^2,$$

for some $\alpha \in \mathbb{Z}[\theta]$ and $y \in \mathbb{Z}$. Let $\phi(\alpha) = x \in \mathbb{Z}_n$. Then, we get

$$x^2 \equiv \phi(\alpha)^2 \equiv \phi(\alpha^2) \equiv \phi\left(\prod_{(a,b) \in S} (a + b\theta)\right)$$

$$\equiv \prod_{(a,b) \in S} \phi(a + b\theta) \equiv \prod_{(a,b) \in S} (a + bm) \equiv y^2 \pmod{n}.$$

If $x \not\equiv \pm y \pmod{n}$, then $\gcd(x - y, n)$ is a non-trivial factor of n.

The NFSM involves a rational factor base and an algebraic factor base. The rational factor base (RFB) consists of the first t_1 primes $p_1, p_2, \ldots, p_{t_1}$, where t_1 is chosen based on a bound B_{rat}. The algebraic factor base (AFB) consists of some primes of small norms in $\mathfrak{O}$. Application of the homomorphism ϕ lets us rewrite the AFB in terms of t_2 rational (integer) primes $p_1, p_2, \ldots, p_{t_2}$, where t_2 is chosen based on a bound B_{alg}.

Now, we describe the rational sieve and the algebraic sieve of the NFSM. Here, we deal with incomplete sieving, that is, higher powers of factor-base primes are not considered in sieving.

Let $T(a, b) = a + bm$. First, we calculate the values of $T(a, b)$ for all b in the range $1 \leqslant b \leqslant u$ and a in the range $-u \leqslant a \leqslant u$. Now, we try to find those (a, b) pairs with $\gcd(a, b) = 1$ and $b \not\equiv 0 \pmod{p}$, for which $T(a, b)$ is B_{rat}-smooth, that is, $T(a, b)$ factors completely into the primes $p_1, p_2, \ldots, p_{t_1}$. The determination whether a small prime p_i divides some $a + bm$ is equivalent to solving the linear congruence $a + bm \equiv 0 \pmod{p_i}$. The sieving bound u is determined based upon certain formulas which probabilistically guarantee that we can obtain the requisite number of relations from the entire sieving process.

We take a two-dimensional array A indexed by a and b. Initially, we store $\log |T(a, b)|$ in $A[a, b]$, truncated after three decimal places. We avoid floating-point operations by storing $\lfloor 1000 \log |T(a, b)| \rfloor$ in $A[a, b]$.

After this initialization, we try to find solutions of the congruence $T(a, b) \equiv 0 \pmod{p}$, where p is a small prime in RFB. For a fixed b, the solutions are $a \equiv -bm \pmod{p}$. Let γ be a solution of $T(a, b) \equiv 0 \pmod{p}$ for a particular b. Then, all the solutions of $T(a, b) \equiv 0 \pmod{p}$ for that b are $\gamma \pm kp$, $k \in \mathbb{N}$. Therefore, we subtract $\lfloor 1000 \log p \rfloor$ from all the array locations $A[a, b]$ such that $a = \gamma \pm kp$. We repeat this procedure for all small primes p in the RFB and for all allowed values of b. After this, the array locations storing $A[a, b] \approx 0$ correspond to the smooth values of $T(a, b)$. We apply trial division on these smooth values.

The algebraic sieve uses the norm function $N : \mathbb{Q}(\theta) \to \mathbb{Q}$. Its restriction to $\mathbb{Z}[\theta]$ yields norm values in $\mathbb{Z}$. For an element of the form $a + b\theta \in \mathbb{Z}[\theta]$, we have the explicit formula:

$$N(a + b\theta) = (-b)^d f(-a/b) = a^d - c_{d-1} a^{d-1} b + \cdots + (-1)^d c_0 b^d,$$

where $f(x) = x^d + c_{d-1} x^{d-1} + \cdots + c_0$.

An element $\alpha \in \mathbb{Z}[\theta]$ is smooth with respect to the small primes of $\mathfrak{O}$ if and only if $N(\alpha) \in \mathbb{Z}$ is B_{alg}-smooth. For each small prime p in the AFB, we compute the set of zeros of f modulo p, that is, all r values satisfying the congruence

$f(r) \equiv 0 \pmod{p}$. For a particular b with $b \not\equiv 0 \pmod{p}$ and $1 \leqslant b \leqslant u$, the norm values with $N(a + b\theta) \equiv 0 \pmod{p}$ correspond to the a values given by $a \equiv -br \pmod{p}$ for some root r of f modulo p. It follows that the same sieving technique as discussed for the rational sieve can be easily adapted to the case of the algebraic sieve.

An (a, b) pair for which both $a + bm$ and $a + b\theta$ are smooth gives us a relation. When sufficiently many relations are obtained from the two sieves, they are combined using linear algebra to get the set S of (a, b) pairs such that $\prod_{(a,b) \in S}(a + bm) = y^2$ and $\prod_{(a,b) \in S}(a + b\theta) = \alpha^2$.

3 Implementation Details

In this section, we describe our work on SIMD-based implementations of the sieving step of the MPQSM and that of the NFSM. We assume that the integer to be factored is odd (because powers of 2 can be easily factored out from an even integer). The largest integer factored using a general-purpose algorithm is RSA768 (768 bits, 232 decimal digits). It was factored by Kleinjung et al. on December 12, 2009 [16]. So, we consider integers having up to 250 decimal digits. We have implemented incomplete sieving for the NFSM. Here, we take $d = 3$ if the number of digits in n is less than 80, and $d = 5$ otherwise [3,17]. We have experimented with two integers n_1 (having 60 digits) and n_2 (having 120 digits), where

$$n_1 = 433351150461357208194113824776813009031297329880309298881453$$

is a product of two 30-digit primes, and

$$n_2 = 6337354302474689465336944839067992729056329122332339606907495845\backslash$$
$$279708185676334289089791539738517232800233047583258907971$$

is a product of two 60-digit primes. Such composite products are frequently used in RSA cryptosystems.

3.1 Sequential Implementation

The sequential implementation is rather straightforward for both the MPQSM and the NFSM.

MPQSM. We take a small prime p from the factor base. Let H be the small integer, up to which there exists a solution of Eqn (4) with $c \in [-M, M]$. For each such $h \in \{1, 2, \ldots, H\}$, we take the precomputed solutions, and for each such solution s, we sieve the array A, that is, subtract $\lfloor 1000 \log p \rfloor$ from the array locations c such that $c = s \pm kp^h$ for some k. We repeat this procedure for all primes in the factor base.

NFSM. We carry out the rational and the algebraic sieves independently on two two-dimensional arrays. The pairs (a, b) indicating smoothness in both the sieves are finally subjected to the test $\gcd(a, b) = 1$. If this gcd is one, then a relation is located. By varying the sieving bound u, we obtain different numbers of relations. We have not attempted to find a complete solvable system. But then, since different cores in one or multiple machine(s) can handle different sieving ranges, and our objective is to measure the benefits of SIMD parallelization, this is not an important issue.

3.2   SIMD-Based Implementation

In our SIMD-based implementations, we have effectively parallelized index calculations. We are provided with 128/256-bit SIMD registers. We want to do one vector addition for 32-bit operands (integers or floating-point numbers) on these registers. For this, two such SIMD registers are loaded with four (or eight) operands each (this is called packing). Then, a single SIMD addition instruction with these two registers as input operands is used to obtain four (or eight) sums in another SIMD register. The four (or eight) results are then extracted from this output register (this is known as unpacking). We carry out this SIMD-based implementation using SSE2 and AVX instruction sets. Notice that unpacking of the output register is necessary for obtaining the four (or eight) indices to subtract log values. However, it is not necessary to repack these indices so long as the sieving bound is not exceeded in these array indices. Unpacking does not destroy the content of an SIMD register, so we can reuse the packed output register as an input during the next parallel index increment.

Implementation on SSE2. While using the SSE2 instruction set, we use 128-bit registers.

MPQSM

- The Basic Idea: This method is similar to the sequential implementation. The major difference is that when we get four integer solutions s_i, we sieve four array locations simultaneously for these four solutions. The four s_i values need not correspond to the same p and/or the same h. However, the s_i values are taken as the minimum solutions in the range $[-M, M]$. We perform four $s_i + kp_i^{h_i}$ operations on 128-bit SIMD registers storing array indices (see Fig. 1), and subtract $\log p$ values from the corresponding array locations.
  A drawback of this method is that four p^h values may vary considerably. For each solution modulo p^h, we sieve at roughly $\lfloor (2M+1)/p^h \rfloor$ locations. If one $p_i^{h_i}$ is larger than other p^h values in a register, the number of iterations of data-parallel sieving is restricted by $\lfloor (2M+1)/p_i^{h_i} \rfloor$, leading to some loss of efficiency. Moreover, if the p^h values in a register are considerably different from one another, the spatial proximity of their sieving locations decreases, and this potentially increases the number of cache misses.

$$
\begin{bmatrix} s_1 \\ s_2 \\ s_3 \\ s_4 \end{bmatrix} + \begin{bmatrix} p_1^{h_1} \\ p_2^{h_2} \\ p_3^{h_3} \\ p_4^{h_4} \end{bmatrix} = \begin{bmatrix} s_1 + p_1^{h_1} \\ s_2 + p_2^{h_2} \\ s_3 + p_3^{h_3} \\ s_4 + p_4^{h_4} \end{bmatrix}, \quad \begin{bmatrix} s_1 + p_1^{h_1} \\ s_2 + p_2^{h_2} \\ s_3 + p_3^{h_3} \\ s_4 + p_4^{h_4} \end{bmatrix} + \begin{bmatrix} p_1^{h_1} \\ p_2^{h_2} \\ p_3^{h_3} \\ p_4^{h_4} \end{bmatrix} = \begin{bmatrix} s_1 + 2p_1^{h_1} \\ s_2 + 2p_2^{h_2} \\ s_3 + 2p_3^{h_3} \\ s_4 + 2p_4^{h_4} \end{bmatrix}, \quad \dots
$$

Fig. 1. Parallel index increments during sieving in the MPQSM

- Improvements: The above problems can be reduced to some extent using the following improvement techniques.
  - So far, we have fixed p (a small prime in the factor base) and varied h in the solutions of $T(c) \equiv 0 \pmod{p^h}$. The sieving locations corresponding to different values of h vary considerably. If, on the other hand, we fix h and allow p to vary, the variation in sieving locations is significantly reduced. In other words, we first consume the solutions of $T(c) \equiv 0 \pmod{p_i}$ for $i = 1, 2, 3, \dots, t$ in groups of four. Next, we process solutions of $T(c) \equiv 0 \pmod{p_i^2}$ for $i = 1, 2, 3, \dots, t$, again in groups of four, and so on. Now, the quantity $\lfloor (2M + 1)/p^h \rfloor$ is roughly of the same order for all of the four p^h values packed in a register. So, the number of iterations in the sieving loop is optimized. Moreover, the probability to hit the same cache line, while accessing locations in A, increases somewhat (particularly, for small values of p and h).
  - If $p^h \geqslant 2M + 1$ and $T(c) \equiv 0 \pmod{p^h}$ has a solution $s \in [-M, M]$, then this is the unique solution for c in the range $-M \leqslant c \leqslant M$. We carry out no index calculations $s + kp^h$, but substract $\log p$ only from $A[s]$.
  - If the overhead associated with packing and unpacking dominates over the benefits of parallelization itself, then data parallelization should be avoided. More precisely, for large values of p^h, we have a very few array locations to sieve, and obtaining these sieving locations using SIMD instructions is not advisable to avoid the packing and unpacking overheads. The threshold, up to which parallelizing solutions modulo p^h remains beneficial, depends on M and B, and is determined experimentally.
  - Usually, the congruence $T(c) \equiv 0 \pmod{p^h}$ has two solutions (for an odd prime p). In the rare case where there is a unique solution of this congruence, we perform sieving with respect to this solution sequentially. Indeed, even numbers of solutions are aligned in pairs in 4-segment SIMD registers. An odd number of solutions disturbs this alignment, making the implementation less efficient.

NFSM. Here we do not take into account the exponents h of the small primes in the factor bases. We process four integer solutions for four different p, and we sieve four array locations simultaneously for these four solutions. The initial solutions γ are chosen to be as small as possible in the range $[-u, u]$. We perform four $\gamma + kp$ operations on 128-bit SIMD registers storing array indices, and subtract $\log p$ values from the corresponding array locations. Fig. 2 demonstrates

$$
\begin{bmatrix} \gamma_1 \\ \gamma_2 \\ \gamma_3 \\ \gamma_4 \end{bmatrix} + \begin{bmatrix} p_1 \\ p_2 \\ p_3 \\ p_4 \end{bmatrix} = \begin{bmatrix} \gamma_1 + p_1 \\ \gamma_2 + p_2 \\ \gamma_3 + p_3 \\ \gamma_4 + p_4 \end{bmatrix}, \quad \begin{bmatrix} \gamma_1 + p_1 \\ \gamma_2 + p_2 \\ \gamma_3 + p_3 \\ \gamma_4 + p_4 \end{bmatrix} + \begin{bmatrix} p_1 \\ p_2 \\ p_3 \\ p_4 \end{bmatrix} = \begin{bmatrix} \gamma_1 + 2p_1 \\ \gamma_2 + 2p_2 \\ \gamma_3 + 2p_3 \\ \gamma_4 + 2p_4 \end{bmatrix}, \quad \cdots .
$$

Fig. 2. Parallel index increments during sieving in the NFSM

these parallel index calculations. We again emphasize that unpacking to obtain the individual array indices $\gamma_i + kp_i$ is needed. However, both the packed registers can be reused in all these SIMD additions so long as the primes p_i remain constant, and the array indices $\gamma_i + kp_i$ remain within the sieving bound u.

A similar procedure is followed for the algebraic sieve where solutions of four different (r, p) pairs are taken at a time.

Implementation on AVX. We follow the same basic idea in conjunction with the improvements discussed above. Sandy Bridge comes with 256-bit SIMD registers, using which we can perform vector operations on eight single-precision floating-point data at a time. The AVX instruction set does not support 256-bit vector integer operations. In order to exploit the power of 256-bit registers, we make floating-point index calculations. But then, we also need conversions between floating-point numbers and integers, since array indices must be integers.

Implementation Issues. Some points concerning our parallel implementations (SSE2 and AVX) are listed below.

- To utilize the SIMD registers properly, we break them into 32-bit segments, and vector operations on 32-bit integers and single-precision floating-point numbers are used such that four addition operations take place using a single instruction. We avoid 64-bit vector operations (only two operations at the cost of one instruction) because packing and unpacking overheads can outperform the gain from parallelization. Moreover, in typical factoring algorithms, array indices safely fit in 32-bit unsigned integer values.
- AVX does not provide instructions for 256-bit vector integer operations, so we transform 32-bit integers to 32-bit single-precision floating-point numbers, and conversely. The mantissa segment of 32-bit single-precision floating-point numbers is only 23 bits long (IEEE Floating-Point Standard). This restricts the choice of M, B, u, B_{rat}, and B_{alg}. For example, array indices can be as large as 2^{23} only. However, since this is already a value which is not too small, this restriction is not unreasonable. In fact, we work with these restrictions in our sequential and 128-bit SIMD implementations also. Indeed, only for very large-scale implementations, we need array indices larger than 2^{23}. Even then, this limitation is not a problem so long as each individual core handles a sieving range no larger than 2^{23}.

```
__m128i xmm_p = _mm_load_si128 (__m128i *P);
__m128i xmm_l = _mm_load_si128 (__m128i *L);
__m128i xmm_l = _mm_add_epi32 (__m128i xmm_l, __m128i xmm_p);
_mm_store_si128 (__m128i *L, __m128i xmm_l);
```

Fig. 3. SSE2 intrinsics used for index calculations

```
__m256 ymm_p = _mm256_load_ps (float *P);
__m256 ymm_l = _mm256_load_ps (float *L);
__m256 ymm_l = _mm256_add_ps (__m256 ymm_l, __m256 ymm_p);
_mm256_store_ps (float *L, __m256 ymm_l);
```

Fig. 4. AVX intrinsics used for index calculations

- Fig. 3 shows the SSE2 intrinsics used in our implementation.[1] The header file emmintrin.h contains the definition of the data type __m128i (representing 128-bit registers) and the declarations for the intrinsics _mm_load_si128, _mm_add_epi32 and _mm_store_si128. The registers xmm_p (for p^h or p values) and xmm_l (for s or γ values) are packed each with four contiguous 32-bit integers starting from the locations P and L, respectively, using _mm_load_si128. Then, they are added with a single vector instruction corresponding to _mm_add_epi32. Finally, the output SIMD register xmm_l is unpacked and its content is stored in the location L. However, unpacking is not destructive, that is, we can reuse this output register later, if required. Now, we subtract the log values from the array locations stored in L[0], L[1], L[2] and L[3]. To use the intrinsics _mm_load_si128 and _mm_store_si128, it is necessary that the addresses P and L are 16-byte aligned. If they are not, we have to use the more time-consuming intrinsics _mm_loadu_si128 and _mm_storeu_si128. Another important point is that the packing overhead is high if we attempt to pack from four non-contiguous locations using _mm_set_epi32 or similar intrinsics. So, we avoid them in our implementations.
- The intrinsics we employ in our implementation using AVX are shown in Fig. 4. The header file immintrin.h contains the definition of the data type __m256 (representing 256-bit registers) and the declarations for the intrinsics _mm256_load_ps, _mm256_add_ps and _mm256_store_ps. Two 256-bit SIMD registers (ymm_p and ymm_l) are packed each with eight contiguous 32-bit floating-point numbers starting from the locations P and L, respectively, using _mm256_load_ps. A single vector instruction corresponding to _mm256_add_ps is used to add them. The individual results in the output SIMD register ymm_l are then extracted in the location starting from the address L. Now, we need to convert the floating-point values L[0], L[1],

---

[1] Only the intrinsics are shown in the figure. The loop structure and other non-SIMD instructions are not shown. The first two intrinsics are used before the sieving loop, whereas the last two intrinsics are used in each iteration of the sieving loop.

`L[2]`, `L[3]`, `L[4]`, `L[5]`, `L[6]` and `L[7]` to integers to obtain the array locations for sieving. If the addresses P and L are not 32-byte aligned, we need to use the slower intrinsics `_mm256_loadu_ps` and `_mm256_storeu_ps`. We avoid using `_mm256_set_ps` or similar intrinsics which are used to pack eight floating-point numbers from arbitrary non-contiguous locations.

4 Experimental Results and Analysis

4.1 Experimental Setup

Version 4.6.3 of GCC supports SSE2 and AVX intrinsics. Our implementation platform is a 2.40GHz Intel Xeon machine (Sandy Bridge microarchitecture with CPU Number E5-2609). The GP/PARI calculator (Version 2.5.0) is used to calculate the log values of large integers, to find the zeros of f modulo p (for NFSM), and to validate the results. We use the optimization flag `-O3` with GCC for all sequential and parallel implementations. To avoid the AVX-SSE and SSE-AVX conversions, we use the flag `-mavx` in the AVX implementation. To handle large integers and operations on them, we use the GMP library (Version 5.0.5) [18].

4.2 Speeding Up Implementations of the MPQSM Sieve Using SSE2 and AVX

Timing and speedup figures for the implementations of the MPQSM sieve are summarized in Table 1. Timings are reported in milliseconds, and for each n, M, B values we have used in our experiments, we take the average of the times taken by fifty executions. We have incorporated all the improvement possibilities discussed in Section 3.2. The rows in the same cluster have the same values for M and B, but differ in the count of digits in the integer being factored.

From Table 1, we observe that the speedup is higher for smaller values of B, and increases when the sieving limit M increases. This is expected, since larger sieving bounds or smaller factor base bounds allow parallel index calculations to proceed for a larger number of iterations. On an average, speedup varies between 20–35%, except in the last two clusters where M and B are large. The speedup with AVX is below the expected result and it happens to be almost the same as that with SSE2, despite the use of 256-bit SIMD registers for AVX. The explanation is that, in the AVX implementation, we have to do a lot of conversions between integer and floating-point formats.

4.3 Speeding Up Implementations of the NFSM Sieve Using SSE2 and AVX

Timing and speedup figures for the implementations of the NFSM sieve (in case of n_1 and n_2) are summarized in Table 2 and Table 3, respectively. Timings are measured in milliseconds. For each data set, we record the average of the times

Table 1. Timing and speedup figures for the MPQSM sieve

Number of digits in n	Sieving limit M	Bound on small primes B	Sequential Time (in ms)	SSE2 Parallelization Time (in ms)	SSE2 Parallelization Speedup (in %)	AVX Parallelization Time (in ms)	AVX Parallelization Speedup (in %)
39	500000	46340	9.14	7.00	23.38	7.02	23.17
100	500000	46340	10.66	8.40	21.22	8.45	20.74
152	500000	46340	15.21	10.65	29.99	11.46	24.68
247	500000	46340	10.34	7.84	24.24	7.97	22.97
89	2000000	46340	69.37	49.54	28.59	49.86	28.12
187	2000000	46340	76.51	49.67	35.08	50.08	34.55
247	2000000	46340	85.59	56.19	34.35	58.31	31.88
93	5000000	46340	319.63	216.38	32.30	228.93	28.38
152	5000000	46340	398.74	260.60	34.64	262.27	34.22
241	5000000	46340	196.84	156.62	20.44	160.11	18.66
65	3000000	300000	120.36	92.22	23.38	94.57	21.43
158	3000000	300000	206.41	124.75	39.56	124.88	39.50
241	3000000	300000	115.81	91.59	20.91	92.35	20.26
100	5000000	463400	333.82	265.41	20.49	259.05	22.40
187	5000000	463400	258.99	193.09	25.45	194.93	24.74
241	5000000	463400	217.96	177.25	18.67	179.33	17.72
65	5000000	803400	231.10	187.93	18.68	189.14	18.16
158	5000000	803400	370.68	264.92	28.53	256.66	30.76
247	5000000	803400	295.03	253.97	13.92	256.43	13.08
65	4000000	4000000	211.23	183.36	13.19	192.86	8.70
187	4000000	4000000	248.04	207.85	16.21	208.36	16.00
251	4000000	4000000	260.76	211.87	18.75	212.01	18.70
65	5000000	5000000	274.38	242.38	11.66	244.66	10.83
158	5000000	5000000	370.98	312.51	15.76	312.53	15.76
241	5000000	5000000	256.53	238.41	7.06	240.24	6.35

Table 2. Timing and speedup figures for the NFSM sieve for n_1

	Sieving limit u	Bound on small primes B'	Sequential Time (in ms)	SSE2 Parallelization Time (in ms)	SSE2 Parallelization Speedup (in %)	AVX Parallelization Time (in ms)	AVX Parallelization Speedup (in %)
Rational Sieve	500000	50000	95.59	79.40	16.93	79.11	17.24
	3000000	50000	1677.30	1208.97	27.92	1206.97	28.04
	3000000	300000	1816.98	1358.18	25.25	1354.13	25.47
Algebraic Sieve	500000	50000	90.49	71.69	20.78	71.66	20.81
	3000000	50000	1564.31	1116.66	28.62	1118.55	28.50
	3000000	300000	1700.84	1266.34	25.55	1260.98	25.86

Table 3. Timing and speedup figures for the NFSM sieve for n_2

	Sieving limit u	Bound on small primes B'	Sequential Time (in ms)	SSE2 Parallelization		AVX Parallelization	
				Time (in ms)	Speedup (in %)	Time (in ms)	Speedup (in %)
Rational Sieve	600000	60000	126.32	100.02	20.82	101.59	19.58
	2000000	60000	970.24	607.13	37.42	605.07	37.64
	2000000	200000	993.67	666.97	32.88	663.11	33.27
Algebraic Sieve	600000	60000	111.50	83.10	25.47	83.52	25.10
	2000000	60000	866.23	523.22	39.60	527.01	39.16
	2000000	200000	912.86	581.89	36.26	579.06	36.57

taken over fifty executions. We take $B_{rat} = B_{alg} = B'$ as the bounds on the small primes in the two sieves. We document the results for $1 \leqslant b \leqslant 10$.

From Table 2 and Table 3, we make the following observations. On an average, we get a speedup between 15–40%. The speedup increases with the increase in the sieving limit u. The speedup is found to be somewhat higher for the algebraic sieve (compared to the rational sieve), although we cannot supply a justifiable explanation for this experimental observation.

5   Conclusion

In this work, we have implemented the sieving phase of the MPQSM and that of the NFSM efficiently, using SSE2 and AVX instruction sets. In general, we get a non-negligible performance gain over the sequential (non-SIMD) implementations. This work can be extended in many ways.

– So far, we have implemented only index calculations in a data-parallel fashion. Our efforts on data-parallelizing the subtraction operations have not produced any benefit. More investigation along this direction is called for. Unlike the index-calculation stage, the subtraction stage cannot reuse its output SIMD register.
– In case of the MPQSM, improving the performance of our SIMD-based implementations for large values of M and B deserves further attention.
– In case of the NFSM, the sieving we implemented here is called *line sieving*. A technique known as *lattice sieving* is proposed as an efficient alternative [10]. Data-parallel implementations of lattice sieving are worth studying.
– Our implementations of the MPQSM and NFSM sieves are not readily portable to polynomial sieves used in the computation of discrete logarithms over finite fields of small characteristics (for example, see [19,20]). Fresh experimentation is needed to investigate the effects of SIMD parallelization on polynomial sieves.

References

1. Pomerance, C.: The quadratic sieve factoring algorithm. In: Beth, T., Cot, N., Ingemarsson, I. (eds.) EUROCRYPT 1984. LNCS, vol. 209, pp. 169–182. Springer, Heidelberg (1985)
2. Dixon, B., Lenstra, A.K.: Factoring integers using SIMD sieves. In: Helleseth, T. (ed.) EUROCRYPT 1993. LNCS, vol. 765, pp. 28–39. Springer, Heidelberg (1994)
3. Bernstein, D.J., Lenstra, A.K.: A general number field sieve implementation. In: The Development of the Number Field Sieve. Lecture Notes in Mathematics, vol. 1554, pp. 103–126 (1993)
4. Dixon, J.D.: Asymptotically fast factorization of integers. Mathematics of Computation 36, 255–260 (1981)
5. Lehmer, D.H., Powers, R.E.: On factoring large numbers. Bulletin of the American Mathematical Society 37, 770–776 (1931)
6. Morrison, M.A., Brillhart, J.: A method of factoring and the factorization of F_7. Mathematics of Computation 29, 183–205 (1975)
7. Silverman, R.D.: The multiple polynomial quadratic sieve. Mathematics of Computation 48, 329–339 (1987)
8. Lenstra, A.K., Lenstra, H.W., Manasse, M.S., Pollard, J.M.: The number field sieve. In: STOC, pp. 564–572 (1990)
9. Buhler, J.P., Lenstra, H.W., Pomerance, C.: Factoring integers with the number field sieve. In: The Development of the Number Field Sieve. Lecture Notes in Mathematics, vol. 1554, pp. 50–94 (1993)
10. Pollard, J.M.: The lattice sieve. In: The Development of the Number Field Sieve. Lecture Notes in Mathematics, vol. 1554, pp. 43–49 (1993)
11. Coppersmith, D., Odlyzko, A.M., Schroeppel, R.: Discrete logarithms in $GF(p)$. Algorithmica 1(1), 1–15 (1986)
12. Lenstra, H.W.: Factoring integers with elliptic curves. Annals of Mathematics 126, 649–673 (1987)
13. Montgomery, P.L.: A block Lanczos algorithm for finding dependencies over $GF(2)$. In: Guillou, L.C., Quisquater, J.-J. (eds.) EUROCRYPT 1995. LNCS, vol. 921, pp. 106–120. Springer, Heidelberg (1995)
14. Microsoft Corporation: Streaming SIMD Extensions 2 Instructions: Microsoft Specific, http://msdn.microsoft.com/en-us/library/kcwz153av=vs.80.aspx
15. Intel Corporation: Intrinsics for Intel(R) Advanced Vector Extensions, http://software.intel.com/sites/products/documentation/hpc/composerxe/en-us/2011Update/cpp/lin/intref_cls/common/intref_bk_advectorext.htm
16. Kleinjung, T., et al.: Factorization of a 768-bit RSA modulus. In: Rabin, T. (ed.) CRYPTO 2010. LNCS, vol. 6223, pp. 333–350. Springer, Heidelberg (2010)
17. Briggs, M.E.: An introduction to the general number field sieve. Master's thesis, Virginia Polytechnic Institute and State University (1998)
18. Free Software Foundation: The GNU Multiple Precision Arithmetic Library, http://gmplib.org/
19. Adleman, L.M., Huang, M.D.A.: Function field sieve method for discrete logarithms over finite fields. Information and Computation 151(1-2), 5–16 (1999)
20. Gordon, D.M., McCurley, K.S.: Massively parallel computation of discrete logarithms. In: Brickell, E.F. (ed.) CRYPTO 1992. LNCS, vol. 740, pp. 312–323. Springer, Heidelberg (1993)

Strong Security and Privacy of RFID System for *Internet of Things* Infrastructure

Manik Lal Das

DA-IICT, Gandhinagar, India
maniklal_das@daiict.ac.in

Abstract. RFID (Radio Frequency IDentification) system has found enormous applications in retail, health care, transport, and home appliances. Over the years, many protocols have been proposed for RFID security using symmetric key and public key cryptography. Based on the nature of RFID tags' usage in various applications, existing RFID protocols primarily focus on tag identification or authentication property. *Internet of Things* (IoT) is emerging as a global network in which every object in physical world would be able to connect to web of world via Internet. As a result, IoT infrastructure requires integration of several complimentary technologies such as sensor networks, RFID system, embedded system, conventional desktop environment, mobile communications and so on. It is prudent that RFID system will play significant roles in IoT infrastructure. In that context, RFID system should support more security properties, such as mutual authentication, key establishment and data confidentiality for its wide-spread adoption in future Internet applications. In this paper, we present a strong security and privacy of RFID system for its suitability in IoT infrastructure. The proposed protocol provides following security goal:

- mutual authentication of tags and readers.
- authenticated key establishment between tag and reader.
- secure data exchange between tag-enabled object and reader-enabled things.

The protocol provides *narrow-strong* privacy and forward secrecy.

Keywords: Internet of Things, RFID security, identification, security, privacy, elliptic curves.

1 Introduction

Internet of Things (IoT) is envisioned as a general evolution of the Internet "from a network of interconnected entities to a network of interconnected objects" [1]. In IoT infrastructure, all physical objects (e.g. human, home appliances, vehicles, chemical reactors, consumer goods) would be able to interact to web of world with the help of software, hardware, and virtual entities through Internet, Bluetooth, and/or Satellite. A high-level view of IoT scenarios and applications is depicted in Figure 1. It is prudent that IoT infrastructure requires

B. Gierlichs, S. Guilley, and D. Mukhopadhyay (Eds.): SPACE 2013, LNCS 8204, pp. 56–69, 2013.
© Springer-Verlag Berlin Heidelberg 2013

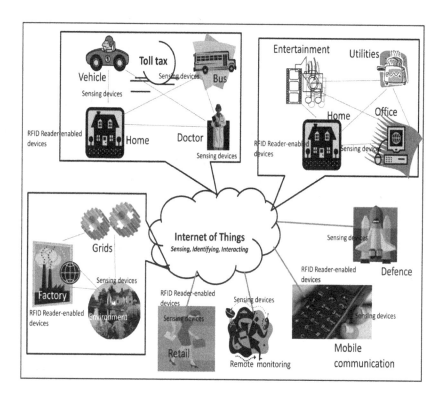

Fig. 1. *Internet of Things* scenarios and applications

integration several complimentary technologies such as sensor networks, RFID system, embedded system, conventional LAN setup with client-server environment, Grid system, cloud computing, mobile communications and so on. In order to address its core issues, IoT infrastructure should resolve some major challenges [2], as listed below.

- Standards: Standards and specifications by international forums are the foremost requirement in order to see IoT in its desired shape. Although European communities have been investing significant efforts towards IoT mission, a collective effort by IEEE, NIST, ITU, ISO/IEC, IETF could probably make this mission effective, implementable and deliverables.
- Identity management: While integrating trillions of objects in IoT infrastructure, managing identities would become a major task in IoT. Both addressing and uniqueness issues have to be resolved suitably. Some existing technologies such as smart cards, RFID tags [3], IPv6, are going to play important roles for identifying objects in IoT infrastructure.
- Privacy: One of the major challenges in global acceptance of IoT is the privacy of objects. The privacy issue involves object privacy, location privacy,

and human privacy. Indeed, object privacy and location privacy can link to human privacy.

- Security: In IoT, the primary means of communication is based on public channel like Internet. Therefore, IoT applications must be safeguarded from both passive and active attackers. In addition, IoT infrastructure needs substantial security measures for Intranet security, data security, system security, hardware security, and physical security.
- Trust and Ownership: IoT infrastructure should support interaction among hosts, intermediate systems and end-entity devices. As a result, trust relationship among entities is a key factor that should exist implicitly or explicitly. At the same time, data ownership is an important concern when one system relies on other system in order to serve some tasks.
- Integration: The main hurdle of IoT infrastructure is the integration of heterogeneous technologies and devices ranging from physical world to web of world. The factors that link to integration issue are computation, bandwidth, storage, interoperability and security.
- Scalability: IoT has a wider spectrum than the conventional Internet-based computing system. Therefore, basic functionalities like communication and service discovery need to function efficiently in both small scale and large-scale environments.
- Regulation: In order see IoT in its desired shape, regulatory issues are the key implementation issues for application and software that use public and/or proprietary technology. Every country has its own Information Technology Act and one could enforce certain regulatory norms before allowing a party to implement some application that has larger interest to its citizens. Roughly speaking, this is perhaps the most crucial and complex agenda in many countries in order to agree or disagree on IoT's adoption for future Internet applications.

RFID system will contribute significantly in IoT infrastructure. An RFID system consists of a set of tags, readers and a back-end server. A tag is basically a microchip with limited memory along with a transponder. Every tag has a unique identity, which is used for its identification purpose. A reader is a device used to interrogate RFID tags. The reader also consists of one or more transceivers which emit radio waves by which passive tags respond back to the reader. The back-end server is assumed to be a trusted server that maintains tags and readers information in its database. In IoT, RFID-enabled things require to talk to other things such as sensors, mobile devices and embedded systems through RFID reader-enabled capability (assume that other devices are RFID reader-enabled). As a result, security is an important concern when RFID-enabled things interact with other system (and vice-versa). In that context, in addition to identification of RFID tags, reader authentication, key establishment and data confidentiality are to be addressed suitably in RFID system for secure integration of them into IoT scenarios and applications.

In recent times, many security protocols have been proposed for RFID system; however, most of them discuss about tags identification and tracking issues

based on the nature of RFID applications. Feldhofer *et al* [4] proposed a protocol based on challenge-response mechanism using block cipher. A family of HB
protocols and improvements have been appeared in literature [5], [6], [7], [8].
Subsequently, many protocols using hash function or symmetric-key algorithm
have been proposed for RFID security [9], [10], [11], [12], each having specific
security and privacy properties. After Vaudenay's [13] remark on the privacy
notion of RFID system, public key cryptographic primitive, specifically elliptic
curve cryptography (ECC) [14], is being realized for RFID security [15], [16],[17],
[18], [19], [20], [21], [22], [23]. Recent progresses on RFID security are fast and we
refer interested readers to [24] for a comprehensive list of recent developments
in RFID security.

Our Contributions. RFID security in the context of IoT needs to evolve further
to support additional security properties such as mutual authentication, key
establishment and data confidentiality. However, the requirement of security
service(s) depends on applications where RFID system is going to act. In this
paper we present a protocol for RFID security using ECC in the context of IoT
scenarios and applications. The protocol aims to provide following security goals.

- mutual authentication of tags and readers.
- key establishment between tag and reader.
- secure data exchange between tag-enabled object and reader-enabled things.

The protocol provides *narrow-strong* privacy and forward secrecy.

Organization of the Paper. The remainder of the paper is organized as follows. In Section 2 we give some perspectives of IoT, RFID security and elliptic
curves arithmetic. In Section 3 we present our protocol. In Section 4 we analyze
the protocol. We conclude the paper in Section 5.

2   Preliminaries

In this section we briefly discuss some preliminaries of RFID security and privacy issues with a brief review of elliptic curves arithmetic and some standard
computational assumptions.

2.1   Security and Privacy Challenges in RFID System

An RFID system aims to achieve following attributes.
Security: Ensuring that fake tags are rejected.

- Identification: Identification of tags ensures its legitimacy to reader. Depending on application requirement, tags' identification or tag-reader mutual
identification is achieved in RFID system.
- Integrity: Integrity allows receiver to detect data tampering/alteration upon
receiving data from sender. As tag-reader communication takes place over
radio waves, RFID security protocol must ensure data integrity property.

Data confidentiality and Key establishment: Data confidentiality aims to prevent unauthorized data access. Data confidentiality under dynamic session key is a classic approach for its additional security measures like forward secrecy, data unlinkability. Even though these properties are not required in the present scenarios of RFID system, when we integrate RFID system in IoT then RFID system may demand session key establishment and data confidentiality for future Internet applications.

Privacy: Ensuring that legitimate tags are protected from compromising privacy.

RFID tags are small and thus, can be attached to consumer goods, library books, home appliances for identification and tracking purposes. In case of any misuse (e.g. stolen RFID-enabled items), the reader can trigger an appropriate message to seller/vendor/owner of the item. The privacy issue can be categorized into following:

- Object Privacy: The use of radio waves makes adversary's task easy for eavesdropping tag-reader communication and thereby, the information relating to the tag is an easy target to the adversary.
- Location Privacy: The tag of an object can be tracked or monitored wherever the object is lying, as the tag-embedded object carries information about the object, object owner, manufacturer, and so on.

In addition to above two privacy concerns, human privacy comes into picture in RFID system. On one hand, person who carries tag-enabled item will be tracked by the reader, which could compromise person's privacy. On the other hand, RFID tags' can trace tag-enabled criminals or suspicious objects in a controlled way, which could save money, national assets and human lives.

2.2   Elliptic Curves Arithmetic

An elliptic curve E over a field F is a cubic curve [14] with no repeated roots. The general form of an elliptic curve is $Y^2 + a_1 XY + a_3 Y = X^3 + a_2 X^2 + a_4 X + a_5$, where $a_i \in F$, $i = 1, 2, \cdots, 5$. The set $E(F)$ contains all points $P(x, y)$ on the curve, such that x, y are elements of F along with an additional point called the *point at infinity*$(\mathcal{O})$. The set $E(F)$ forms an abelian group under elliptic curve point addition operation with $\mathcal{O}$ as the additive identity. For all $P, Q \in E(F)$, let F_q be a finite field with order prime q. The number of points in the elliptic curve group $E(F_q)$, represented by $\#E(F_q)$, is called the *order of the curve* E over F_q. The order of a curve is determined by calculating $q + 1 - t$, where $|t| \leq \sqrt{q}$ is the trace of the Frobenius [14]. The order of a point $P \in E(F_q)$ is the smallest positive integer r, such that $rP = \mathcal{O}$. Without loss of generality, the elliptic curve equation can be simplified as $y^2 = x^3 + ax + b \pmod{q}$, where $a, b \in F_q$ satisfy $4a^3 + 27b^2 \neq 0$, if the characteristic of F_q is neither 2 nor 3. There are two operations on ECC, point addition and scalar multiplication of point, which are commonly used ECC-based security protocol.

Point Addition. The line joining of points P, Q intersects the curve at another point R. This is an interesting feature of ECC and one has to choose a suitable elliptic curve to obtain an elliptic curve group of order sufficiently large to accommodate cryptographic keys.

Scalar Multiplication of a Point. For a scalar n, multiplication of a curve point P by n is defined as n-fold addition of P, i.e., $nP = P + P + \cdots + P$ (n-times).

Map-to-Point: Map-to-Point is an algorithm for converting an arbitrary bit string into an elliptic curve point. Firstly, the string has to be converted into an integer and then a mapping is required from that integer onto an elliptic curve point. There are fast algorithms [14] for computation of scalar multiplication of point and map-to-point operation.

Computational Assumptions

Elliptic Curve Discrete Logarithm Problem (ECDLP). Elliptic Curve Discrete Logarithm Problem (ECDLP) is a standard assumption in which ECC-based cryptographic algorithm can rely upon. The ECDLP is stated as: given two elliptic curves points P and $Q(=xP)$, finding scalar x is an intractable problem with best known algorithms and available computational resources.

Decisional Diffie-Hellman (DDH) assumption: Let P be a generator of $E(F_q)$. Let $x, y, z \in_R Z_q$ and $A = xP$, $B = yP$. The DDH assumption states that: the distribution $< A, B, C(=xyP) >$ and $< A, B, C(=zP) >$ is computationally indistinguishable.

3   The Proposed Protocol

The protocol consists of two phases - (i) Setup phase and (ii) Authentication, Key establishment and Data confidentiality phase.

3.1   Setup Phase

System Setup: The system has three types of entities, namely, a back-end server, readers and tags. We assume that the back-end server is a trusted entity and connected to reader(s) securely. The back-end server chooses a suitable elliptic curve $E(F_q)$ over a finite field F_q where q is a prime number sufficiently large enough to accommodate cryptographic keys. Let $P \in E(F_q)$ be the generator of $E(F_q)$. We assume that the back-end server is configured with m number of tags and n number of readers. The parameters $E(F_q)$, q and P are made public.

SetupTag: For $i = 1, 2, \cdots, m$, the back-end server personalizes i^{th} tag with a private key x_i. The corresponding public key X_i $(=x_iP)$ is stored in tag and readers memory. We note that X_i provides identity information of the ith tag during tag-reader communication.

SetupReader: For $j = 1, 2, \cdots, n$, the back-end server personalizes j^{th} reader with a private key y_j. The corresponding public key Y_j ($=y_j P$) is stored in reader and tags memory.

3.2 Authentication, Key Establishment and Data Confidentiality Phase

This phase works as follows.

1. Tag chooses a random number $n_t \in_R Z_q$ and computes $N_t = n_t P$. Tag sends N_t to the reader.
2. Reader chooses a random $n_r \in_R Z_q$ and computes
   $$N_r = n_r P$$
   $$d = \text{xcord}[yN_t + n_r X]$$
   $$k = \text{xcord}[n_r N_t]$$
   $$C_r = PRF(d\|X\|Y\|N_t\|N_r\|k)$$
   Reader sends N_r, C_r to the tag. Here, $PRF()$ is a pseudo-random function that provides similar properties of a cryptographic hash function.
3. Upon receiving $< N_r, C_r >$, tag computes
   $$d = \text{xcord}[xN_r + n_t Y]$$
   $$k = \text{xcord}[n_t N_r]$$
   $$C_r' = PRF(d\|X\|Y\|N_t\|N_r\|k)$$
   then checks whether $C_r' = C_r$. If it holds, then reader's authentication is confirmed. Now, tag computes $C_t = PRF(k\|Y\|X\|N_r\|N_t\|d)$ and sends C_t to the reader.
4. Reader computes $C_t' = PRF(k\|Y\|X\|N_r\|N_t\|d)$ and checks whether $C_t' = C_t$. If it holds, then tag's authentication is confirmed.

The shared key $SK = PRF(X, k, Y)$ between tag and reader is established after successful authentication of each other. This shared key SK can be used for data confidentiality for that session. Once the session is expired, the ephemeral secrets n_r and n_t will be erased from the respective local system.

We note that in Step 2, reader uses tag's public key X to compute d. The information of tag's X needs to be provided along with the message in Step 1. This can be done in multiple ways. For example, a separate parameter $\alpha = n_t Y \oplus X \oplus Y$ can be communicated in the Step 1. The reader retrieves X by computing $\alpha \oplus Y \oplus yN_t$. Now, the reader checks its database for any entry of X. If so, the reader picks that X and proceeds further, else, rejects tag's request. Other possible solution could be of using a $PRF()$, secrets and nonce for generating a checksum for X in Step 1 that should convey the message to the reader for choosing the correct X for the communicating tag.

4 Security Analysis

Assumptions. Although, RFID system can have multiple readers, while analysing the protocol we simplify this by considering that the protocol has one reader and a set of tags $\mathcal{T} = \{T_1, T_2, \cdots, T_m\}$. Initially, $\mathcal{T}$ is empty, but tags are added as and when needed. The reader maintains a database of tuples $< ID_i, x_i, X_i >$, one for every tag $T_i \in \mathcal{T}$ with identity ID_i for $i = 1, 2, \cdots, m$. Every tag T_i maintains an internal state S_i.

Adversarial Model. We consider a *narrow-strong* adversary [13] for analyzing the privacy of our protocol. The adversary is capable of intercepting communication between tag and reader, and can inject data, alter content and delete data. The adversary has ability to use a virtual tag *vtag* in order to refer to a genuine tag that is in readers' vicinity. The adversary can invoke following oracles (the definition of the oracles is taken from [13], [25]).

$T_i \leftarrow$ CreateTag(ID): on input a tag ID, this oracle creates a tag with the given ID and corresponding secrets, and registers the new tag with the reader. A reference T_i to the new tag is returned.

$vtag \leftarrow$ DrawTag(T_i, T_j): on input a pair of tag references, this oracle generates a *vtag* and stores the tuple (*vtag*, T_i, T_j) in a table $\mathcal{L}$ in reader database. If the drawing tag reference is already in the table $\mathcal{L}$ then the oracle returns $\bot$; otherwise, it returns *vtag*.

Free($vtag_b$): on input *vtag*, this oracle retrieves the tuple (*vtag*, T_i, T_j) from the table $\mathcal{L}$. If $b = 0$, it resets the tag T_i. Otherwise, it resets the tag T_j. Then, it removes the entry (*vtag*, T_i, T_j) from $\mathcal{L}$. When a tag is reset, its volatile memory is erased. The non-volatile memory that contains the state **S** is preserved.

$C_t \leftarrow$ Launch: this oracle launches a new protocol run with the reader. It returns a session identifier *sid*, generated by the reader.

$\lambda' \leftarrow$ SendTag($\lambda, vtag_b$): on input *vtag*, this oracle retrieves the tuple (*vtag*, T_i, T_j) from the table $\mathcal{L}$ and sends the message λ to either T_i (if $b = 0$) or T_j (if $b = 1$). It returns λ'. If the above tuple is not found in $\mathcal{L}$, it returns $\bot$.

$\lambda' \leftarrow$ SendReader(λ, sid): on input λ and *sid*, this oracle sends the message λ to the reader in session *sid* and returns λ' from the reader.

Result(*sid*): on input *sid*, this oracle returns a bit indicating whether or not the reader accepted *sid* as a protocol run that resulted in successful authentication of the tag. If there exists no session with identifier *sid*, then $\bot$ is returned.

Corrupt(T_i): on input a tag reference T_i, this oracle returns the complete internal state S_i of T_i.

In our protocol, the adversary can execute all oracles except the Result oracle.

4.1 Privacy Experiment

The goal of the adversary in this experiment is to distinguish between two different tags. The experiment consists of a challenger $\mathcal{C}$ and an adversary $\mathcal{A}$. The adversary $\mathcal{A}$ controls the communication channel between the reader and every tag. The experiment is defined as follows.

$\quad$ Exp$^b_{\mathcal{S},\mathcal{A}}(k')$:
$\quad\quad$ 1. $b \in_R \{0, 1\}$
$\quad\quad$ 2. SetupReader(k')

3. $g \leftarrow \mathcal{A}^{Queries}(narrow\text{-}strong\ capability)$
4. Check whether $g = b$

The challenger $\mathcal{C}$ presents to $\mathcal{A}$ the system where either T_i (if $b = 0$) or T_j (if $b = 1$) are selected when returning a virtual tag reference through the DrawTag oracle. Here, k' is the security parameter.

The adversary $\mathcal{A}$ is allowed to query the oracles any number of times and then outputs a guess bit g. We say that $\mathcal{A}$ breaks the privacy of the protocol if and only if $g = b$, that is, if it correctly identifies which of the tags was active. The advantage of the adversary is defined as

$$\mathrm{Adv}_{\mathcal{A}}(k') = \Pr\left[\mathrm{Exp}^0_{\mathcal{S},\mathcal{A}}(k') = 1\right] + \Pr\left[\mathrm{Exp}^1_{\mathcal{S},\mathcal{A}}(k') = 1\right] - 1$$

Theorem 1. *The proposed protocol is narrow-strong private under the DDH assumption.*

Proof. Assume that an adversary $\mathcal{A}$ can break *narrow-strong* privacy of the protocol. That is, $\mathcal{A}$ is able to distinguish a tag from different instances of the protocol runs.

Setup phase:

- Personalize reader with its secret key y and public keys $(X_1, X_2, \cdots, X_m)$ of m tags.
- Personalize each tag with key x_i for $i = 1, 2, \cdots, m$ and with the public key Y of the reader.

Learning phase:
$\mathcal{A}$ calls following oracles in any order:

- SendReader oracle for q_r times (note that $\mathcal{A}$ can call this oracle any number of times, but for simplicity we assume that he calls it for q_r times). With these queries, $\mathcal{A}$ can gather (N_{r_i}, C_{r_i}) for $i = 1, 2, \cdots, q_r$.
- SendTag oracle, say for q_t times. With these queries, $\mathcal{A}$ can gather (N_{t_i}, C_{t_i}) for $i = 1, 2, \cdots, q_t$.
- Corrupt oracle for any $m - 2$ tags (except 2 tags). He then obtains the non-volatile memory state $\mathcal{S}$ of $m - 2$ tags. For simplicity, we assume that tags $T_3, T_4, \cdots, T_m$ are being compromised and tags T_1 and T_2 are not compromised. In other words, $\mathcal{A}$ has knowledge of $m - 2$ tags secrets $x_3, x_4, \cdots, x_m$, but no knowledge of x_1 and x_2.

Challenge phase:
- $\mathcal{A}$ selects two tags T_1 and T_2 on which he did not execute Corrupt oracles.
- $\mathcal{C}$ picks $b \in_R \{1, 2\}$ and submits following to the adversary $\mathcal{A}$:

$\mathrm{Exp}^b_{\mathcal{S},\mathcal{A}}(k')$:
    1. $n_b \in_R Z_q$
    2. $N_b, C_{b,real} \leftarrow$ SendTag$(\cdot, x_b)$
    3. $C_{b,real} \leftarrow$ SendTag$_{real}(\cdot, x_b)$
    4. Return $T_{b,real}$

$\mathrm{Exp}^b_{\mathcal{S},\mathcal{A}}(k')$:
    1. $n_b \in_R Z_q$
    2. $N_b, C_{b,random} \leftarrow$ SendTag$(\cdot, r)$
    3. $C_{b,random} \leftarrow$ SendTag$_{random}(\cdot, r)$
    4. Return $T_{b,random}$

Now, $\mathcal{A}$'s task is to guess whether $C_{b,r} \in \{T_1, T_2\}$, where $r \in \{real, random\}$.

$\mathcal{A}$ can use his database that he gathered in *Learning phase* to check whether $C_{b,real}$ and $C_{b,random}$ match to any records in his database. None of the record in $\mathcal{A}$'s database can find any mapping to $C_{b,real}$ or $T_{b,random}$, as $\mathcal{A}$'s database contains all T_i for tags $i = 3, 4, \cdots, m$ which are created by the corresponding tags' secret key x_i.

If $\mathcal{A}$ can distinguish $C_{b,real}$ and $C_{b,random}$ then he can break the privacy of the protocol. Firstly, it is computationally infeasible for $\mathcal{A}$ to find any clue of n_b from N_b (as $N_b = n_b P$). Secondly, $C_{b,real}$ is an authentication code, computed by a cryptographically secure pseudo-random function with secret parameters of the reader and a transient secret n_b. Without knowing x_b, it is computationally infeasible to guess (with probability not significantly $> \frac{1}{2}$) whether $C_{b,r}$ belongs to T_1 or T_2. As a result, if $\mathcal{A}$ aims to distinguish $C_{b,real}$ and $C_{b,random}$, then he has to first obtain the pre-image of $PRF()$ and then solve the ECDLP, which are infeasible problems. Therefore, $\mathcal{A}$ cannot break the privacy of the protocol. In other words, the advantage $\mathtt{Adv}_{\mathcal{A}}(k')$ of the privacy experiment that $\mathcal{A}$ can have is negligible in k'.   □

4.2   Security Experiment

Assume that the adversary $\mathcal{A}$ can convince the reader to accept a fake tag. In order to convince the reader, $\mathcal{A}$ requires to compute a valid authentication code on a target tag (say, T_{target}). Note that T_{target} has not participated in SendTag and Corrupt oracles. Without these two queries, $\mathcal{A}$ cannot have x_{target}. As a result, he cannot compute d_{target} and k_{target}.

Theorem 2: *The protocol is secure if for any adversary, the advantage that the adversary guesses a session key is negligible in security parameter k'.*

Proof: Suppose that the adversary $\mathcal{A}$ can successfully guess a session key with a non-negligible advantage ξ. Let $\mathcal{D}$ be a distinguisher who can distinguish the distribution spaces Q_R and Q_S, where Q_R is a set of random numbers and Q_S is a set of real session keys. Suppose that $\mathcal{D}$ acts as the adversary while making the target-session query[1] interacting with reader and tag. At the start of the experiment, $\mathcal{D}$ is given $SK \in \{$reader, tag, $r\}$. Here, r is a random number or a session key, each with probability $\frac{1}{2}$. $\mathcal{D}$'s goal is to predict if SK is the real session key between reader and tag with non-negligible advantage in security parameter k'. That is, $\mathcal{D}$ outputs 0 if it says $SK \in Q_R$ and 1 if $SK \in Q_S$. The experiment works as follows.

1) assume that $\mathcal{D}$ has gathered l numbers of the real session keys SK_i between reader and tag for $i = 1, 2, \cdots, l$.
2) $\mathcal{D}$ chooses a target session and invokes $\mathcal{A}$ (who can win the target-session query with non-negligible probability ξ) to interact with tag and reader during the target session.

---

[1] Target-session query: Target-session query is pertaining to any unexpired session and unexposed session. A session is termed exposed if either the local state of the tag or the session key of a session is known or the tag is corrupt.

3) $\mathcal{D}$ acts as a simulator for $\mathcal{A}$ and does following:

- $\mathcal{A}$ activates the session i. Then $\mathcal{D}$ sends the message (N_r, C_r) to the tag, acting as the reader. Upon receiving (N_r, C_r) tag responds with (N_t, C_t). Now $\mathcal{D}$ sends (N_t, C_t) to reader pretending as the tag.
- Whenever $\mathcal{A}$ issues Corrupt query on tags (except the tag which participates in the target-session query), $\mathcal{D}$ learns the corresponding private-public keys (x_i, X_i) along with the state S_i.
- If $\mathcal{A}$ issues a target-session query on T_{target} then $\mathcal{D}$ obtains the local secrets from the reader and computes $SK = n_r N_{target}$. Now, $\mathcal{D}$ gives SK to $\mathcal{A}$ as a challenge. Then, $\mathcal{D}$ outputs whatever $\mathcal{A}$ outputs and halts.
- If $\mathcal{A}$ chooses any other session as the target-session, $\mathcal{D}$ outputs random SK and halts.

Now $\mathcal{A}$ tries to guess SK whether $SK \in \{Q_S, Q_R\}$. If $SK \in Q_S$, then SK has the same property as that of the real session key. Otherwise, SK has the property of a random key. As per our assumption, $\mathcal{A}$ can output his guess with probability $\frac{1}{2} + \xi$, where ξ is non-negligible in k'.

When $\mathcal{A}$ picks i as its target-session, $\mathcal{D}$ outputs the same output as that of $\mathcal{A}$. Therefore, $\mathcal{D}$ wins with the probability $\frac{1}{2} + \xi$. Otherwise, $\mathcal{D}$ outputs a random guess with probability $\frac{1}{2}$. But, the case of $\mathcal{A}$ choosing i as its target-session occurs with a probability of $\frac{1}{l}$. Therefore, total probability of $\mathcal{D}$ wins the experiment is $(\frac{1}{l}(\frac{1}{2} + \xi) + (1 - \frac{1}{l})\frac{1}{2}) = (\frac{1}{2} + \frac{\xi}{l})$. As l is a large number, $\frac{\xi}{l}$ is negligible in k'. As a result, $\mathcal{D}$'s advantage to win the experiment is negligible in k'. Therefore, the adversary cannot guess a session key with non-negligible probability in k'. $\square$

Theorem 3. *The proposed protocol provides strong security, as no polynomial-time adversary can distinguish corrupt and uncorrupt tags with non-negligible advantage in security parameter k'.*

Proof. Suppose that the adversary has invoked Corrupt oracle on the target tag, say T_c. He then knows x_c and Y. Assume that the adversary can track T_c whenever T_c communicates to reader further. This implies that the adversary can distinguish T_c and any uncorrupt tags.

When the corrupt tag T_c communicates to the reader in a new session, the adversary can intercept parameters (N_t, N_r, C_r), where $N_t = n_t P$, $N_r = n_r P$ and $C_r = PRF(d\|X\|Y\|N_t\|N_r\|k)$. In order to check whether C_r belongs to X, the adversary has to calculate d and k from x_c, Y, and session specific parameters. However, d and k require the ephemeral secret n_t *(resp. n_r)* for the current session, which he cannot guess with non-negligible probability in security parameter k'. Furthermore, guessing n_t from N_t *(resp. n_r from N_r)* is basically solving the ECDLP, which he cannot solve. As a result, the adversary cannot compute d and k to link C_r to T_c that he has got from the reader. In other words, every C_r from reader looks a random string which the adversary cannot distinguish with the captured C_r from previous runs of the protocol using the same tag. $\square$

Forward Secrecy. The proposed protocol provides forward secrecy. If the adversary gets hold of the private keys of tag and reader, he cannot learn any previous session keys, because the session key $SK = PRF(X\|k\|Y)$, where $k = \text{xcord}[n_t n_r P]$, involves the ephemeral secrets n_t and n_r chosen by tag and reader, respectively. The ephemeral secrets are erased from the local state of tag and reader once the session is expired. Furthermore, the adversary cannot guess n_t from n_T (resp. n_r from N_r), as it relies on ECDLP. As a result, even though the adversary knows the private key x_t of tag and/or x_r of reader, he cannot compute k of previous session without having the corresponding n_t or n_r, and thereby, he cannot compute any previous session keys. Therefore, the protocol provides *forward secrecy*.

4.3   Efficiency

There are many authentication protocols for RFID system based on elliptic curves arithmetic. Bringer *et al* [19] proposed a randomized RFID protocol, which is based on the Schnorr's identification protocol [26]. Subsequently, several protocols [17], [15], [23] have been proposed based on the Schnorr's identification protocol. However, most of them suffer from tracking attacks [20], [22]. The main reason behind the tracking attacks is that their protocol's security strength did reduce to Schnorr's identification protocol, but they failed to support claimed privacy preserving. An adversary can intercept some previous messages and then would be able to link to a tag by manipulating intercepted messages. As far as efficiency is concerned, communication and storage cost of our protocol is as efficient as [19], [17], [15], [23]. Our protocol takes little more computation cost than [19], [17], [15], [23]. However, the protocols [19], [17], [15], [23] failed to support strong security and privacy which are important concerns in RFID system. Whereas, our protocol supports strong privacy and security.

5   Conclusions

Internet of Things (IoT) is projecting as a global network that could connect every object around us. RFID system is one of the core components in IoT infrastructure. In order to make secure communication in several complementary technologies in IoT infrastructure, integration of RFID system in IoT infrastructure requires strong security and privacy notion. We proposed a protocol for RFID security and privacy in the context of IoT scenarios and applications. The proposed protocol provides mutual authentication, key establishment and data confidentiality. While writing this paper, RFID system needs only authentication property, but key establishment and data confidentiality are additional security properties provided by the protocol for their usage in future Internet applications. We have showed that the proposed protocol is secure and provides *narrow-strong* privacy.

Acknowledgement. This work was supported in part by Department of Science and Technology, Ministry of Science & Technology, Government of India through DST/INT/SPAIN/P-6/2009 Indo-Spanish Joint Programme of Cooperation in Science and Technology.

References

1. European Commission: Internet of Things – An action plan for Europe,
   `http://eur-lex.europa.eu/LexUriServ/`
   `LexUriServ.do?uri=COM:2009:0278:FIN:EN:PDF`
2. Roman, R., Najera, P., Lopez, J.: Securing the Internet of Things. IEEE Computer 44(9), 51–58 (2011)
3. ISO/IEC 14443-2:2001. Identification cards – Contactless integrated circuit(s) cards – Proximity cards – Part 2: Radio frequency power and signal interface
4. Feldhofer, M., Dominikus, S., Wolkerstorfer, J.: Strong Authentication for RFID Systems using the AES Algorithm. In: Joye, M., Quisquater, J.-J. (eds.) CHES 2004. LNCS, vol. 3156, pp. 357–370. Springer, Heidelberg (2004)
5. Hopper, N., Blum, M.: Secure Human Identification Protocols. In: Boyd, C. (ed.) ASIACRYPT 2001. LNCS, vol. 2248, pp. 52–66. Springer, Heidelberg (2001)
6. Juels, A., Weis, S.A.: Authenticating Pervasive Devices with Human Protocols. In: Shoup, V. (ed.) CRYPTO 2005. LNCS, vol. 3621, pp. 293–308. Springer, Heidelberg (2005)
7. Gilbert, H., Robshaw, M., Sibert, H.: An Active Attack Against HB+ - a Provably Secure Lightweight Authentication Protocol. IET Electronic Letters 41(21), 1169–1170 (2005)
8. Bringer, J., Chabanne, H., Dottax, E.: HB++: a Lightweight Authentication Protocol Secure against Some Attacks. In: proceedings of Security, Privacy and Trust in Pervasive and Ubiquitous Computing, pp. 28–33 (2006)
9. Avoine, G., Oechslin, P.: RFID Traceability: A Multilayer Problem. In: S. Patrick, A., Yung, M. (eds.) FC 2005. LNCS, vol. 3570, pp. 125–140. Springer, Heidelberg (2005)
10. Peris-Lopez, P., Hernandez-Castro, J.C., Estevez-Tapiador, J.M., Ribagorda, A.: An Efficient Authentication Protocol for RFID Systems Resistant to Active Attacks. In: Denko, M.K., et al. (eds.) EUC-WS 2007. LNCS, vol. 4809, pp. 781–794. Springer, Heidelberg (2007)
11. Peris-Lopez, P., Hernandez-Castro, J.C., Tapiador, J.M.E., Li, T., van der Lubbe, J.C.A.: Weaknesses in Two Recent Lightweight RFID Authentication Protocols. In: Bao, F., Yung, M., Lin, D., Jing, J. (eds.) Inscrypt 2009. LNCS, vol. 6151, pp. 383–392. Springer, Heidelberg (2010)
12. Hernandez-Castro, J.C., Peris-Lopez, P., Phan, R.C.-W., Tapiador, J.M.E.: Cryptanalysis of the David-Prasad RFID Ultralightweight Authentication Protocol. In: Ors Yalcin, S.B. (ed.) RFIDSec 2010. LNCS, vol. 6370, pp. 22–34. Springer, Heidelberg (2010)
13. Vaudenay, S.: On privacy models for RFID. In: Kurosawa, K. (ed.) ASIACRYPT 2007. LNCS, vol. 4833, pp. 68–87. Springer, Heidelberg (2007)
14. Hankerson, D., Menezes, A., Vanstone, S.: Guide to Elliptic Curve Cryptography. Springer (2004)
15. Lee, Y.K., Batina, L., Verbauwhede, I.: Untraceable RFID Authentication Protocols: Revision of EC-RAC. In: Proceedings of the IEEE International Conference on RFID, pp. 178–185 (2009)
16. Hein, D., Wolkerstorfer, J., Felber, N.: ECC Is Ready for RFID – A Proof in Silicon. In: Avanzi, R.M., Keliher, L., Sica, F. (eds.) SAC 2008. LNCS, vol. 5381, pp. 401–413. Springer, Heidelberg (2009)
17. Lee, Y.K., Sakiyama, K., Batina, L., Verbauwhede, I.: Elliptic Curve Based Security Processor for RFID. IEEE Transactions on Computer 57(11), 1514–1527 (2008)

18. Oren, Y., Feldhofer, M.: A Low-resource Public-key Identification Scheme for RFID Tags and Sensor Nodes. In: Proceedings of the ACM Conference on Wireless Network Security, pp. 59–68 (2009)
19. Bringer, J., Chabanne, H., Icart, T.: Cryptanalysis of EC-RAC, a RFID Identification Protocol. In: Franklin, M.K., Hui, L.C.K., Wong, D.S. (eds.) CANS 2008. LNCS, vol. 5339, pp. 149–161. Springer, Heidelberg (2008)
20. Deursen, T., Radomirovic, S.: Attacks on RFID Protocols. Cryptology ePrint Archive: listing for 2008(2008/310) (2008)
21. van Deursen, T., Radomirović, S.: EC-RAC: Enriching a Capacious RFID Attack Collection. In: Ors Yalcin, S.B. (ed.) RFIDSec 2010. LNCS, vol. 6370, pp. 75–90. Springer, Heidelberg (2010)
22. Fan, J., Hermans, J., Vercauteren, F.: On the Claimed Privacy of EC-RAC III. In: Ors Yalcin, S.B. (ed.) RFIDSec 2010. LNCS, vol. 6370, pp. 66–74. Springer, Heidelberg (2010)
23. Lee, Y.K., Batina, L., Singelee, D., Verbauwhede, I.: Low-Cost Untraceable Authentication Protocols for RFID (extended version). In: Proceedings of the ACM Conference on Wireless Network Security (WiSec), pp. 55–64 (2010)
24. RFID Security & Privacy Lounge, `http://www.avoine.net/rfid/`
25. Hermans, J., Pashalidis, A., Vercauteren, F., Preneel, B.: A new RFID privacy model. In: Atluri, V., Diaz, C. (eds.) ESORICS 2011. LNCS, vol. 6879, pp. 568–587. Springer, Heidelberg (2011)
26. Schnorr, C.P.: Efficient identification and signatures for smart cards. In: Brassard, G. (ed.) CRYPTO 1989. LNCS, vol. 435, pp. 239–252. Springer, Heidelberg (1990)

Correlation-Immune Boolean Functions for Leakage Squeezing and Rotating S-Box Masking against Side Channel Attacks

Claude Carlet

LAGA, Universities of Paris 8 and Paris 13; CNRS, UMR 7539;
Department of Mathematics,University of Paris 8, 2 rue de la liberté
93526 Saint-Denis cedex 02, France
claude.carlet@univ-paris8.fr

Boolean functions, from $\mathbb{F}_{2^n}$ to $\mathbb{F}_2$, have been playing an important role in stream ciphers, because they can be used in their pseudo-random generators to combine the outputs to several LFSR (in the so-called combiner model). Recall that the keystream (which is bitwise added to the plaintext for producing the ciphertext) is in such framework the sequence output by the function during a sufficient number of clock-cycles. The combiner Boolean function must then be balanced, that is, have uniform output distribution, for avoiding some straightforward distinguishing attack; and it should be *correlation-immune* of highest possible order.

An n-variable Boolean function $f(x_1, \ldots, x_n)$ is correlation-immune of some order $m < n$ (in brief, m-CI) if fixing at most m of the n input variables $x_1, \ldots, x_n$ does not change the output distribution of the function, whatever are the positions chosen for the fixed variables and the values chosen for them (a balanced m-CI function is called m-resilient). Such m-th order correlation immunity allows resisting the Siegenthaler attack [15] at the order m, which is a divide and conquer cryptanalysis using the existence of a correlation between the output to the function and m input bits $x_{i_1}, \ldots, x_{i_m}$, to make an exhaustive search of the initialization of the LFSRs of indices $i_1, \ldots, i_m$ (given a sub-sequence of the keystream), without needing to know the initialization of the other LFSRs. The initialization of these other LFSRs can subsequently be recovered by diverse methods, allowing rebuilding the whole keystream. Of course, a correlation attack at the order $m + 1$ is possible if the function is not $(m + 1)$-CI, but the attacker needs then to know a longer part of the keystream for recovering the initialization of $m + 1$ LFSR in order to rebuild the rest of the keystream. The function must also have large algebraic degree for allowing resistance to the Berlekamp-Massey attack [12] and lie at large Hamming distance from affine functions, that is, have large nonlinearity, for allowing resistance to the fast correlation attack [13] and its variants.

These constraints were roughly the only ones needed on the combiner function at the end of the last century (recall that all that can be done for asserting the security of a stream cipher is to ensure that it resists all the known attacks and has enough randomness for hoping resisting future attacks; indeed, no attempt has been successful for building an efficient stream cipher whose security

B. Gierlichs, S. Guilley, and D. Mukhopadhyay (Eds.): SPACE 2013, LNCS 8204, pp. 70–74, 2013.
© Springer-Verlag Berlin Heidelberg 2013

could be proved like for block ciphers). Since the beginning of this century, a series of cryptanalyses called algebraic attacks has been discovered: the standard algebraic attack [9], the fast algebraic attack [8] and the Rønjom-Helleseth attack [14] (see a survey in [2] recalling the corresponding constraints on Boolean functions). No construction of infinite classes of resilient functions allowing resistance to all attacks on the combiner model is known yet, even when the notion of correlation-immunity is weakened as proposed in [7]. The study of CI functions has become then (maybe temporarily) more theoretical than really practical, from cryptographic viewpoint.

A new role in cryptography for correlation-immune functions, which renews their interest in cryptography, has appeared very recently in the framework of *side channel attacks* (in brief, SCA).

The implementation of cryptographic algorithms over devices like smart cards, FPGA, ASIC, leaks information on the secret data, leading to very efficient SCA. These attacks allow recovering the key from few plaintext-ciphertext pairs in a few seconds if no counter-measure is included in the algorithm and/or the device. Recall that for being considered robust, a cryptosystem should not be cryptanalysed by an attack needing less than 2^{80} elementary operations (which represent thousands of centuries of computation with a modern computer) and less than billions of plaintext-ciphertext pairs. This high level of security is achievable when the attacker has no information on the data processed by the algorithm when the cryptosystem is run. This model of attack is called the *black box* cryptanalysis model. In practice, as soon as the cryptosystem runs over some device, some information on this data leaks through electromagnetic waves or power consumption; a more appropriate model is then that of *grey box* cryptanalysis, in which the attacker does not have access to the exact data processed by the device (this would correspond to a white box model) but to a partial information on this data, which can be for instance a noisy version of the Hamming weight of some *sensitive variable* depending on a few bits of the secret key. He can then measure the leakage during a series of implementations with the same key and different plaintexts, and apply statistical methods to determine the most probable values of these few bits. This is particularly problematic when the cipher is implemented in smart cards or in hardware. And it is particularly true for iterative ciphers like block ciphers since it is then possible to attack the first round, when the diffusion is not yet optimal.

Fortunately, counter-measures exist, but they are costly in terms of running time (more in software applications), of implementation area (in hardware applications) and program executable file size (in software), all the more if they need to resist higher order side channel attacks (the d-th order attack computes the variance of the d-th power of the leakage for determining the most probable value of the sensitive variable; the complexity of the attack is exponential in the order). In fact, the cost overhead is then too high for real-world products.

The most commonly used counter-measure is a secret-sharing method called *masking*. It is efficient both for implementations in smart cards (which are software implementations including a part of hardware) and FPGA or ASIC (hardware implementation). The principle of masking is to replace every sensitive variable Z by a number of *shares* $M_0, \ldots, M_d$ such that the knowledge of some of them, but not all, gives no information on the value of Z, and the knowledge of all of them allows recovering this value. In other words, Z is a deterministic function of all the M_i, but is independent of $(M_i)_{i \in I}$ if $|I| \leqslant d$. The simplest way of achieving this is to draw $M_1, \ldots, M_d$ at random (they are then called *masks*) and to take M_0 such that $M_0 + \cdots + M_d$ equals the sensitive variable, where $+$ is a relevant group operation (in practice, the bitwise XOR). This counter-measure allows resisting the SCA of order d.

Correlation immune functions allow reducing, at least in two possible ways, the overhead of masking while keeping the same resistance to d-th order SCA, when the leak is simply (a noisy version of) a linear combination over the reals of the bits of the sensitive variable (such asumption is quite realistic in general):

- by applying a method called *leakage squeezing*, which allows achieving with one single mask the same protection as with d ones, with d strictly larger than 1. This method has been introduced in [11] and further studied in [10]; it has been later generalized in [3] to several masks. In its original single-mask version, it uses a bijective vectorial function F; the mask M_1 is not processed as is in the device, but in the form of $F(M_1)$. The condition for achieving resistance to d-th order SCA is that the graph indicator of F, that is, the $2n$-variable Boolean function whose support equals the graph $\{(x, y)/y = F(x)\}$ of F, is d-CI. Such graph is a *complementary information set* code (CIS code for short), in the sense that it admits (at least) two information sets which are complement of each other. The condition that the indicator of this CIS code is m-CI is equivalent to saying that the dual distance of this code is at least $d + 1$.
- an alternative way of resisting higher order SCA with one single mask consists in avoiding processing the mask M_1 at all: for every sensitive variable Z which is the input to some box S in the block cipher, Z is replaced by $Z + M_1$ where M_1 is drawn at random, and $Z + M_1$ is the input to a "masked" box S_{M_1} whose output is $S(Z)$ (or more precisely, is a masked value of $S(Z)$, since the process of masking must continue during the whole implementation). This method, called *Rotating Sbox Masking* (RSM), obliges, for each box S in the cipher, to implement a look-up table for each masked box S_{M_1} (in fact, this is costly in practice only for nonlinear boxes). To reduce the corresponding cost, M_1 is not drawn at random in the whole set of binary vectors of the same length as Z, but in a smaller set of such vectors. The condition for achieving resistance to d-th order SCA is that the indicator of this set is a d-CI function. Of course, given d, we wish to choose this non-zero d-CI function with lowest possible weight, since the size of the overhead due to the masked look-up tables is proportional to the Hamming weight of this d-CI function (note however that if the cipher is made like the AES, with identical substitution boxes up to affine equivalence, the substitution layer can be slightly modified so as to be masked at no extra cost: the affine equivalent boxes are replaced by masked versions of a same box). Moreover, with

RSM, some keys are indistinguishable; specifically, the attacker recovers the affine space equal to the set of null linear structures of the indicator of the masks, translated by the correct key. This means that an exhaustive search is required to finish the side-channel analysis [6].

In both cases, this needs to use correlation-immune functions of low weights (with a particular shape in the case of leakage squeezing since the function must then be the indicator of the graph of a permutation). Most of the numerous studies made until now on CI functions dealt with resilient functions, and it happens that the known constructions of resilient functions do not work for constructing low weight CI functions. We shall review what is known on CI functions in this framework and on CIS codes, basing us on the survey work [1] on minimal weight CI functions in at most 13 variables and on the papers on CIS codes [5,4]; we shall investigate constructions.

Acknowledgement. All the work on counter-measures to side channel attacks has been made in collaboration with Sylvain Guilley. I take this opportunity to thank him deeply for our exciting collaboration.

References

1. Bhasin, S., Carlet, C., Guilley, S.: Theory of masking with codewords in hardware: low weight d-th order correlation-immune functions. IACR ePrint Archive 303 (2013)
2. Carlet, C.: Boolean functions for cryptography and error-correcting codes, in Boolean Models and Methods in Mathematics, Computer Science, and Engineering, ser. In: Crama, Y., Hammer, P.L. (eds.) Encyclopedia of Mathematics and its Applications, ch. 8, vol.134, pp. 257–397. Cambridge University Press, Cambridge (2010), http://www.math.univ-paris13.fr/carlet/pubs.html
3. Carlet, C., Danger, J.-L., Guilley, S., Maghrebi, H.: Leakage Squeezing of Order Two. In: Galbraith, S., Nandi, M. (eds.) INDOCRYPT 2012. LNCS, vol. 7668, pp. 120–139. Springer, Heidelberg (2012)
4. Carlet, C., Freibert, F., Guilley, S., Kiermaier, M., Kim, J.-L., Solé, P.: Higher-order CIS codes. IEEE Transactions on Information Theory (Submitted 2013)
5. Carlet, C., Gaborit, P., Kim, J.-L., Solé, P.: A new class of codes for Boolean masking of cryptographic computations. IEEE Transactions on Information Theory 58(9), 6000–6011 (2012)
6. Carlet, C., Guilley, S.: Side-channel indistinguishability. In: Proceedings of HASP 2013, 2nd International Workshop on Hardware and Architectural Support for Security and Privacy, Tel Aviv, Israel, pp. 9:1-9:8. ACM, New York (June 2013)
7. Carlet, C., Guillot, P., Mesnager, S.: On immunity profile of Boolean functions. In: Gong, G., Helleseth, T., Song, H.-Y., Yang, K. (eds.) SETA 2006. LNCS, vol. 4086, pp. 364–375. Springer, Heidelberg (2006)
8. Courtois, N.T.: Fast Algebraic Attacks on Stream Ciphers with Linear Feedback. In: Boneh, D. (ed.) CRYPTO 2003. LNCS, vol. 2729, pp. 176–194. Springer, Heidelberg (2003)
9. Courtois, N., Meier, W.: Algebraic Attacks on Stream Ciphers with Linear Feedback. In: Biham, E. (ed.) EUROCRYPT 2003. LNCS, vol. 2656, pp. 346–359. Springer, Heidelberg (2003)

10. Maghrebi, H., Carlet, C., Guilley, S., Danger, J.-L.: Optimal first-order masking with linear and non-linear bijections. In: Mitrokotsa, A., Vaudenay, S. (eds.) AFRICACRYPT 2012. LNCS, vol. 7374, pp. 360–377. Springer, Heidelberg (2012)
11. Maghrebi, H., Guilley, S., Danger, J.-L.: Leakage Squeezing Countermeasure against High-Order Attacks. In: Ardagna, C.A., Zhou, J. (eds.) WISTP 2011. LNCS, vol. 6633, pp. 208–223. Springer, Heidelberg (2011)
12. Massey, J.L.: Shift-register analysis and BCH decoding. IEEE Transactions on Information Theory 15, 122–127 (1969)
13. Meier, W., Staffelbach, O.: Fast correlation attacks on stream ciphers. In: Günther, C.G. (ed.) EUROCRYPT 1988. LNCS, vol. 330, pp. 301–314. Springer, Heidelberg (1988)
14. Rønjom, S., Helleseth, T.: A new attack on the filter generator. IEEE Transactions on Information Theory 53(5), 1752–1758 (2007)
15. Siegenthaler, T.: Decrypting a Class of Stream Ciphers Using Ciphertext Only. IEEE Transactions on Computer C-34(1), 81–85 (1985)

A Time Series Approach for Profiling Attack

Liran Lerman[1,2], Gianluca Bontempi[2],
Souhaib Ben Taieb[2], and Olivier Markowitch[1]

[1] Quality and Security of Information Systems, Département d'informatique,
Université Libre de Bruxelles, Belgium
[2] Machine Learning Group, Département d'informatique,
Université Libre de Bruxelles, Belgium

Abstract. The goal of a profiling attack is to challenge the security
of a cryptographic device in the worst case scenario. Though template
attack is reputed as the strongest power analysis attack, they effectiveness is strongly dependent on the validity of the Gaussian assumption.
This led recently to the appearance of nonparametric approaches, often
based on machine learning strategies. Though these approaches outperform template attack, they tend to neglect the potential source of information available in the temporal dependencies between power values. In
this paper, we propose an original multi-class profiling attack that takes
into account the temporal dependence of power traces. The experimental
study shows that the time series analysis approach is competitive and
often better than static classification alternatives.

Keywords: side-channel attack, power analysis, machine learning, time
series classification.

1 Introduction

Embedded devices such as smart cards, mobile phones, and RFID tags are widely
used in our everyday lives. These devices implement cryptographic operations
allowing to secure, for example, bank transfers, buildings and cars. A modern
bank card embeds securely a secret information allowing *in fine* to transfer
cash. This operation is allowed by the smart card when it receives the right
PIN code. During the verification of the PIN code, a PIN-related information
(associated to the right PIN) is processed by the device. This secret information
could be retrieved by physical attacks that analyze the power consumption [24],
the processing time [23], or the electromagnetic emanation [15] of the device.
In this work, we focus on attacks based on power consumption analysis. These
attacks aim to infer the key-related information (label) from a time series of
power measurements called trace.

Differential Power Analysis (DPA) [24] is an example of physical attack which
first models the theoretic power consumption for each secret information. Then
the real and the predicted power consumption are compared by using metrics,
also known as distinguishers, such as the correlation coefficient [12], the difference
of means [24], the mutual information [16], or the Kolmogorov-Smirnov Test [40].

B. Gierlichs, S. Guilley, and D. Mukhopadhyay (Eds.): SPACE 2013, LNCS 8204, pp. 75–94, 2013.
© Springer-Verlag Berlin Heidelberg 2013

The rationale is that the likelihood of a secret information is related to the degree of similarity between the predicted and the real power consumption.

Profiling attack (PA), and more precisely Template Attack (TA) [11], makes another step forward in the use of statistical modelling of power consumption; it estimates the conditional density function of the time series for each key-related information by using a Gaussian parametric model. Thereafter, the time series are classified under a maximum likelihood approach. If the assumption of gaussianity holds, it can be considered as the strongest power analysis in an information theoretic sense [11]. TA is particularly suitable (1) to analyze the security of a cryptographic device in the worst case scenario and (2) when the attacker is only able to observe a single use of the key (e.g. in stream ciphers).

In recent years the cryptographic community explored new approaches based on machine learning models. These methods demonstrate that template attacks underestimate the security of embedded devices. Lerman et al. [26, 27] compared a template attack with a binary machine learning approach, based on non-parametric methods, against a cryptographic device (FPGA Xilinx Spartan XC3s5000) implementing 3DES. In this work the authors dealt with a limited number of traces (between 125 and 256 samples) and a very high number of dimensions (between 6,000 and 10,000 points per trace) by adopting a robust dimensionality reduction methods. Hospodar et al. [20, 21] analyzed a software implementation of a portion of the AES algorithm. Their experiments support the idea that non-parametric techniques can be competitive and sometimes better (i.e. less number of traces in the attack phase) than state-of-the-art approaches when simplistic assumptions do not hold. Heuser et al. [19] generalized this idea by analyzing multi-class classification models in several contexts (e.g. varying the signal-to-noise ratio by an additional Gaussian noise, and varying the number of required traces in the attack phase to achieve a fixed guessing entropy). In the same year Bartkewitz et al. [3] applied a multi-class machine learning model allowing to improve the attack success with respect to the binary approach.

However, all the attacks proposed so far tend to disregard the potential source of information available in the temporal dependencies between power values. We aim to fill this gap by proposing an original multi-class profiling attack based on the adoption of a time series approach. The idea is to adopt a time series prediction algorithm (notably the Lazy Learning algorithm [1, 6, 9]) i) to characterize the temporal dependencies in the traces associated to each target value (related to a secret key) and ii) to design a classifier based on the temporal likelihood of the new traces.

We make a detailed assessment of the proposed approach by considering 6 datasets with different signal-to-noise ratios. The experimental results confirm that the classical template attack is not optimal in several contexts [3, 19–21, 26, 27, 29]. At the same time we show that our time series profiling attack is competitive (or better) with state-of-the-art approaches. Our interpretation is that the proposed method allows a more compact way to address the issue of large dimensionality. So far classification techniques in side-channel attack focus on a set of values associated to relevant parts of the trace. Given the noise and the large number of collected values, this demands the adoption of feature selection techniques which have to deal with a large dimensionality issue. This is no more the case in our approach where the time series is no more seen as a very large set of independent values but rather as an auto-regressive stochastic process which can be described by a low dimensional mapping.

This paper is organized as follows. Section 2 reviews the state-of-the-art of profiling attacks including the well-known template attack and the profiling attack based on machine learning classification models. Section 3 introduces our original attack based on time series modeling. Section 4 illustrate the power of our proposal with several datasets. We conclude the paper in Section 5.

2 Profiling Attack

2.1 Preliminaries

Let e be an encryption algorithm (a block-cipher) that transforms plaintext $m \in \mathcal{M}$ into ciphertext $c \in \mathcal{C}$ under the control of a secret key $O_i \in \mathcal{O}$ where $\mathcal{O} = \{O_1, O_2, ..., O_K\}$. More formally

$$e : \mathcal{O} \times \mathcal{M} \to \mathcal{C}$$
$$c = e_{O_i}(m)$$

Let d be the decryption algorithm such that

$$d : \mathcal{O} \times \mathcal{C} \to \mathcal{M}$$
$$m = d_{O_i}(c)$$

Traditional cryptanalysis techniques search relations between plaintexts, ciphertexts and the corresponding used keys. On the other hand, profiling attacks analyze the implementation of cryptographic operations. In particular they perform the worst-case security evaluation of cryptographic devices with the most powerful adversary in the information theoretic sense, by analyzing the relation between the leaked information (i.e. the power consumption) and the secret key O_i.

During the encryption, a function $f_{O_i}(m)$ called a sensitive variable [37] (f in short) is executed. Examples of this function are:

$$f_{O_i}(m) = \qquad O_i \qquad\qquad (1)$$
$$f_{O_i}(m) = \qquad m \oplus O_i \qquad\qquad (2)$$
$$f_{O_i}(m) = \mathrm{SBox}(m \oplus O_i) \qquad\qquad (3)$$

where $\oplus$ is the exclusive-or and SBox is a nonlinear function.

The attacker focuses on a single (or combined [14]) function f in order to recover the key. In order to be close to the power consumption, the value of f is mapped with a leakage model to another value $Q \in \mathcal{Q}$ where $\mathcal{Q} = \{Q_1, Q_2, ..., Q_K\}$. Examples of leakage models are the identity, the Hamming weight (HW), and the Hamming distance (HD) [31].

For each value of this function let us observe N times the power consumption of a device (identically to the one that the attacker wants to target) over a time interval of length n and denote by *trace* the series of observations. Let $^jT_i = \left\{^j_tT_i \in \mathbb{R} \mid t \in [1; n]\right\}$ be the j-th trace associated to the target value Q_i and $\mathcal{T}$ be a set of traces.

Profiling Attack approaches model the stochastic dependency between the value of Q_i and a trace ^jT_i. More precisely, they estimate the probability distribution $P(Q_i|^jT_i; \theta_i)$ (where θ_i is the parameter of the distribution) on the basis of a set of traces (training set) associated to each target value (also known as class).

Two criteria are typically used to assess the quality of a profiling attack: (1) the number of required traces (the lower the better) (2) the success rate (the higher the better) of the model. We chose the second but both methods allow to know which attack is faster to recover the key. Note that these two criteria are related since a high success rate allows the adoption of a low number of traces during the attacking phase. In the following, the accuracy of an attack represents its success rate. More precisely, the accuracy relates to the probability that the correct target value is returned by the attack.

2.2   Template Attack

In order to classify a trace, the Template Attack strategy estimates a template $P(Q_i|^jT_i; \theta_i)$ for each target value Q_i. By making the assumption of normality, each template's estimation demands the estimation of the means μ_i and the covariance matrix Σ_i from traces associated to the i-th target value. This set of traces is measured on a controlled device similar to the target chip.

Once a template is estimated for each target value, the attacker classifies a new trace T (measured on the target device) by computing the value $\hat{Q} \in \mathcal{Q}$ which maximizes the *a posteriori* probability

$$\hat{Q} = \arg\max_Q P(Q|T) \tag{4}$$

$$= \arg\max_Q \frac{P(T|Q) \times P(Q)}{P(T)} \tag{5}$$

$$= \arg\max_Q \hat{P}(T|Q; \hat{\mu}_i, \hat{\Sigma}_i) \times \hat{P}(Q) \tag{6}$$

where the *apriori* probabilities $\hat{P}(Q)$ are estimated by the user accordingly.

If a set $\mathcal{T}$ of traces for a constant secret key are available, the attacker uses the equation (or the log-likelihood rule):

$$\hat{P}(Q|\mathcal{T}) = \frac{(\prod_{T \in \mathcal{T}} \hat{P}(T|Q)) \times \hat{P}(Q)}{\sum_{q \in \mathcal{Q}} (\prod_{T \in \mathcal{T}} \hat{P}(T|q)) \times \hat{P}(q))} \tag{7}$$

2.3   Profiling Attack Based on Machine Learning

In recent years we have assisted to a growing use of machine learning for profiling attack. These techniques do not require the adoption of any parametric or normal assumption and are more suitable to deal with very large dimensional noisy datasets. A conventional machine learning approach to classification relies on two main steps: the dimensionality reduction and the model building.

Dimensionality Reduction. Dimensionality reduction (also known as feature selection or points of interest) aims to extract a subset of p informative variables out of the original n variables [2, 35, 36]. There are plenty of advantages in dimensionality reduction: speed up of the learning process, enhancement of model interpretability, reduction of the amount of storage and improvement of the quality of models by mitigating the curse of dimensionality [4].

The curse of dimensionality is a well known problem in machine learning which states that by increasing dimensionality, the sparsity of data increases at an exponential rate, too. This is a problem when considering classifiers which have to group traces associated to the same target value.

There are several feature selection methods in the literature but we restrict ourselves to three methods. The MAX method selects a set of highest values in a trace.

Another feature selection is the minimum Redundancy Maximum Relevance (mRMR). It was first proposed in the bioinformatics literature [34] in order to deal efficiently with configurations where the number of points in each trace is much larger than the number of traces in the learning set. Its purpose is to rank variables by prioritizing the ones which have a low mutual dependence (i.e., low redundancy) while still providing a large amount of information about the output (i.e., large relevance). The method starts by selecting the variable $r = \left\{ {}_t^j T_i \mid i \in [1; K] ; j \in [1; N] \right\}$ having the highest mutual information about the target variable $Q = \{ Q_i \mid i \in [1; K] \}$. Given a set of selected variables R, the criterion updates this set by adding the variable $t = \left\{ {}_t^j T_i \mid i \in [1; K] ; j \in [1; N] ; t \notin R \right\}$ that maximizes the mutual information with the target variable and that minimizes the mutual information with the already selected variables.

Another feature selection method is the Sum of Squared Pairwise t-differences (SOST) [17] based on the T-Test. The T-Test assesses whether the weighted means of traces associated to two different classes are significantly different from each other at time t. More precisely it is expressed by:

$$\frac{{}_t\mu_i - {}_t\mu_j}{\frac{\sqrt{{}_t\sigma_i{}^2}}{N_i} + \frac{\sqrt{{}_t\sigma_j{}^2}}{N_j}} \tag{8}$$

where ${}_t\mu_i$, ${}_t\sigma_i$ and N_i are respectively the means, the standard deviation and the number of traces at time t that are associated to the class Q_i.

The SOST method selects the most relevant components t that have the highest values according to:

$$\sum_{j>i=0}^{K} \left(\frac{t\mu_i - t\mu_j}{\frac{\sqrt{t\sigma_i^2}}{N_i} + \frac{\sqrt{t\sigma_j^2}}{N_j}} \right)^2 \tag{9}$$

Model Building. Machine learning literature proposes plenty of nonparametric algorithms to estimate $P(Q_i|^jT_i;\theta_i)$ on the basis of data. Two well-known examples are Random Forest (RF) [10] and a Support Vector Machine (SVM) [13]. These two techniques allow to remove the Gaussian assumption and to infer in a data driven manner the model which best fits the stochastic dependency between target value and power consumption.

SVM. In a binary classification setting (e.g. $Q_1 = -1$ and $Q_2 = 1$), if the two classes are separable, the SVM algorithm is able to compute from a set of traces the separating hyperplane with the maximal margin, where the margin is the sum of the distances from the hyperplane to the closest traces of each of the two classes.

The SVM classification computes the parameters b (the bias) and w (the weight vector) of the separating hyperplane $[w^\top T + b]$ by solving the following convex optimisation problem:

$$\min \frac{1}{2}(w^\top w) \tag{10}$$

subject to

$$Q_i(w^{\top j}T_i + b) \geq 1 \; \forall i \in [1;2], j \in [1;N] \tag{11}$$

A trace T is assigned to class Q_1 if $w^\top T + b < 0$ and to Q_2 otherwise.

In a setting where the two classes cannot be linearly separated the formulation is changed by introducing a set of slack variables $\xi_j^i \geq 0$ with $i \in [1;2], j \in [1;N]$ then leading to the problem

$$\min_{w} \frac{1}{2}(w^\top w) + C\sum_{i=1}^{2}\sum_{j=1}^{N} \xi_j^i \tag{12}$$

subject to

$$Q_i(w^{\top j}T_i + b) \geq 1 - \xi_j^i \; \forall i \in [1;2], j \in [1;N] \quad\quad C \geq 0 \quad\quad \xi_j^i \geq 0 \tag{13}$$

A larger C means that a higher penalty to classification errors is assigned.

SVM is also modifiable to nonlinear classification tasks by performing a nonlinear transformation κ of traces. This function is named kernel function and can have several forms (e.g. linear, polynomial, radial basis function, sigmoid).

Its purpose is to find a linear separation in a higher dimension if there are no linear separation in the initial dimension. We refer to [19] for a discussion about the role of the kernel function in Equation 13. We used the kernel Radial Basis Function in our experiments.

Several extensions for constructing a multi-class SVM are possible such as one-against-one and one-against-all [22]. We used the one-against-one strategy in our experiments since all methods perform similarly [25].

RF. The Random Forest algorithm was introduced by Breiman in 2001 to address the problem of instability in large decision trees, where by instability we denote the sensitivity of a decision tree structure to small changes in the training set. In other words, large decision trees prone to high variance resulting in high prediction errors.

Let DT_i be a decision tree. In order to reduce the variance, this method relies on the principle of model averaging by building a set of B $(B > 1)$ approximately unbiased decision trees $(\{DT_1, DT_2, ..., DT_B\})$ and returning the most consensual prediction. This means that the target value $\hat{Q}$ of an unlabeled observation T is calculated through a majority vote of the set of trees. More formally,

$$\hat{Q} = f_{\text{majority}}\left(DT_1(T), DT_2(T), ..., DT_B(T)\right) \tag{14}$$

where f_{majority} is the majority vote function and DT_i is the i-th classification tree which returns its prediction for T.

RF is based on two aspects. First each tree is constructed with a different set of traces through the boostrapping method. This method builds a bootstrap sample for each decision tree by resampling (with replacement) the original data set. Observations in the original data set that do not occur in a bootstrap sample are called out-of-bag observations and are used as a validation set. Secondly, each tree is built by adopting a random partitioning criterion. This idea allows to obtain decorrelated trees, thus improving the accuracy of the resulting RF model. The number of trees (B) in the random forest has to be large enough to create diversity among the predictions. In our experiment we use 500 trees which as a rule of thumb is considered as a sufficient number for obtaining accurate prediction.

In conventional decision trees each node is split using the best split among all variables. In the case of a random forest, each node is split using the best among a subset of variables randomly chosen at that node. Also, unlike conventional decision trees, the trees of the random forest are fully grown and are not pruned. In other words, each node contains traces associated to a value of the key. This implies null training error but large variance and consequently a large test error for each single tree. The averaging of the single trees represents a solution to the variance issue without increasing the bias, and allows the design of an overall accurate predictor. Hence the improvements in prediction obtained by random forests are solely a result of variance reduction.

3   A Time Series Approach for Profiling Attacks

Power analysis deals with time series representing the power consumption of a cryptographic device over time. A time series represents a sequence of data points. The most distinctive aspect of a time series is the existence of a stochastic dependency between past and future values. This section introduces our original approach to take into account such a dependency during a profiling attack.

State-of-the-art approaches assume that this dependency is negligible [3, 19–21, 26, 27]. They start with a feature selection step (before a classification step) by projecting traces in new dimensions where (1) the new dimensions correlate highly with the target value and, optionally, (2) the new dimensions correlate weakly between them. We intend to show that in fact such temporal dependence is relevant and can be used in order to improve the success rate of the attack.

Let $y = \{y_1, y_2, ..., y_n\}$ be a time series made of n observations. In the time series literature, the autoregressive formalism is the conventional way to represent the stochastic dependency in a time series [7, 30]. According to this formalism there exists a dependency between the future value y_{t+1} and a set of p past values $\{y_t, y_{t-1}, ..., y_{t-p+1}\}$. More formally it is assumed that each time series has been generated by an autoregressive process of the form

$$y_{t+1} = f_\theta (y_t, y_{t-1}, ..., y_{t-p+1}) + \varepsilon_{t+1} \tag{15}$$

where ε_t is the additive noise at time t and f is the autoregressive function parametrized by θ. For instance f can be a linear function defined as

$$f_\theta (y_t, y_{t-1}, ..., y_{t-p+1}) = c + \sum_{i=0}^{p-1} a_i y_{t-i} \tag{16}$$

where $\theta = [c, a_0, a_1, ..., a_{p-1}]$ is the parameter of the model.

The fitting error of $\hat{f}$ represents the difference between the observed values y and the fitted values $\hat{y}$ provided by the estimated model $\hat{f}_{\hat{\theta}}$, i.e.

$$r(\hat{f}_{\hat{\theta}}, y) = \frac{1}{n - p} \sum_{t=p}^{n-1} \left(\hat{f}_{\hat{\theta}} (y_t, y_{t-1}, ..., y_{t-p+1}) - y_{t+1} \right)^2 \tag{17}$$

In our case the time series y is a trace ${}^j T_i$. A trace contains a succession of consumptions peaks related to the rising and falling edge of the clock (see Figure 5). The data processed inside the cryptographic device are supposed to influence the amplitude of these peaks. As a result, it is expected that the parameter θ describing these peaks is related to the secret (or target) information.

In order to take into account the temporal dependence we fit a time series model $\hat{f}_{\hat{\theta}_i}$ for each class i. The embedding step allows to estimate the parameter θ_i by transforming each time series (related to the i-th class) in a set of $n - p$ time series. More precisely this step transforms each time series $\{y_1, y_2, ..., y_n\}$ into

$$\begin{bmatrix} y_{p+1} \\ y_{p+2} \\ \cdots \\ y_n \end{bmatrix} \begin{bmatrix} y_p & \cdots & y_2 & y_1 \\ y_{p+1} & \cdots & y_3 & y_2 \\ \cdots & \cdots & \cdots & \cdots \\ y_{n-1} & \cdots & y_{n-p+1} & y_{n-p} \end{bmatrix} \tag{18}$$

where the matrix $(n-p) \times 1$ represents the expected output value of the regression model f_θ given the other matrix $(n - p) \times p$. Then the learning step selects the value of θ_i that minimizes the fitting error on the set of transformed time series (by the embedding step) related to the i-th class.

Once a time series model is fitted for each class, we use them to perform a classification of a new trace T. Our technique returns the class by mapping the fitting errors of each regression model to the real class with a classifier h. Examples of classifier h are the random forest, the support vector machine and the arg min function. The arg min function is formalized by

$$\hat{Q} = \arg \min_i r(\hat{f}_{\hat{\theta}_i}, T) \tag{19}$$

The resulting method presents two main advantages with respect to the state-of-the-art: (1) it allows to take into account the natural temporal ordering of data, and (2) it reduces the variance of the feature selection step. This is expected to reduce the complexity of the resulting method with respect to static classifiers since a time series model considers a few number of points ($p - 1$ points instead of n) at a time. As a consequence the new approach has a lower variance and leads to a more robust method against noise.

During the attacking phase of a target device, the main expensive step is the computation of the fitting error of each regression model on a trace T. Its complexity is $O(K \times (n - p))$ where K is the number of regression models. In practice the proposed approache can be easily made parallel: each time series model can be executed on different processors allowing to speed up the attacking phase.

4   Experiments

In order to assess the quality of the time series approach, we benchmarked it against template attacks and profiling attacks based on static classification models and three feature selection strategies. We used several datasets with different signal-to-noise ratios. The parameters of each classification and time series models are estimated with a learning set made of 80% of the original dataset. For each model we search the best number of inputs per clock cycle of the crypto device (between 2 and 5 since additional points in the same clock cycle do not provide additional information [35]) by using a validation set. Finally a test set (independent of the learning and the validation set) is used to compare the accuracy of each approach.

4.1   Target Implementation

In order to easily reproduce the results, the experiments were carried out on power leakages that are freely available on the DPAContest V1 website [38] where the cryptographic device (a SecmatV1 SoC in ASIC) implements the unprotected block-cipher DES. Note that the proposed profiling attack is generalizable to other crypto algorithms.

The target value represents the Hamming distance between the left input block and left output block of the last round. Since we have no control on the crypto device (the keys/plaintexts was randomly chosen) we focused on the target values of 7 to 25 in order to have at least several traces per class. However since all the attacks are assessed on the same datasets, this should not have any impact on the results. We choose this target value because (1) it is highly correlated with the traces, (2) it allows to recover 48 bits of the secret key[1] when a plaintext-ciphertext pair is known, and (3) it is good enough in order to compare several approaches.

In the worst case we need $\binom{32}{16} \times 8$ (less than 2^{38}) tests to find all the secret key when the target value is known (in the best case we need only 8 tests to find the secret key). In order to reduce the number of tests an attacker can target the Hamming weight (or the Hamming distance) of a byte (which involves a worse success rate due to a decreasing of the signal-to-noise ratio). Another solution is to use this Hamming distance as an input to other attacks such as an Algebraic Side-Channel Attack [32] or a classical DPA combined with a template attack approach [33]. But the purpose of this section is essentially to compare several approaches in several contexts with real datasets and, therefore, to validate the theoretical presentation performed in previous sections.

4.2   Measurement Setup

In order to generate the traces of the DPAContest V1 an oscilloscope collected 81,089 traces (see a trace in Figure 5), each composed of 20,000 points. A more detailed description of the attacked implementation and the measurement setup can be found in [38]. A fairly standard way of applying power analysis is to focus on one round of the crypto algorithm (where the trace and the target value are dependent) [31]. As a result, we reduced the size of each trace by zooming on the time interval when the target value is manipulated. For this we computed the Pearson correlation between each time of 500 traces and their relatively target values (see Figure 6). We selected a time interval of 100 where the first significant correlation is obtained (a trace in this time interval is plotted in Figure 7).

As stated in the previous section, we focused on the target values (i.e. de HD) between 7 and 25. We reduced the size of the dataset to 8095 by computing the average of 10 traces (associated to the same target value) in order to reduce the

---

[1] The last 8 bits of the key are searched with a brute-force strategy that requires plaintext-ciphertext pairs.

noise[2]. Table 1 shows the number of traces per target value. It is worth to note that the number of traces per class is strongly imbalanced.

We added a Gaussian noise in order to analyze the signal-to-noise impact on the prediction of each approach[3]. The Gaussian noise follows a Gaussian distribution with a mean of 0 and a standard deviation varying by 0.001 between 0 and 0.005. It allows to confront several models against 6 different contexts. Another approach would be to reduce the number of traces involved in the average. We decided to use the first approach in order to have the same number of traces in each dataset while controlling the noise level with a good precision. The limit of 0.005 for the noise level was mainly based on the result of Figure 8 which shows the impact of the added noise to two traces associated to two different target values. In other words, the noise level was selected according to the difficulty to distinguish traces associated to different target values. A higher noise level does not allow to distinguish classes which include more than 70% of traces of the dataset. This is corroborated in our experiments where several profiling attacks behave as a random model with a noise level of 0.005.

Table 1. Number of traces per target value

Target value	7	8	9	10	11	12	13	14	15	16
Number of traces	6	21	51	122	245	435	666	880	1064	1128

Target value	17	18	19	20	21	22	23	24	25	
Number of traces	1067	873	675	423	239	127	51	16	6	

4.3 Model Selection

We tried several autoregressive models, classification models and feature selection algorithms. For the sake of conciseness we report only the most successful models. We tested the RF, the SVM and the TA as static classification models with the feature selection algorithms MAX, SOST and mRMR. For the time series approach, we considered the Lazy Learning autoregressive model [1, 6, 9] (LL) with the classifiers arg min (see Equation 19), RF and SVM.

The LL model proved to be a very effective technique in a number of academic and industrial case studies [8] as it can be applied for a nonlinear regression case. Each lazy model keeps in memory the learning set in order to predict the output value by interpolating the samples in the neighborhood of the input value. The rationale is that it is the neighbors of the input value that are the more relevant for the interpolation problem and, more precisely, to build a regression model.

In order to search the neighbors of the input value we used the euclidean metric. The final performance is extremely sensitive to the choice of the number

---

[2] We used 6482 traces in the profiling phase and 1613 traces in the test set during the attacking phase.

[3] The Shapiro-Wilk test (with a significance level of 5%) corroborates that the noise on the collected traces follows a univariate Gaussian distribution.

of neighbors: a too small value allows to fit an eventual nonlinearity but at the cost of a high variance; a too high value leads to a large modeling bias. The local regression model tunes automatically the best number of neighbors on the basis of a fast leave-one-out procedure.

4.4   Experimental Results

We first check the quality of the time series fit. Figure 1 shows the fitting returned by three LL models[4] associated to the 7-th, the 16-th and the 25-th HD and with a p equal to 2 (see Equation 15). As it can be seen, each time series model predicts values close to the actual data.

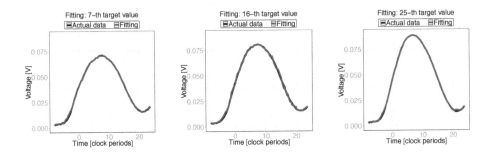

Fig. 1. Fitting of three traces (associated with classes 7, 16 and 25) by three lazy models (with a p equal to 2)

The second experiment compares the template attack against the time series approach. Clearly, from Figure 2, it can be observed that the success rates are similar when the traces contain a high signal-to-noise ratio. Moreover, as expected, the higher is the level of noise, the lower is the performances of both approaches due to the fact that there are less information leakage available. However the time series approach outperforms the state-of-the-art approach when the noise increases. Another important advantage of the time series approach over TA is that the higher the noise the higher the difference between their success rates. It confirms the robustness of the new approach against noise and therefore the model parameters are expected to be more reliably estimated.

The third experiment assesses the time series approach vs. a static classification strategy based on random forest. The results are shown in Figure 3. Random forest allows a higher success rate than template attack in high noise level while their results are similar in the high signal-to-noise ratio context. It confirms the results of previous research [3, 19–21, 26, 27, 29] that template attack is not optimal on several contexts. Nevertheless the success rates of the random forest is lower than the time series approach when the level of noise increases.

---

[4] We used the implementation available on CRAN [5].

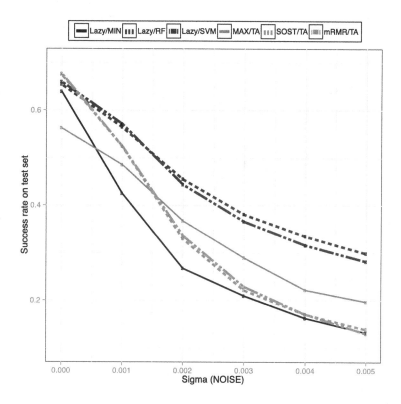

Fig. 2. Success rate per noise level on test set using time series approaches vs template attacks. A/B symbolizes the use of the preprocessing method A with the classifier B.

The last experiment compares the time series approach to a classifier based on support vector machine. The result is plotted in Figure 4. It highlights a similar performance between both approaches when we pick out the best feature selection method for each noise level. However our approach allows a higher success rate (in a noisy context) without the drawback of selection of the best feature selection for each noise level. Note that the selection step of the classification model (both in the regression and in the classification approach) influences the success rate.

4.5   Discussion and Open Questions

The experimental results of the previous sections suggest some considerations. The first one concerns accuracy. We show that for several datasets our approach improves the accuracy of the power analysis attack with respect to conventional template attack as well as to static classification model approach in low signal-to-noise ratio settings.

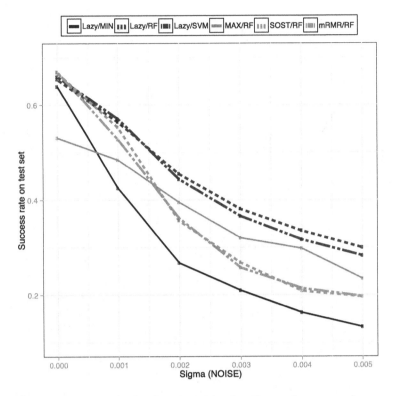

Fig. 3. Success rate per noise level on test set using time series approaches vs random forest. A/B symbolizes the use of the preprocessing method A with the classifier B.

The time series models and the feature selection methods can be seen as a pre-processing step where traces are projected in new dimensions. Their influences in the success rate can be described in terms of the Bias-Variance trade-off [18]. An increase in the complexity of the model leads to an increase of its variance which in turns induces a high sensitivity to noise. On the other hand, in a low noise context where the variance of models does not influence its success rate a more complex model is advantageous due to the fact that its low bias improves its success rate. As a result, a low (resp. high) complex model is favorable in the case of a low (resp. high) signal-to noise context. This reasoning is supported by our experiments: the pre-processing model with the lowest complex outperforms the others in the noisy case. More precisely, the MAX function as well as the time series models lead to higher success rates when we use a RF or a SVM for the classification step. In contrast the SOST and the mRMR seem to outperform the MAX function when the noise is low. As a result the choice of a feature selection should be related to the level of noise on the collected traces. Surprisingly the lazy models combined with the RF or the SVM have a high success rate compared to the presented methods in low and high signal-to-noise case. This is motivated by its low bias rate and its low variance rate.

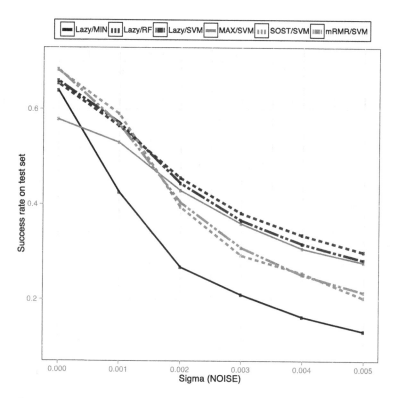

Fig. 4. Success rate per noise level on test set using time series approaches vs support vector machine. A/B symbolizes the use of the preprocessing method A with the classifier B.

An interesting open problem concerns the selection of the classification model in the time series approach. Our results suggest that a random forest or a support vector machine allow to improve the accuracy compared to a MIN function. We could guess that the reason is related to the estimation's accuracy of the error of fitting of each time series model. This estimation is linked to the number of traces used in the learning set of each time series model. A higher number of trace leads to a better estimation of each parameter [39]. As the number of traces in each class is not uniformly distributed (i.e. the number of traces in each class is imbalanced), some time series models estimate better their error of fitting compared to other. As a result, the error of fitting of each time series model should be weighted with the accuracy of their model. We speculate that the RF and the SVM estimate these weight values which allow them to outperform the MIN function. Another issue is that there are some classes that are more difficult to fit than other. Indeed Figure 9 shows that the distribution of the fitting's errors is different for each class. As a result an important question for further research is to determine whether we can improve the success rate by varying the p value for each time series model or at least to rebalance the learning set.

5   Conclusion

Profiling attacks are useful tools in the evolution of leaking cryptographic devices in a worst case scenario. In this paper, we first proposed a new and efficient profiling attack in a multi-class problem. More precisely we introduced a transformation of traces to new dimensions by taking into account the temporal dependence of traces. This new approach offers several starting points for further work with other time series models in the profiling attacks.

We showed that the choice of a feature selection should be related to the level of noise in the collected traces. It led to discuss the advantage of our new proposed technique from a theoretical point of view based on the bias-variance trade-off [18]. We put forward that such profiling attack is less sensitive to noise thanks to its lower variance compared to the presented attacks. Therefore, our method can be carried out in all scenarios where the previously profiling attacks are relevant.

The theoretical point of view is confirmed with several experiments where the new approach allows to improve (significantly) the success rate in several contexts (with several levels of noise). Eventually we discussed the results that lead to interesting open questions such that the impact of differences between the distributions, for each class, of fitting errors in the time series approach. Another interesting question concerns the effect of the number of traces in the learning set for each approach. A more robust model against noise needs less traces in the learning set. As a result, future works will verify whether our proposal outperforms the previous models in a high dimensionality context where the number of traces is less than the number of components in each trace.

In summary this paper confirms that template attack can be improved with machine learning models by designing automatically models from data. More precisely a more powerful adversary is obtained by taking into account the temporal dependence of traces. Hence, practically secure crypto implementations would clearly require to be analyzed with the time series approach. In order to make the time series approach easier to reproduce, an open-source program has been made publicly available [28].

Acknowledgements. Gianluca Bontempi acknowledges the support of the Communauté Francaise de Belgique (ARC project).

References

1. Aha, D.W.: Editorial. Artificial Intelligence Review 11, 7–10 (1997)
2. Archambeau, C., Peeters, E., Standaert, F.-X., Quisquater, J.-J.: Template attacks in principal subspaces. In: Goubin, L., Matsui, M. (eds.) CHES 2006. LNCS, vol. 4249, pp. 1–14. Springer, Heidelberg (2006)
3. Bartkewitz, T., Lemke-Rust, K.: Efficient template attacks based on probabilistic multi-class support vector machines. In: Mangard, S. (ed.) CARDIS 2012. LNCS, vol. 7771, pp. 263–276. Springer, Heidelberg (2013)

4. Bellman, R.: Dynamic Programming, 1st edn. Princeton University Press, Princeton (1957)
5. Birattari, M., Bontempi, G.: Lazy: Lazy Learning for Local Regression, R package version 1.2-14 (2003)
6. Birattari, M., Bontempi, G., Bersini, H.: Lazy learning meets the recursive least squares algorithm. In: Proceedings of the 1998 Conference on Advances in Neural Information Processing Systems II, pp. 375–381. MIT Press, Cambridge (1999)
7. Bisgaard, S., Kulahci, M.: Time Series Analysis and Forecasting by Example. Wiley Series in Probability and Statistics. John Wiley Sons (2011)
8. Bontempi, G., Birattari, M., Bersini, H.: Lazy learners at work: The lazy learning toolbox. In: EUFIT 1999: The 7th European Congress on Intelligent Techniques and Soft Computing, Abstract Booklet with CD Rom, Aachen, Germany. ELITE Foundation (1999)
9. Bontempi, G., Birattari, M., Bersini, H.: Lazy Learning: A local method for supervised learning. In: Jain, L.C., Kacprzyk, J. (eds.) New Learning Paradigms in Soft Computing, pp. 97–137. Springer, Heidelberg (2001)
10. Breiman, L.: Random forests. Machine Learning 45, 5–32 (2001)
11. Chari, S., Rao, J., Rohatgi, P.: Template attacks. In: Kaliski Jr., B.S., Koç, Ç.K., Paar, C. (eds.) CHES 2002. LNCS, vol. 2523, pp. 13–28. Springer, Heidelberg (2003)
12. Coron, J.-S., Naccache, D., Kocher, P.: Statistics and secret leakage. ACM Trans. Embed. Comput. Syst. 3, 492–508 (2004)
13. Cortes, C., Vapnik, V.: Support-vector networks. Machine Learning, 273–297 (1995)
14. Elaabid, M.A., Meynard, O., Guilley, S., Danger, J.-L.: Combined side-channel attacks. In: Chung, Y., Yung, M. (eds.) WISA 2010. LNCS, vol. 6513, pp. 175–190. Springer, Heidelberg (2011)
15. Gandolfi, K., Mourtel, C., Olivier, F.: Electromagnetic Analysis: Concrete Results. In: Koç, Ç.K., Naccache, D., Paar, C. (eds.) CHES 2001. LNCS, vol. 2162, pp. 251–261. Springer, Heidelberg (2001)
16. Gierlichs, B., Batina, L., Tuyls, P., Preneel, B.: Mutual Information Analysis - A Generic Side-Channel Distinguisher. In: Oswald, E., Rohatgi, P. (eds.) CHES 2008. LNCS, vol. 5154, pp. 426–442. Springer, Heidelberg (2008)
17. Gierlichs, B., Lemke-Rust, K., Paar, C.: Templates vs. stochastic methods. In: Goubin, L., Matsui, M. (eds.) CHES 2006. LNCS, vol. 4249, pp. 15–29. Springer, Heidelberg (2006)
18. Hastie, T., Tibshirani, R., Friedman, J.: The elements of statistical learning: data mining, inference and prediction, 2nd edn. Springer (2009)
19. Heuser, A., Zohner, M.: Intelligent machine homicide - Breaking cryptographic devices using support vector machines. In: Schindler, W., Huss, S.A. (eds.) COSADE 2012. LNCS, vol. 7275, pp. 249–264. Springer, Heidelberg (2012)
20. Hospodar, G., Gierlichs, B., Mulder, E.D., Verbauwhede, I., Vandewalle, J.: Machine learning in side-channel analysis: a first study. J. Cryptographic Engineering 1(4), 293–302 (2011)
21. Hospodar, G., Mulder, E.D., Gierlichs, B., Vandewalle, J., Verbauwhede, I.: Least Squares Support Vector Machines for Side-Channel Analysis, pp. 99–104. Center for Advanced Security Research Darmstadt (2011)
22. Hsu, C.-W., Lin, C.-J.: A comparison of methods for multiclass support vector machines. Trans. Neur. Netw. 13(2), 415–425 (2002)

23. Kocher, P.C.: Timing attacks on implementations of diffie-hellman, RSA, DSS, and other systems. In: Koblitz, N. (ed.) CRYPTO 1996. LNCS, vol. 1109, pp. 104–113. Springer, Heidelberg (1996)
24. Kocher, P.C., Jaffe, J., Jun, B.: Differential power analysis. In: Wiener, M. (ed.) CRYPTO 1999. LNCS, vol. 1666, pp. 388–397. Springer, Heidelberg (1999)
25. KreBel, U.H.-G.: Pairwise classification and support vector machines. In: Advances in Kernel Methods, pp. 255–268. MIT Press, Cambridge (1999)
26. Lerman, L., Bontempi, G., Markowitch, O.: Side Channel Attack: an Approach Based on Machine Learning, pp. 29–41. Center for Advanced Security Research Darmstadt (2011)
27. Lerman, L., Bontempi, G., Markowitch, O.: Power analysis attack: an approach based on machine learning. International Journal of Applied Cryptography (to appear, 2013)
28. Lerman, L., Bontempi, G., Markowitch, O.: sideChannelAttack: Side Channel Attack, R package version 1.0-7 (2013)
29. Lerman, L., Fernandes Medeiros, S., Veshchikov, N., Meuter, C., Bontempi, G., Markowitch, O.: Semi-supervised template attack. In: Prouff, E. (ed.) COSADE 2013. LNCS, vol. 7864, pp. 184–199. Springer, Heidelberg (2013)
30. Makridakis, S., Wheelwright, S., Hyndman, R.J.: Forecasting: Methods and Applications. Wiley series in management. Wiley (1998)
31. Mangard, S., Oswald, E., Popp, T.: Power analysis attacks - revealing the secrets of smart cards. Springer (2007)
32. Oren, Y., Renauld, M., Standaert, F.-X., Wool, A.: Algebraic side-channel attacks beyond the hamming weight leakage model. In: Prouff, E., Schaumont, P. (eds.) CHES 2012. LNCS, vol. 7428, pp. 140–154. Springer, Heidelberg (2012)
33. Oswald, E., Mangard, S.: Template Attacks on Masking-Resistance Is Futile. In: Abe, M. (ed.) CT-RSA 2007. LNCS, vol. 4377, pp. 243–256. Springer, Heidelberg (2006)
34. Peng, H., Long, F., Ding, C.: Feature selection based on mutual information criteria of max-dependency, max-relevance, and min-redundancy. IEEE Transactions on Pattern Analysis and Machine Intelligence 27(8), 1226–1238 (2005)
35. Rechberger, C., Oswald, E.: Practical template attacks. In: Lim, C.H., Yung, M. (eds.) WISA 2004. LNCS, vol. 3325, pp. 440–456. Springer, Heidelberg (2005)
36. Reparaz, O., Gierlichs, B., Verbauwhede, I.: Selecting time samples for multivariate DPA attacks. In: Prouff, E., Schaumont, P. (eds.) CHES 2012. LNCS, vol. 7428, pp. 155–174. Springer, Heidelberg (2012)
37. Rivain, M., Dottax, E., Prouff, E.: Block ciphers implementations provably secure against second order side channel analysis. In: Nyberg, K. (ed.) FSE 2008. LNCS, vol. 5086, pp. 127–143. Springer, Heidelberg (2008)
38. DPAContest V1 (February 2013), http://www.dpacontest.org/home/
39. Wallace, B.C., Dahabreh, I.J.: Class probability estimates are unreliable for imbalanced data (and how to fix them). In: Zaki, M.J., Siebes, A., Yu, J.X., Goethals, B., Webb, G.I., Wu, X. (eds.) ICDM, pp. 695–704. IEEE Computer Society (2012)
40. Whitnall, C., Oswald, E., Mather, L.: An exploration of the kolmogorov-smirnov test as a competitor to mutual information analysis. In: Prouff, E. (ed.) CARDIS 2011. LNCS, vol. 7079, pp. 234–251. Springer, Heidelberg (2011)

Appendix

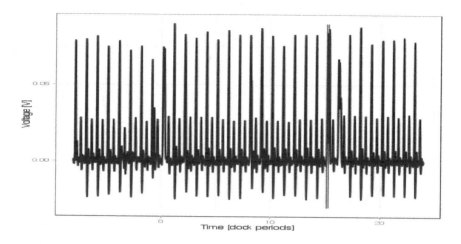

Fig. 5. A trace from the DPAContest V1 where the blue lines represent the time interval where the target value is manipulated

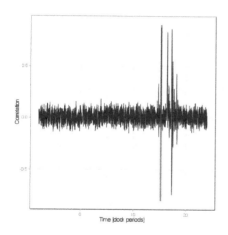

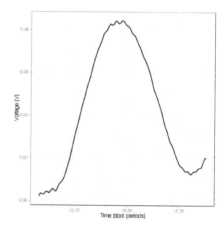

Fig. 6. Correlation between traces and the target value for each time

Fig. 7. A zoom on a trace when the target value is manipulated

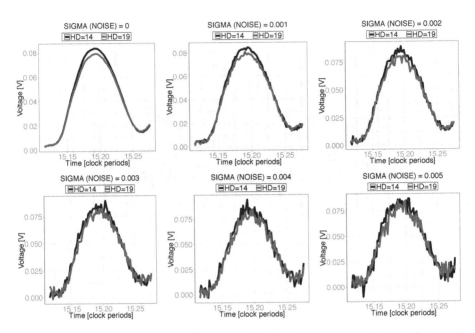

Fig. 8. Each figure shows two traces associated to two different target values (i.e. 14-th and 19-th HD) with a different noise level

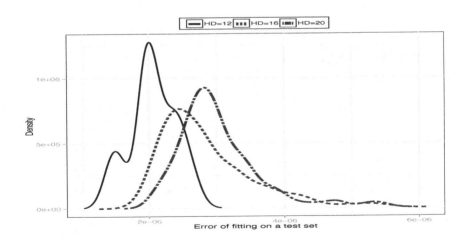

Fig. 9. Three errors densities of fitting on a testing set by different lazy models (where p equal to 2) for classes 9, 16 and 20

Algorithms for Switching between Boolean and Arithmetic Masking of Second Order

Praveen Kumar Vadnala and Johann Großschädl

University of Luxembourg,
Laboratory of Algorithmics, Cryptology and Security (LACS),
6, rue Richard Coudenhove-Kalergi, 1359 Luxembourg
{praveen.vadnala,johann.groszschaedl}@uni.lu

Abstract. Masking is a widely-used countermeasure to thwart Differential Power Analysis (DPA) attacks, which, depending on the involved operations, can be either Boolean, arithmetic, or multiplicative. When used to protect a cryptographic algorithm that performs both Boolean and arithmetic operations, it is necessary to change the masks from one form to the other in order to be able to unmask the secret value at the end of the algorithm. To date, known techniques for conversion between Boolean and arithmetic masking can only resist first-order DPA. This paper presents the first solution to the problem of converting between Boolean and arithmetic masking of second order. To set the context, we show that a straightforward extension of first-order conversion schemes to second order is not possible. Then, we introduce two algorithms to convert from Boolean to arithmetic masking based on the second-order provably secure S-box output computation method proposed by Rivain et al (FSE 2008). The same can be used to obtain second-order secure arithmetic to Boolean masking. We prove the security of our conversion algorithms using similar arguments as Rivain et al. Finally, we provide implementation results of the algorithms on three different platforms.

Keywords: Differential power analysis, Second-order DPA, Arithmetic masking, Boolean Masking, Provably secure masking.

1 Introduction

Side-channel cryptanalysis exploits information leakage from the execution of a concrete implementation of a cryptographic algorithm [12]. Therefore, this kind of attack is methodically very different from "traditional" cryptanalysis, which essentially focuses on finding secret keys in a black box model given only pairs of plaintexts and ciphertexts. The first form of side-channel attacks discussed in the literature are timing attacks, i.e. attacks exploiting measurable differences in the execution time of a cryptographic algorithm or a specific operation it is based upon [13,11]. A more sophisticated class of attacks are power analysis attacks, which aim to deduce information about the secret key from the power consumption of the device while a certain operation is carried out [15]. A third

B. Gierlichs, S. Guilley, and D. Mukhopadhyay (Eds.): SPACE 2013, LNCS 8204, pp. 95–110, 2013.
© Springer-Verlag Berlin Heidelberg 2013

class are electromagnetic (EM) attacks, which exploit the relationship between secret data and EM emanations produced by the device [1].

Power analysis attacks received extensive attention from the cryptographic community ever since Kocher and his team published them for the first time in their seminal paper *Differential Power Analysis* [14]. These attacks allow one to recover the full secret key with relatively few measurements and it is close to impossible to totally circumvent them with current semiconductor technologies [15]. While Simple Power Analysis (SPA) attacks try to recover a secret value by directly "comparing" the power measurements with the corresponding operations, Differential Power Analysis (DPA) attacks are much more sophisticated and aim to reveal a secret value by applying statistical techniques on multiple measurements of the same operation. Masking is a widely-used countermeasure to thwart DPA attacks, which involves using random variables, called masks, to reduce the correlation between the secret value and the obtained leakage [2]. In order to circumvent first-order DPA attacks [15] that involve a single operation using masking, we divide the secret value into two shares: a mask generated randomly and the masked value of the secret. However, this approach can still be attacked via a second-order DPA involving two operations corresponding to the two shares of the secret [16,19]. In general, a d-th order masking scheme is vulnerable to a $(d + 1)$-th order DPA attack involving all $d + 1$ shares of the secret. These attacks are called Higher-Order DPA attacks (HODPA).

Depending on the operation to be protected, a masking scheme can either be Boolean (using logical XOR), arithmetic (using modular addition/subtraction) or multiplicative (using modular multiplication). To successfully "unmask" the variable at the end of the algorithm, one has to track the change of the masked secret value during the execution of the algorithm. If an algorithm contains two of the three afore-mentioned operations (i.e. XOR, modular addition/subtraction, modular multiplication), the masks have to be converted from one form to the other, keeping this conversion free from any leakage. Goubin introduced secure methods to convert between first-order Boolean and arithmetic masks in [10]. Coron and Tchulkine improved the method for switching from arithmetic to Boolean masking in [5], which was recently further improved by Debraize in [6]. While solutions exist for converting between arithmetic and multiplicative masking of higher order [7,8,9], the conversion between Boolean and arithmetic masking is currently limited to first order. We aim to fill this gap by presenting algorithms to switch between Boolean and arithmetic masks of second order.

In the context of second-order masking, a sensitive variable x is represented by three shares; these are $x_1 = x \oplus x_2 \oplus x_3$, x_2 and x_3 in the case of Boolean masking, and $A_1 = x - A_2 - A_3$, A_2 and A_3 for arithmetic masking [15]. The problem is to convert between Boolean and arithmetic masking without introducing any first-order or second-order leakage. Unfortunately, it is not possible to extend the existing first-order secure conversion schemes to second order as we will show later. Therefore, we employ techniques proposed by Rivain et al in [21] to arrive at the first solution for converting second-order masks from one form to the other. In [21], the authors describe two provably secure methods to compute S-box outputs without first or second-order leakage. By applying these methods, we present a total of four algorithms, two for each conversion type.

The rest of the paper is organized as follows. We review some of the existing solutions for a first-order conversion as well as the paper of Rivain et al in Section 2. Then, we show that a straightforward application of Goubin's method is insecure for second-order conversion in Section 3. We introduce our algorithms for Boolean to arithmetic conversion in Section 4. The algorithms to convert in the opposite direction (i.e. arithmetic to Boolean) can be derived similarly and are described in Section 5. We prove the security of our algorithms in Section 6 for a device leaking in the Hamming weight model. Section 7 summarizes some implementation results and, finally, Section 8 concludes the paper.

2   Previous Work

This section provides an overview of recent results that will be used later in the paper. We first summarize existing methods for switching between arithmetic and Boolean masking of first order. Then, we describe two techniques proposed by Rivain et al at FSE 2008 to compute S-box outputs secure against second-order DPA attacks [21].

2.1   Securing Conversions against First-Order DPA

The first solution to the problem of Boolean to arithmetic mask conversion was presented by Messerges in [17], which was later proven to be insecure by Coron and Goubin in [4]. At CHES 2001, Goubin proposed an algorithm for switching between Boolean and arithmetic masks secure against first-order DPA attacks [10]. His algorithm to convert from Boolean to arithmetic masking is based on the following fact: for $I = \{0, 1, \ldots, 2^n - 1\}$ with $n \geq 1$ and $x' \in I$, the function $\phi_{x'}(r) : I \to I$ defined as $\phi_{x'}(r) = (x' \oplus r) - r \bmod 2^n$ is affine over the field $GF(2)$. Therefore, the function $\psi_{x'} = \phi_{x'} \oplus \phi_{x'}(0)$ is linear over $GF(2)$ and, as a result, $x = x' \oplus r$ with Boolean shares (x', r) can be converted to the equivalent arithmetic shares (A, r) for any random γ via the following relation:

$$
\begin{aligned}
A &= \phi_{x'}(r) = \psi_{x'}(r) \oplus x' \\
&= \psi_{x'}(\gamma) \oplus \psi_{x'}(r \oplus \gamma) \oplus x' \\
&= [(x' \oplus \gamma) - \gamma] \oplus x' \oplus [(x' \oplus (r \oplus \gamma)) - (r \oplus \gamma)]
\end{aligned}
$$

This method is highly efficient, requiring only a constant number of elementary operations. Goubin's arithmetic to Boolean conversion is based on the following fact: $x' = (A + r) \oplus r$ is equivalent to $x' = A \oplus u_{n-1}$, where

$$
\begin{cases}
u_0 = 0 \\
u_{i+1} = 2[u_i \wedge (A \oplus r) \oplus (A \wedge r)] \ \forall \ i \geq 0
\end{cases}
$$

Unfortunately, this method is far less efficient since the number of operations is proportional to the size of the registers.

Algorithm 1. Secure second-order S-box output computation: First variant

---

Input: Three input shares: $(x_1 = x \oplus x_2 \oplus x_3, x_2, x_3) \in \mathbb{F}_{2^n}$, two output shares: $(y_1, y_2) \in \mathbb{F}_{2^m}$, and an (n, m)-bit S-box lookup function S
Output: Masked S-box output: $S(x) \oplus y_1 \oplus y_2$
 1: Randomly generate n-bit number r
 2: $r' \leftarrow (r \oplus x_2) \oplus x_3$
 3: **for** a from 0 to $2^n - 1$ **do**
 4:     $a' \leftarrow a \oplus r'$
 5:     $T[a'] \leftarrow ((S(x_1 \oplus a) \oplus y_1) \oplus y_2)$
 6: **end for**
 7: **return** $T[r]$

In 2003, Coron and Tchulkine proposed a new algorithm for conversion from arithmetic to Boolean masking [5]. To convert two n-bit ($n = p \cdot k$) arithmetic shares A and R with $x = A + R \bmod n$ into two Boolean shares x' and R such that $x = x' \oplus R$, the algorithm works on each k-bit word independently. Therefore, A and R are divided into p words of k bits: $A = A_1 \,\|\, A_2 \,\|\, \ldots \,\|\, A_{p-1}$ and $R = R_1 \,\|\, R_2 \,\|\, \ldots \,\|\, R_{p-1}$. Now, the Boolean share equivalent to the i-th word of the arithmetic share A_i is computed as $x'_i = (A_i + R_i + c_{i+1}) \oplus R_i$, where c_{i+1} is the carry bit produced from the previous k-bit word. The algorithm precomputes two small tables of 2^k entries each, and reuses them several times in the course of the conversion. The first table serves to convert each arithmetic-share word independently to the equivalent Boolean-share word. This table contains the entries $(z + r) \oplus r$ for all possible values of $z \in [0, 2^k - 1]$ and the random value $r \in [0, 2^k - 1]$. The correct value for the i-th word can be obtained when $z = (A_i - r + R_i) + c_{i+1}$. The second table is used to mask the carry that needs to be passed from one word to the next-higher. Even though this increases the memory requirements, the conversion time is reduced significantly. Neiße and Pulkus [18] modified the algorithm so as to reduce the memory needed to store the tables. At CHES 2012, Debraize discovered a bug in the Coron-Tchulkine algorithm and devised a new variant that is also more efficient [6].

2.2 Generic Countermeasure against Second-Order DPA

At FSE 2008, Rivain et al proposed two algorithms to protect the computation of S-box outputs against second-order attacks [21]. Given three input shares of a secret value x, namely $x_1 = x \oplus x_2 \oplus x_3$, x_2, and x_3 (which are all in $\mathbb{F}_{2^n}$) and two output shares $y_1, y_2 \in \mathbb{F}_{2^m}$ along with an (n, m) S-box lookup function S, they compute the third share y_3 such that $y_1 \oplus y_2 \oplus y_3 = S(x)$. Hence, we have $y_3 = S(x) \oplus y_1 \oplus y_2$. The algorithms compute $(S(x_1 \oplus a) \oplus y_1) \oplus y_2$ for all possible values of a (i.e. $0 \leq a \leq 2^{n-1}$), among which the correct value can be obtained when $a = x_2 \oplus x_3$. We recall these algorithms below.

Algorithm 1 uses a table of 2^n entries to store $(S(x_1 \oplus a) \oplus y_1) \oplus y_2$ for all possible values of a. Here, the value $(x_2 \oplus x_3)$ is masked via a random variable r, the result of which is assigned to r'. Thereafter, the entry corresponding to

Algorithm 2. Secure second-order S-box output computation: Second variant

---

Input: Three input shares: $(x_1 = x \oplus x_2 \oplus x_3, x_2, x_3) \in \mathbb{F}_{2^n}$, two output shares: $(y_1, y_2) \in \mathbb{F}_{2^m}$, and an (n, m)-bit S-box lookup function S

Output: Masked S-box output: $S(x) \oplus y_1 \oplus y_2$

1: Randomly generate one bit b
2: **for** a **from** 0 **to** $2^n - 1$ **do**
3:    $cmp \leftarrow compare_b(x_2 \oplus a, x_3)$
4:    $R_{cmp} \leftarrow ((S(x_1 \oplus a) \oplus y_1) \oplus y_2)$
5: **end for**
6: **return** R_b

$(S(x_1 \oplus a) \oplus y_1) \oplus y_2$ will be stored at location $a' = a \oplus r'$. The correct value of the third share y_3 can be retrieved by accessing the value stored in the table at location $T[r]$. As $r = a'$, the value of a becomes $a = r \oplus r' = x_2 \oplus x_3$, thus yielding the desired result.

The security of Algorithm 1 can be proven by showing that it is impossible to recover x by combining any pair of intermediate variables computed by the algorithm. We refer the interested reader to Section 3.1 in [21] for the complete proof. In Section 6, we will use the same approach to prove the security of our conversion techniques. Algorithm 1 requires a table of 2^n words (each having a length of m bits) in RAM, and is, therefore, not suitable for low-cost devices. To overcome this issue, Rivain et al introduced another algorithm consuming less memory at the expense of executing more operations.

Algorithm 2 specifies the second solution proposed by Rivain et al in [21] to securely compute an S-box output. In this variant, they use a function called $compare_b(x, y)$, which returns b if $x = y$ and $\bar{b}$ otherwise. A first-order secure implementation of $compare_b$ is necessary to guarantee the security of the algorithm. To this end, Rivain et al [21] presented a method for implementing the $compare_b$ function, shown in Algorithm 3. The secure S-box computation works as follows: First, a random bit b is generated, which is one of the inputs to the $compare_b$ function. Then, for each possible value of a, the algorithm computes $(S(x_1 \oplus a) \oplus y_1) \oplus y_2$, which will be written to either R_b or $R_{\bar{b}}$, depending on the actual output of the $compare_b$ function. The inputs to the $compare_b$ function are $x_2 \oplus a$ and x_3. When $a = x_2 \oplus x_3$, $compare_b(x_2 \oplus a, x_3)$ returns b, thus the result is stored in R_b. In all other cases, the returned value is $\bar{b}$, so the result is stored in the register $R_{\bar{b}}$. At the end of the algorithm, the value stored in R_b is $S(x) \oplus y_1 \oplus y_2$, which is exactly what we wanted to achieve.

Note that Algorithm 2 needs only 2^n bits in RAM, namely for the function $compare_b$. Thus, it requires m times less memory than Algorithm 1, though the execution time is longer due to multiple calls to the $compare_b$ function.

3   Applying Goubin's Conversion to Second Order

In this section, we demonstrate that a straightforward application of Goubin's conversion technique [10] to the second order does not work. Assume we have

---

Algorithm 3. Computation of the *compare*$_b$ function

Input: x, y, b, n
Output: b if $x = y$, $\bar{b}$ otherwise
1: $r_3 \leftarrow rand(n)$
2: $T[0 : 2^n - 1] \leftarrow \bar{b}, \bar{b}, \ldots, \bar{b}$
3: $T[r_3] \leftarrow b$
4: **return** $T[(x \oplus r_3) \oplus y]$

---

three Boolean shares x_1, x_2, x_3 whereby $x = x_1 \oplus x_2 \oplus x_3$. We need to find the arithmetic shares A_1, A_2, and A_3 such that $x = A_1 + A_2 + A_3 \bmod 2^n$. To do so, we can iteratively compute A_1, A_2, A_3 as follows:

$$x = A_1 + (x_2 \oplus x_3)$$
$$x = A_1 + A_2 + x_3$$
$$A_1 = x - (x_2 \oplus x_3)$$
$$A_2 = (x_2 \oplus x_3) - x_3$$
$$A_3 = x_3$$

Based on the above, we can compute A_1 in the following way:

$$A_1 = x_1 \oplus (x_2 \oplus x_3) - (x_2 \oplus x_3) = \phi_{x_1}(x_2 \oplus x_3)$$
$$= \phi_{x_1}(x_2) \oplus \phi_{x_1}(x_3) \oplus x_1.$$

One could try to securely compute $\phi_{x_1}(x_2)$ and $\phi_{x_1}(x_3)$ as follows:

$$\phi_{x_1}(x_2) = \phi_{x_1}(x_2 \oplus r) \oplus \phi_{x_1}(r) \oplus x_1$$
$$\phi_{x_1}(x_3) = \phi_{x_1}(x_3 \oplus r) \oplus \phi_{x_1}(r) \oplus x_1.$$

This means,

$$A_1 = \phi_{x_1}(x_2 \oplus r) \oplus \phi_{x_1}(r) \oplus \phi_{x_1}(x_3 \oplus r) \oplus \phi_{x_1}(r) \oplus x_1$$
$$= \phi_{x_1}(x_2 \oplus r) \oplus \phi_{x_1}(x_3 \oplus r) \oplus x_1$$
$$= ((x_1 \oplus x_2 \oplus r) - (x_2 \oplus r)) \oplus ((x_1 \oplus x_3 \oplus r) - (x_3 \oplus r)) \oplus x_1.$$

But we can combine the leakages from $x_1 \oplus x_2 \oplus r$ and $x_3 \oplus r$ to get $x_1 \oplus x_2 \oplus x_3 = x$, inducing a second order attack. Similarly, we can combine the leakages from $x_1 \oplus x_3 \oplus r$ and $x_2 \oplus r$ to get $x_1 \oplus x_2 \oplus x_3 = x$. Now, let us consider the case where we use a different random r_i for computing each $\phi_{x_i}(x_j)$, i.e.

$$\phi_{x_1}(x_2) = \phi_{x_1}(x_2 \oplus r_1) \oplus \phi_{x_1}(r_1) \oplus x_1$$
$$\phi_{x_1}(x_3) = \phi_{x_1}(x_3 \oplus r_2) \oplus \phi_{x_1}(r_2) \oplus x_1.$$

This means,

$$A_1 = \phi_{x_1}(x_2 \oplus r_1) \oplus \phi_{x_1}(r_1) \oplus \phi_{x_1}(x_3 \oplus r_2) \oplus \phi_{x_1}(r_2) \oplus x_1.$$

Now, when computing A_1, regardless of what sequence we choose, we would be leaking the secret x while combining the results. For example, assume that we calculate according to the following sequence:

$$\phi_{x_1}(r_1) \oplus \phi_{x_1}(x_3 \oplus r_2) \oplus \phi_{x_1}(r_2) = \phi_{x_1}(x_3 \oplus r_1)$$
$$= ((x_1 \oplus x_3 \oplus r_1) - (x_3 \oplus r_1))$$

Let us further assume that $\phi_{x_1}(x_2 \oplus r_1)$ is calculated as follows:

$$\phi_{x_1}(x_2 \oplus r_1) = ((x_1 \oplus x_2 \oplus r_1) - (x_2 \oplus r_1))$$

Then, we can combine the leakages from $x_1 \oplus x_2 \oplus r_1$ and $x_3 \oplus r_1$ to find the value of x. From this, we conclude that the straightforward application of the method of Goubin does not work for second order.

4   Second-Order Boolean to Arithmetic Masking

This section addresses the problem of securely converting second-order Boolean shares to the corresponding arithmetic shares without any second-order or first-order leakage. To start with, we are given three Boolean shares x_1, x_2, x_3 such that $x = x_1 \oplus x_2 \oplus x_3$ where x is a sensitive variable. The goal is to find three arithmetic shares A_1, A_2, A_3 satisfying $x = A_1 + A_2 + A_3$ without leaking any information exploitable in a first or second-order DPA attack. We propose two algorithms to achieve this goal; one is based on Algorithm 1 and the second on Algorithm 2. Both of our algorithms use the secure S-box output computation of Rivain et al [21], which simplifies the security proofs.

The first of our variants is given in Algorithm 4; we devised this conversion by modifying Algorithm 1 appropriately. The algorithm generates two shares A_2, A_3 randomly from $[0, 2^n - 1]$ and computes the third share via the relation $A_1 = (x - A_2) - A_3$. The aim of Algorithm 1 was to output $S(x) \oplus y_1 \oplus y_2$ as result. Hence, it computed $(S(x_1 \oplus a) \oplus y_1) \oplus y_2$ for every possible value of the variable a from 0 to $2^n - 1$, and then obtained the correct value for the case $a = x_2 \oplus x_3$. But here, our aim is to compute $(x - A_2) - A_3$, which requires us to modify the table entries to $((x_1 \oplus a) - A_2) - A_3$ so that we can obtain the correct value when $a = x_2 \oplus x_3$. Note that the subtractions are modulo 2^n.

Correctness: When $a' = r$, a becomes $r \oplus r' = x_2 \oplus x_3$. Thus, $T[a'] = T[r] = ((((x_1 \oplus x_2) \oplus x_3) - A_2) - A_3) = (x - A_2) - A_3$, from which follows that $A_1 = (x - A_2) - A_3$ and finally $x = A_1 + A_2 + A_3$.

We devised Algorithm 5 by appropriately adapting Algorithm 2. Again, we first compute the value of $((x_1 \oplus a) - A_2) - A_3$ for all possible values of a and store the result in R_b or $R_{\bar{b}}$, depending on the return value of $compare_b$. When $a = x_2 \oplus x_3$, the value of $x_2 \oplus a$ and x_3 become equal, hence $compare_b$ returns b. Consequently, the correct value of $A_1 = (x - A_2) - A_3$ is stored in R_b. In all other cases (i.e. $a \neq x_2 \oplus x_3$), the value $((x_1 \oplus a) - A_2) - A_3$ is stored in $R_{\bar{b}}$.

Algorithm 4. Boolean to arithmetic conversion of 2nd order: First variant

---

Input: Boolean shares: $x_1 = x \oplus x_2 \oplus x_3$, x_2, x_3
Output: Arithmetic shares: $A_1 = (x - A_2) - A_3$, A_2, A_3
 1: Randomly generate n-bit numbers r, A_2, A_3
 2: $r' \leftarrow (r \oplus x_2) \oplus x_3$
 3: **for** a from 0 to $2^n - 1$ **do**
 4:     $a' \leftarrow a \oplus r'$
 5:     $T[a'] \leftarrow ((x_1 \oplus a) - A_2) - A_3$
 6: **end for**
 7: $A_1 = T[r]$
 8: **return** A_1, A_2, A_3

Algorithm 5. Boolean to arithmetic conversion of 2nd order: Second variant

---

Input: Boolean shares: $x_1 = x \oplus x_2 \oplus x_3$, x_2, x_3
Output: Arithmetic shares: $A_1 = (x - A_2) - A_3$, A_2, A_3
 1: Randomly generate n-bit numbers A_2, A_3
 2: Randomly generate one bit b
 3: **for** a from 0 to $2^n - 1$ **do**
 4:     $cmp \leftarrow compare_b(x_2 \oplus a, x_3)$
 5:     $R_{cmp} \leftarrow ((x_1 \oplus a) - A_2) - A_3$
 6: **end for**
 7: $A_1 = R_b$
 8: **return** A_1, A_2, A_3

---

5   Second-Order Arithmetic to Boolean Masking

In this section, we briefly introduce two algorithms to securely convert second-order arithmetic shares into the "corresponding" Boolean shares, whereby the conversion does not introduce any second-order (or first-order) leakage. More precisely, given three arithmetic shares A_1, A_2, A_3 of a sensitive variable x such that $x = A_1 + A_2 + A_3$, both of these algorithms compute the Boolean shares x_1, x_2, x_3 satisfying $x = x_1 \oplus x_2 \oplus x_3$ without second or first-order leakage.

Algorithm 6 employs a lookup table similar to Algorithm 4. Here, the value of r' is $(A_2 - r) + A_3$, where r is a random value in the range $[0, 2^n - 1]$. The table entries corresponding to $a' = a - r'$ are now $((A1 + a) \oplus x_2) \oplus x_3$ instead of $((x_1 \oplus a) - A_2) - A_3$. Similar to Algorithm 4, the two shares x_2 and x_3 are generated randomly from $[0, 2^n - 1]$, while the third share x_1 is $T[r]$.

Correctness: When $a' = r$, a becomes $r + r' = A_2 + A_3$. Thus, $T[a'] = T[r] = ((((A_1 + A_2) + A_3) \oplus x_2) \oplus x_3) = (x \oplus x_2) \oplus x_3$, from which follows that $x_1 = (x \oplus x_2) \oplus x_3$ and finally $x = x_1 \oplus x_2 \oplus x_3$.

Algorithm 7 shows the other method to convert arithmetic shares of second order to "equivalent" Boolean shares. Among the three Boolean shares, x_2 and x_3 are generated randomly within the range $[0, 2^{n-1}]$. One of the two registers R_0, R_1 serves to store the correct value of x_1 and the other is used for storing

---

Algorithm 6. Arithmetic to Boolean conversion of 2nd order: First variant

---

Input: Arithmetic shares: $A_1 = (x - A_2) - A_3$, A_2, A_3
Output: Boolean shares: $x_1 = x \oplus x_2 \oplus x_3$, x_2, x_3

1: Randomly generate n-bit numbers r, x_2, x_3
2: $r' \leftarrow (A_2 - r) + A_3$
3: **for** a **from** 0 **to** $2^n - 1$ **do**
4:     $a' \leftarrow a - r'$
5:     $T[a'] \leftarrow ((A_1 + a) \oplus x_2) \oplus x_3$
6: **end for**
7: $x_1 = T[r]$
8: **return** x_1, x_2, x_3

Algorithm 7. Arithmetic to Boolean conversion of 2nd order: Second variant

---

Input: Arithmetic shares: $A_1 = (x - A_2) - A_3$, A_2, A_3
Output: Boolean shares: $x_1 = x \oplus x_2 \oplus x_3$, x_2, x_3

1: Randomly generate n-bit numbers x_2, x_3
2: Randomly generate one bit b
3: **for** a **from** 0 **to** $2^n - 1$ **do**
4:     $cmp \leftarrow compare_b(a - A_2, A_3)$
5:     $R_{cmp} \leftarrow ((A_1 + a) \oplus x_2) \oplus x_3$
6: **end for**
7: $x_1 = R_b$
8: **return** x_1, x_2, x_3

---

the incorrect value. The compare instruction compares $(a - A_2)$ with $A3$; when they are equal, $compare_b$ returns b and, thus, the result is stored in R_b. In this case, the result is the correct value of x_1, which means $((A_1 + A_2 + A_3) \oplus x_2) \oplus x_3 = (x \oplus x_2) \oplus x_3$. Otherwise, the result is incorrect and stored in R_b'.

6   Security Analysis

We first review the security model introduced in [21]. Then, based on the same model, we present the security proofs of all our four algorithms against second-order attacks. We assume that the device leaks in the Hamming weight model (i.e. the leakage is proportional to the Hamming weight of the data processed on the device). Below we summarize some basic definitions and results that are used in the proofs for quick reference (partly taken from [21]).

- *Sensitive variable:* An intermediate variable obtained by applying a certain function on a known value (e.g. plaintext) and the secret key.
- *Primitive random variable:* An intermediate variable generated by a random number generator with uniform distribution.
- *Functional dependence:* If an intermediate variable is obtained by applying a discrete function on some other variable X, then it is said to be functionally dependent on X. Otherwise, it is functionally independent.

- *Statistical dependence:* If the statistical distribution of an intermediate variable varies according to some other variable X, then it is said to be statistically dependent on X. Otherwise, it is statistically independent.
- Functional independence implies statistical independence, but the converse is false.
- In second-order DPA, leakages from at most two intermediate variables are allowed to be exploited simultaneously. So, for a cryptographic algorithm to be called second-order secure, it is important that every pair of intermediate variables is statistically independent of any sensitive variable.
- A set of intermediate variables is statistically independent from a variable X if, and only if, all intermediate variables belonging to the set are statistically independent of X.
- Given two sets A and B, $A \times B$ is statistically independent from a variable X if, and only if, all pairs in $A \times B$ are statistically independent of X.
- **Lemma 1.** *For statistically independent random variables X and Y, it holds that for every measurable function f, $f(X)$ is statistically independent of the variable Y.*
- **Lemma 2.** *Let X and Y be statistically independent random variables where Y is uniformly distributed, and Z a variable that is statistically independent of Y and functionally independent of X. In this case, the pair $(Z, X \oplus Y)$ is statistically independent of X.*

Limitations of the Security Proofs: The algorithms in [21], though proven secure against "standard" DPA attacks, suffer from two problems. Firstly, the algorithm not using table computations, i.e. Algorithm 2, is only secure in the Hamming weight model. At COSADE 2012, Coron et al have shown that this algorithm is *not* secure when the device leaks in the Hamming distance model [3]. They also demonstrated that a straightforward conversion of a proof from the Hamming weight model to Hamming distance model by initializing the bus (resp. register) with 0 before every write operation has a second-order flaw. As a consequence, the proof of Algorithm 2 from [21] is not valid anymore in the Hamming distance model. The conversion of a security proof from one leakage model to another is still an open issue. Since Algorithm 5 and Algorithm 7 are similar to Algorithm 2, they suffer from said limitation too. However, a solution to the conversion problem for Rivain et al's generic countermeasure for secure S-box computation would, of course, also apply to our algorithms.

Secondly, some current developments in side-channel cryptanalysis indicate that masking might succumb to a so-called *horizontal side-channel attack* (see e.g. [20,22]). By targeting the table generation phase of a masking scheme, an attacker may succeed to recover the secret key when the signal-to-noise ratio is low. However, these attacks are generic in the sense that they are applicable to essentially any practical masking scheme; our algorithms are no exception. The problem of securely generating the masked table is still an open challenge and requires further attention. Any solution to this problem can be readily applied to our algorithms as well to help them resist horizontal attacks. Hence, despite these limitations, our algorithms are still practically relevant.

Proposition 1. *Algorithm 4 is secure against second-order DPA.*

Proof. We follow the notation of [21] for the sake of simplicity. Each intermediate variable of the algorithm can be seen as a result of applying the function I_j on the loop index a. Assume that $I_{index} = I_{index}(a)$ for $0 \leq a \leq 2^n - 1$ and $I = \bigcup_{index=0}^{num} I_{index}$, whereby num specifies the total number of intermediate variables. We list all intermediate variables used in Algorithm 4 in Table 1.

Table 1. Intermediate variables used in Algorithm 4

index	I_{index}
1	x_2
2	x_3
3	A_2
4	A_3
5	r
6	$r \oplus x_2$
7	$r \oplus x_2 \oplus x_3$
8	a
9	$a \oplus r \oplus x_2 \oplus x_3$
10	$x \oplus x_2 \oplus x_3$
11	$x \oplus x_2 \oplus x_3 \oplus a$
12	$(x \oplus x_2 \oplus x_3 \oplus a) - A_2$
13	$((x \oplus x_2 \oplus x_3 \oplus a) - A_2) - A_3$
14	$(x - A_2) - A_3$

Table 2. Intermediate variables used in Algorithm 5

index	I_{index}
1	x_2
2	x_3
3	A_2
4	A_3
5	b
6	a
7	$x_2 \oplus a$
8	$\delta_0(x_2 \oplus a \oplus x_3) \oplus b$
9	$x \oplus x_2 \oplus x_3$
10	$x \oplus x_2 \oplus x_3 \oplus a$
11	$(x \oplus x_2 \oplus x_3 \oplus a) - A_2$
12	$((x \oplus x_2 \oplus x_3 \oplus a) - A_2) - A_3$
13	$(x - A_2) - A_3$

We recall that, for an algorithm to be secure against second-order DPA, no pair of intermediate variables should be statistically dependent on a sensitive variable. Consequently, we need to prove that $I \times I$ is statistically independent of x. To simplify matters, we divide the set of intermediate variables into three subsets: $E_1 = I_1 \cup I_2 \cup \ldots \cup I_9$, $E_2 = I_{10} \cup I_{11} \cup \ldots \cup I_{13}$, and $E_3 = I_{14}$. The objective now is to prove that all possible combinations of these three sets are statistically independent of x.

1. $\mathbf{E_1 \times E_1}$: All the intermediate variables in E_1 are functionally independent of x. Hence, $E_1 \times E_1$ is statistically independent of x.
2. $\mathbf{E_2 \times E_2}$: It can be seen that $I_{10} = x \oplus x_2 \oplus x_3$ is statistically independent of x. As all elements in $E_2 \times E_2$ are functions of I_{10}, it can be inferred that $E_2 \times E_2$ is statistically independent of x by applying Lemma 2.
3. $\mathbf{E_3 \times E_3}$: It is also straightforward to see that $E_3 \times E_3$ is statistically independent of x since $x - (A_2 - A_3)$ is statistically independent of x.
4. $\mathbf{E_1 \times E_2}$: E_1 is statistically independent of $(x_2 \oplus x_3)$ and functionally independent of x. According to Lemma 2, $E_1 \times \{x \oplus x_2 \oplus x_3\}$ is statistically independent of x. Hence, according to Lemma 1, $E_1 \times E_2$ is statistically independent of x.

5. $\mathbf{E_1} \times \mathbf{E_3}$: Since E_1 is statistically independent of $A_2 - A_3$, the combination $E_1 \times \{x - (A_2 - A_3)\}$ (i.e. $E_1 \times E_3$) is statistically independent of x. As the pair $(x \oplus x_2 \oplus x_3, (x - A_2) - A_3)$ is statistically independent of x, it holds that $(I_{10} \cup I_{11} \cup I_{12}) \times E_3$ is statistically independent of x because all these can be expressed as a function of $(x \oplus x_2 \oplus x_3, (x - A_2) - A_3)$.

6. $\mathbf{E_2} \times \mathbf{E_3}$: We need to prove that $I_{13} \times E_3$ is statistically independent of x to establish that $E_2 \times E_3$ is statistically independent of x. Suppose that $v_1 = (x - A_2) - A_3$ and $v_2 = (x \oplus x_2 \oplus x_3 \oplus a)$. It can be seen that v_1 and v_2 are statistically independent of each other as well as of variable x. We can write $I_{13} \times E_3$ as $\{v_1 + v_2 - x\} \times v_1$, which is statistically independent of x.

From all this it can be concluded that Proposition 1 holds. $\square$

Proposition 2. *Algorithm 5 is secure against second-order DPA.*

Proof. Assume that the Boolean function $\delta_0(x) = 0$ only when $x = 0$. So, the function $compare_b(x, y)$ can be represented as $\delta_0(x \oplus y) \oplus b$. For Algorithm 5 to be secure, it is important that the $compare_b$ function is implemented in a way which prevents any first-order leakage on $compare(x, y)$. One such method is recalled in Algorithm 3 (originally proposed in [21]) and we can construct the proof on this method. The intermediate variables appearing in Algorithm 5 are given in Table 2. It can be easily seen that nearly all intermediate variables are identical to those in Algorithm 4. Thus, we can prove the security of Algorithm 5 by using the same arguments as given in the proof of Proposition 1. $\square$

Table 3. Intermediate variables used in Algorithm 6

Table 4. Intermediate variables used in Algorithm 7

index	I_{index}
1	x_2
2	x_3
3	A_2
4	A_3
5	r
6	$A_2 - r$
7	$A_2 - r + A_3$
8	a
9	$a - A_2 + r - A_3$
10	$x - A_2 - A_3$
11	$x - A_2 - A_3 + a$
12	$(x - A_2 - A_3 + a) \oplus x_2$
13	$(x - A_2 - A_3 + a) \oplus x_2 \oplus x_3$
14	$x \oplus x_2 \oplus x_3$

index	I_{index}
1	x_2
2	x_3
3	A_2
4	A_3
5	b
6	a
7	$a - A_2$
8	$\delta_0((a - A_2) \oplus A_3) \oplus b$
9	$x - A_2 - A_3$
10	$x - A_2 - A_3 + a$
11	$(x - A_2 - A_3 + a) \oplus x_2$
12	$(x - A_2 - A_3 + a) \oplus x_2 \oplus x_3$
13	$x \oplus x_2 \oplus x_3$

Proposition 3. *Algorithm 6 is secure against second-order DPA.*

Proof. Table 3 lists all intermediate variables appearing in Algorithm 6. We can use similar arguments as in Proposition 1 to prove that no pair of intermediate variables is statistically dependent on x.   □

Proposition 4. *Algorithm 7 is secure against second-order DPA.*

Proof. We show all intermediate variables that appear in Algorithm 7 in Table 4. Again, the security proof can be developed similar to the one of Proposition 1, namely by showing that no pair of the intermediate variables is statistically dependent on x.   □

7 Implementation Results

We implemented all algorithms from Section 4 and Section 5 in Matlab and in ANSI C, whereby we only considered the simplest case of converting between 8-bit masks. The Matlab implementation served as a reference for the C implementation so that we could easily verify the correctness of the latter. We tested our four algorithm individually using 100,000 pseudo-random inputs and found that all of them produce the correct result in all cases. The C implementation generates the random numbers with help of the **rand** function of the standard C library[1]. Although this is sufficient for testing, a real-world implementation would need pseudo-random numbers of better quality. Furthermore, it should be noted that we developed all our implementations primarily for the purpose of having a proof of concept rather than achieving high performance. The implementations can be further optimized, which means the results we report in this section should be seen as upper bounds of the execution time. Also, if the conversions are used in real-world applications, one needs to take care that the compilation process respects the flow of intermediate variables assumed in the security proofs given in Section 6. If this is not the case, it becomes necessary to develop an assembly language implementation.

The implementation of Algorithm 4 and Algorithm 6 is straightforward; we create a table of 256 bytes and, for each of the 256 possible values of a, store the corresponding entry in a byte. The indexing of the table is done via a' and the correct value of the third share is retrieved by accessing the table entry corresponding to r. An optimized implementation of Algorithm 5 and Algorithm 7 has to perform the *compare_b* function as efficiently as possible. We used the following approach to implement this function. First, we create an array of 32 bytes and initialize all the bits to $\bar{b}$. We treat the array as a collection of 256 bits, all initialized to $\bar{b}$. Then, for a random value r_3, we set the corresponding bit position in the array to b. Each call to *compare_b* is now simply replaced by a single look-up into the array. To give an example, *compare_b*(x, y) is obtained by retrieving the value at the bit position $(x \oplus r_3) \oplus y$. The index of the byte containing the bit can be obtained through a logical right-shift operation. The bit itself can be extracted from the byte via a shift operation too.

---

[1] On an 8-bit AVR processor, e.g. ATmega128, calling the **rand** function takes around 800 clock cycles when using the **avr-libc** library of the WinAVR tool suite.

Table 5. Implementation results on an 8, 16 and 32-bit platform

Algorithm	Cycles	RAM (bytes)
8-bit architecture (AVR)		
Algorithm 4	5769	256
Algorithm 5	6742	32
Algorithm 6	5769	256
Algorithm 7	6742	32
16-bit architecture (MSP)		
Algorithm 4	4983	256
Algorithm 5	16706	32
Algorithm 6	4983	256
Algorithm 7	16706	32
32-bit architecture (ARM)		
Algorithm 4	793	256
Algorithm 5	1087	32
Algorithm 6	793	256
Algorithm 7	1087	32

In order to assess the execution time of the algorithms, we compiled them for the 32-bit ARM platform as well as the 8-bit AVR platform and performed simulations with AVR Studio. In addition, we evaluated our four algorithms on a low-power 16-bit micro-controller, the TI MSP430, with the help of a cycle-accurate instruction-set simulator. Table 5 illustrates the simulation results we obtained on these three platforms. The second column of Table 5 specifies the execution time (in clock cycles) needed to convert an 8-bit mask from one form to the other. The third column gives the memory (RAM) requirements of the algorithms in number of bytes. As we can see, the two algorithms using table look-ups, i.e. Algorithm 4 and Algorithm 6, are faster than the ones which do not use tables. This is because of the additional time required to evaluate the $compare_b$ function in the case of Algorithm 5 and Algorithm 7. However, both algorithms based on the table computation method require exactly eight times more memory than their counterparts.

Note that the execution times of Algorithm 5 and Algorithm 7 obtained on the 16-bit platform are somewhat misleading. As can be seen from Table 5, the execution time on the TI MSP430 is by a factor of roughly 2.5 slower than the time on the 8-bit AVR. This can be explained through the fact that the used MSP430 processor does not have a barrel shifter, which means a shift operation by n bit positions takes n clock cycles. On the other hand, the AVR features a fast barrel shifter able to execute all shift operations in one cycle, irrespective of the shift distance.

8   Conclusions

In this paper, we addressed the practical problem of converting between second-order Boolean and arithmetic masking. We introduced two algorithms secure against second-order attacks for each direction by applying the generic second-order secure countermeasure proposed by Rivain et al at FSE 2008. The time complexity of these algorithms is $O(2^n)$, where n is the size of the data to be converted. All algorithms are proven to be secure when the device leaks in the Hamming weight model. Our implementation results show that the algorithms without tables require eight times less memory (i.e. RAM) than the table-based algorithms, but the saving in RAM footprint comes at the expense of increased execution time. The proposed algorithms become costly when the length of the data to be converted exceeds 16 bits. As part of our future research, we aim to improve the efficiency of the conversion methods by devising algorithms with a better time-memory trade-off.

References

1. Agrawal, D., Archambeault, B., Rao, J.R., Rohatgi, P.: The EM side-channel(s). In: Kaliski Jr., B.S., Koç, Ç.K., Paar, C. (eds.) CHES 2002. LNCS, vol. 2523, pp. 29–45. Springer, Heidelberg (2003)
2. Chari, S., Jutla, C.S., Rao, J.R., Rohatgi, P.: Towards sound approaches to counteract power-analysis attacks. In: Wiener, M. (ed.) CRYPTO 1999. LNCS, vol. 1666, pp. 398–412. Springer, Heidelberg (1999)
3. Coron, J.-S., Giraud, C., Prouff, E., Renner, S., Rivain, M., Vadnala, P.K.: Conversion of security proofs from one leakage model to another: A new issue. In: Schindler, W., Huss, S.A. (eds.) COSADE 2012. LNCS, vol. 7275, pp. 69–81. Springer, Heidelberg (2012)
4. Coron, J.-S., Goubin, L.: On boolean and arithmetic masking against differential power analysis. In: Paar, C., Koç, Ç.K. (eds.) CHES 2000. LNCS, vol. 1965, pp. 231–237. Springer, Heidelberg (2000)
5. Coron, J.-S., Tchulkine, A.: A new algorithm for switching from arithmetic to boolean masking. In: Walter, C.D., Koç, Ç.K., Paar, C. (eds.) CHES 2003. LNCS, vol. 2779, pp. 89–97. Springer, Heidelberg (2003)
6. Debraize, B.: Efficient and provably secure methods for switching from arithmetic to boolean masking. In: Prouff, E., Schaumont, P. (eds.) CHES 2012. LNCS, vol. 7428, pp. 107–121. Springer, Heidelberg (2012)
7. Genelle, L., Prouff, E., Quisquater, M.: Secure multiplicative masking of power functions. In: Zhou, J., Yung, M. (eds.) ACNS 2010. LNCS, vol. 6123, pp. 200–217. Springer, Heidelberg (2010)
8. Genelle, L., Prouff, E., Quisquater, M.: Montgomery's trick and fast implementation of masked AES. In: Nitaj, A., Pointcheval, D. (eds.) AFRICACRYPT 2011. LNCS, vol. 6737, pp. 153–169. Springer, Heidelberg (2011)
9. Genelle, L., Prouff, E., Quisquater, M.: Thwarting higher-order side channel analysis with additive and multiplicative maskings. In: Preneel, B., Takagi, T. (eds.) CHES 2011. LNCS, vol. 6917, pp. 240–255. Springer, Heidelberg (2011)
10. Goubin, L.: A sound method for switching between boolean and arithmetic masking. In: Koç, Ç.K., Naccache, D., Paar, C. (eds.) CHES 2001. LNCS, vol. 2162, pp. 3–15. Springer, Heidelberg (2001)
11. Handschuh, H., Heys, H.M.: A timing attack on RC5. In: Tavares, S., Meijer, H. (eds.) SAC 1998. LNCS, vol. 1556, pp. 306–318. Springer, Heidelberg (1999)

12. Kelsey, J., Schneier, B., Wagner, D., Hall, C.: Side channel cryptanalysis of product ciphers. In: Quisquater, J.-J., Deswarte, Y., Meadows, C., Gollmann, D. (eds.) ESORICS 1998. LNCS, vol. 1485, pp. 97–110. Springer, Heidelberg (1998)

13. Kocher, P.C.: Timing Attacks on Implementations of Diffie-Hellman, RSA, DSS, and Other Systems. In: Koblitz, N. (ed.) CRYPTO 1996. LNCS, vol. 1109, pp. 104–113. Springer, Heidelberg (1996)

14. Kocher, P., Jaffe, J., Jun, B.: Differential power analysis. In: Wiener, M. (ed.) CRYPTO 1999. LNCS, vol. 1666, pp. 388–397. Springer, Heidelberg (1999)

15. Mangard, S., Oswald, M.E., Popp, T.: Power Analysis Attacks - Revealing the Secrets of Smart Cards, vol. 54, pp. 1–337. Springer (2007)

16. Messerges, T.S.: Using second-order power analysis to attack DPA resistant software. In: Paar, C., Koç, Ç.K. (eds.) CHES 2000. LNCS, vol. 1965, pp. 238–251. Springer, Heidelberg (2000)

17. Messerges, T.S.: Securing the AES finalists against power analysis attacks. In: Schneier, B. (ed.) FSE 2000. LNCS, vol. 1978, pp. 150–164. Springer, Heidelberg (2001)

18. Neiße, O., Pulkus, J.: Switching blindings with a view towards IDEA. In: Joye, M., Quisquater, J.-J. (eds.) CHES 2004. LNCS, vol. 3156, pp. 230–239. Springer, Heidelberg (2004)

19. Oswald, E., Mangard, S., Herbst, C., Tillich, S.: Practical second-order DPA attacks for masked smart card implementations of block ciphers. In: Pointcheval, D. (ed.) CT-RSA 2006. LNCS, vol. 3860, pp. 192–207. Springer, Heidelberg (2006), http://dx.doi.org/10.1007/11605805_13

20. Pan, J., Hartog, J.I., Lu, J.: You cannot hide behind the mask: Power analysis on a provably secure s-box implementation. In: Youm, H.Y., Yung, M. (eds.) WISA 2009. LNCS, vol. 5932, pp. 178–192. Springer, Heidelberg (2009), http://dx.doi.org/10.1007/978-3-642-10838-9_14

21. Rivain, M., Dottax, E., Prouff, E.: Block ciphers implementations provably secure against second order side channel analysis. In: Nyberg, K. (ed.) FSE 2008. LNCS, vol. 5086, pp. 127–143. Springer, Heidelberg (2008)

22. Tunstall, M., Whitnall, C., Oswald, E.: Masking tables—an underestimated security risk. In: Moriai, S. (ed.) Fast Software Encryption, 20th International Workshop, FSE 2013, Singapore, March 10-13. LNCS, Springer (2013) (Revised Selected Papers)

Identity-Based Identification Schemes from ID-KEMs

Prateek Barapatre and Chandrasekaran Pandu Rangan

Theoretical Computer Science Lab.,
Department of Computer Science and Engineering,
IIT Madras, Chennai, India
{pbarapatre.64,prangan55}@gmail.com

Abstract. Identity-based identification(IBI) schemes are means to achieve entity identification in the identity-based setting in a secure fashion. Quite a large number of IBI schemes exist, but, there is still a need for more efficient(in terms of computation and communication) IBI schemes, especially in domains like mobile devices and smart cards. We propose a generic framework for constructing an IBI scheme from an Identity-Based Key Encapsulation Mechanism(ID-KEM) which is semantically secure against adaptive chosen ciphertext attack on one-wayness(OW-CCA2). The derived IBI scheme will be secure against impersonation under active and concurrent attacks. This framework if applied to ID-KEM can lead to more efficient IBI scheme, as opposed to an IBI scheme developed from scratch, depending on the underlying ID-KEM used. Additionally, we propose a new concrete and efficient IBI scheme secure against concurrent attack based on the q-BDHI hard problem assumption.

Keywords: Identity-based cryptography, Identity-based identification, Key encapsulation mechanism, q-Bilinear Diffie-Hellman inversion, Random oracle model.

1 Introduction

A *Standard Identification(SI)* scheme is an interactive protocol which allows an honest entity, called a *prover*, to prove its identity to a verifying entity, called a *verifier*, in a secure fashion. In this process the secret information of the proving entity is not revealed but the *verifier* gets convinced of the genuineness of the *prover*. It enables a *prover* to convince a *verifier* that he is indeed the same entity which he claims to be. The identification schemes can be both symmetric and asymmetric. We concentrate on asymmetric or the public identity-based identification scheme in this work.

Historically there are basically two types of identification schemes:

1. Challenge-and-Response type, obtained in a natural way from encryption or signature schemes.
2. Σ-protocol type, which is a kind of proof of knowledge [1] consisting of a three-round interactive protocol.

B. Gierlichs, S. Guilley, and D. Mukhopadhyay (Eds.): SPACE 2013, LNCS 8204, pp. 111–129, 2013.

In this work, we focus on Challenge-and-Response type of identification scheme using key encapsulation mechanism. The notion of SI can be extended to the ID-based cryptography setting as proposed by Shamir [2] and is known as identity-based identification(IBI) scheme. In an IBI scheme, there is a central authority called the Private Key Generator(PKG), which generates master secret key, master public key and also generates private key for users from their respective public identity. The *prover*, then can verify himself to a *verifier* using a protocol, where the *verifier* knows only the claimed public identity of the *prover*, the public parameters and the master public key. Identification schemes have a large number of applications in the real world, like in the verification of smart cards, military and defense activities, etc.

To break an identification protocol, the aim of an adversary(impersonator) is to prove himself as an entity which he is not. For this the adversary stands between a *verifier* and a *prover*, and invokes many instances of the *prover* application(*prover* clones), each clone having independent states and random tapes. Interacting in some cheating way, the adversary tries to collect information of the secret key from the *prover* clones while the adversary interacts with the *verifier* simultaneously trying to impersonate as the *prover*. This type of an adversary is called a concurrent active attacker.

Recently, Ananda and Arita [3] proposed a framework to obtain identification schemes from key encapsulation mechanism. We extend their idea to the identity-based settings, where the public key of each party is the entity's identity. Moreover, we also show that one-way CCA2 secure ID-KEM serves the required purpose to achieve security against concurrent attacks for IBI schemes. The generic framework proposed can be applied to any OW-CCA2 secure ID-KEM to obtain an IBI scheme secure against concurrent attacks. The KEM-based identification scheme is advantageous as compared to encryption-based identification scheme. This is because, in the case of KEM, an entity can encapsulate random strings which can be generated by the entity itself, as opposed to the encryption-based scheme where one has to encrypt strings(messages) given as input from the other entity. Consequently, KEM-based schemes have a possibility of having simpler and more efficient protocol than encryption-based identification scheme. There are many IBI schemes existing in the literature like those in [4,5,6,7]. With the increased use of mobile devices there is a need for more efficient and faster cryptographic schemes. In the later half of the paper, we propose a new concrete IBI scheme, and our new scheme is more efficient than the existing schemes(in terms of computation or communication).

Our Contribution. In this paper, we first present our general framework for constructing an IBI scheme secure against concurrent attacks from an OW-CCA2 secure ID-KEM. A *verifier* of the OW-CCA2 secure ID-KEM makes a pair of random strings and its corresponding cipher text using the master public key and the public identity of the *prover*, and then sends only the cipher-text to the *prover*. The *prover* decapsulates the cipher text and returns the result as a response to the *verifier*. The *verifier* checks whether the response received from the *prover* is same as the initial random string he used. This way of identification seems to be very easy and simple and it defines our generic framework in the identity-based model. Following the generic construction, we independently propose a novel IBI scheme based on the q-BDHI hard problem assumption and then prove its security in the random oracle model.

Paper Organization. The paper is organized as follows: In Section 2 we fix some notations and discuss the various preliminaries used in the subsequent sections of the paper. In Section 3 we review the formal definitions and security models of IBI and ID-KEM schemes. In Section 4 we give the generic construction for deriving a new IBI scheme from an OW-CCA2 secure ID-KEM. Section 5 covers the construction of the new two-round IBI scheme in the random oracle model and its security proof in the random oracle model. We compare the efficiency of our scheme with the existing schemes in Section 6. Finally we conclude our work in Section 7.

2   Preliminaries

In this section, we discuss the primitives required, including bilinear pairings, their properties and some of the associated hard problems.

2.1   Bilinear Groups and Assumptions

The scheme proposed will require groups equipped with a bilinear map. We review the necessary facts about bilinear maps and associated groups in a similar fashion as that given in Boneh et al [8].

- $\mathbb{G}_1$, $\mathbb{G}_2$, $\mathbb{G}_T$ are multiplicative cyclic groups of prime order p.
- u_1 is a generator of $\mathbb{G}_1$ and u_2 is a generator of $\mathbb{G}_2$.
- ϕ is an isomorphism from $\mathbb{G}_2$ to $\mathbb{G}_1$ with $u_1 = \phi(u_2)$.
- $\hat{e}$ is a map, $\hat{e} : \mathbb{G}_1 \times \mathbb{G}_2 \to \mathbb{G}_T$.

The bilinear map $\hat{e}$ must satisfy the following properties:

- *Bilinearity*: For all $u \in \mathbb{G}_1$, all $v \in \mathbb{G}_2$ and all $a,b \in \mathbb{Z}$ we have $\hat{e}(u^a, v^b) = \hat{e}(u,v)^{ab}$.
- *Non-degeneracy*: $\hat{e}(u_1, u_2) \neq 1$.
- *Computable*: There is an efficient algorithm to compute $\hat{e}(u,v)$, for all $u \in \mathbb{G}_1$ and $v \in \mathbb{G}_2$.

There are many hard problems studied pertaining to bilinear maps. The following are some of the hard problems associated with bilinear maps which we will use in proving the security of our scheme.

Definition 2.1. (*Computational Bilinear Diffie-Hellman (BDH)*) *problem [9] - Given group elements $(g_1,\ g_2,\ g_2^x,\ g_2^y,\ g_2^z)$ for $x, y, z \in_R \mathbb{Z}_P$, compute $\hat{e}(g_1, g_2)^{xyz}$.*

Definition 2.2. (*q-Bilinear Diffie-Hellman inversion (q-BDHI)*) *problem [10] - Given the group elements $(g_1, g_2, g_2^x, g_2^{x^2}, g_2^{x^3}, \ldots, g_2^{x^q})$ with $x \in_R \mathbb{Z}_P$, compute $\hat{e}(g_1, g_2)^{1/x}$.*

3   Formal Definition and Security Models

In this section, we formally describe IBI and ID-KEM along with their security models.

3.1   Identity Based Identification(IBI) Scheme

An IBI system consists of four Probabilistic Polynomial Time(PPT in short) algorithms (*Setup 'S', Extract 'E', Prove 'P' and Verify 'V'*) [7,6] where,

1. *Setup(S)*: The trusted key issuing authority(PKG) takes as input 1^t, where t is the security parameter, and generates the system parameters, the master public key M_{pk} and the master secret key M_{sk}. It publishes the system parameters and M_{pk} while keeps the secret M_{sk} to itself.
2. *Extract(E)*: For a user A, the PKG takes in the public identity of the user $ID_A \in \{0,1\}^*$, M_{sk} and returns the corresponding user secret key (d_{ID_A}).
3. *Identification Protocol(P and V)*: The *prover* with identity ID_A, runs the interactive *Prover(P)* algorithm with initial state as the user secret key d_{ID_A}, whereas the *verifier* runs the *Verifier(V)* algorithm with initial state as the public identity of the user ID_A and the master public key M_{pk}. At the end of the protocol, the *verifier* outputs either 1 or 0(Accept/Reject).

In the random oracle model, the three algorithms - E, P and V have access to functions H whose range may depend on M_{pk}. It is required that for all $t \in \mathbb{N}$, $ID_i \in \{0,1\}^*$, $M_{sk}, M_{pk} \in S(1^t)$, the functions H with appropriate domain and range, and $d_{ID_i} \in E(M_{sk}, ID_i : H)$, the interaction between P and V is accepted with probability one.

3.2   Security Model for IBI

We consider the security notion for IBI as proposed in [11,6]. We consider three types of attacks on the *honest prover*, namely passive attack, active attack and concurrent attack. The goal of an adversary towards an *IBI* scheme is impersonation. An impersonator is considered successful, if it interacts with an *honest verifier* as a *cheating prover* and manages to convince him with a high probability that he is the actual *prover*. In this case the IBI scheme is said to be broken and hence insecure.

We describe in general three types of attacks which an impersonator can mount on IBI schemes:

1. *Passive Attack*: This type of adversary merely listens to the transcript queries between an *honest verifier* and *honest prover*, and tries to extract information from them. The adversary only taps the channel between the *honest prover* and *verifier*. It is the most easy and weak type of attack.
2. *Active attack*: In this type of attack the adversary interacts with the *prover* as a *cheating verifier* and tries to gain knowledge using extraction queries and decapsulation of various cipher texts. After he has gathered sufficient information he acts as a *cheating prover* to convince an *honest verifier*. If he succeeds in doing so, then he has successfully broken the scheme.

3. *Concurrent Attack*: This type of adversary is similar to the active adversary, but with the difference that here he can invoke multiple *prover* instances and interacts with them at the same time.

The impersonation attack between an impersonator I and the challenger is described as a two-phased attack game described below:

- **Setup.** The challenger takes the security parameter and runs the Setup algorithm 'S'. It gives the impersonator I the system parameters and master public key M_{pk} and keeps the master secret key M_{sk} to itself.
- **Phase 1**
  1. I issues polynomial number of key extraction queries for identities ID_1, $ID_2,\ldots,ID_q$. The challenger responds to the queries by running the extract algorithm and replies by returning the corresponding private key for the public identity queried.
  2. I issues transcript queries and some identification queries on ID_j.
  3. The queries in above steps are interleaved and asked adaptively by I. Also it is assumed that I will not query the same ID_i in the identification/transcript queries for which it has already queried the algorithm E.
- **Phase 2**
  1. I outputs a challenge identity $ID^* \neq \{ID_i$ in the extraction queries$\}$ on which it wishes to impersonate. I now plays the role of a *cheating prover*, trying to convince an *honest verifier*.
  2. I can still continue to issue extract, identification and transcript queries, with the restriction that the challenge identity is not queried for a key extract.

We say that I succeeds in impersonating if it can make an *honest verifier* accept with non-negligible probability.

Definition 3.1. *We say that an IBI scheme is (T, q_1, ϵ)-secure under passive, active and concurrent attacks if for any passive/active/concurrent impersonator I who runs in time T,*

$$Pr[I \text{ can impersonate}] < \epsilon,$$

where I can make at most q_1 key extraction queries.

We now proceed to give more formal definitions for the IBI scheme under passive, active and concurrent settings. Let $\mathcal{A}(CP, CV)$ be an adversary consisting of two PPT algorithms, CP(*cheating prover*) and CV(*cheating verifier*) and let $t \in \mathbb{N}$ be the security parameter. There are four oracles namely *Initialize oracle*(INIT), *Corrupt oracle*(CORR), *Conversation oracle*(CONV) and *Prover oracle*(PROV) as shown in Figure 1, the access to which for the adversary depends on the type of attack as depicted in Figure 2. The adversary can initialize and corrupt identities of its own choice using the INIT and CORR oracles. In case of passive attacks(*pa*), the adversary gets access to the CONV oracle, which

Oracle INIT(ID_i)
If $ID_i \in CU \cup HU \cup AU$ then return $\perp$
$d_{ID_i} \overset{R}{\leftarrow} S(M_{sk}, ID_i);\ \ HU \leftarrow HU \cup \{ID_i\}$
Return 1

Oracle CORR(ID_i)
If $ID_i \notin HU \backslash AU$ then return $\perp$
$CU \leftarrow CU \cup ID_i; HU \leftarrow HU \backslash \{ID_i\}$
Return d_{ID_i}

Oracle CONV(ID_i)
If $ID_i \notin HU$ then return $\perp$
$(C, d) \overset{R}{\leftarrow} \mathbf{Run}[P(d_{ID_i}) \leftrightarrow V(M_{pk}, ID_i)]$
Return C

Oracle PROV(ID_i, s, M_{in})
If $ID_i \notin HU \backslash AU$ then return $\perp$
If$(ID_i, s) \notin PS$ then
If $atk = Active\ Attack$ then $PS \leftarrow (ID_i, s)$
If $atk = Concurrent\ Attack$ then $PS \leftarrow PS \cup (ID_i, s)$
Pick random bits ρ for prover algorithm P
$St_P[ID_i, s] \leftarrow (d_{ID_i}, \rho)$
$(M_{out}, St_P[ID_i, s]) \leftarrow P(M_{in}, St_P[ID_i, s])$
Return M_{out}.

Fig. 1. Oracles given to an adversary attacking IBI scheme

when queried with the identity ID_i of the honest and initialized user, returns a transcript of ID_i and the *verifier*, each time using fresh random bits. When an identity is initialized, it is issued a secret key by the authority. When an (honest) identity is corrupted, its secret key is returned to the adversary. CU is the set of corrupted users, HU is the set of honest users, and AU is the set of users under attack.

In the case of active attacks(aa) or concurrent attacks(ca), the adversary gets additional access to PROV. Its arguments are an identity ID_i, a session number, and a message that the adversary, playing the role of *verifier*, sends to ID_i in its role as a *prover*. The oracle maintains state for the *prover* for each active session, but allows only one session to be active at any point if the attack is an active one, rather than a concurrent one. At the end of its execution, CV transfers its state to CP and outputs an uncorrupted identity ID^*. In the second stage, CP will try to impersonate ID^*. A point in this definition worth noting is that we have allowed CP to query the same oracles as CV. This allows CP to initialize, corrupt, interact with, or see conversations involving certain identities depending on the challenge it gets from the *verifier*. The only restriction is that CP cannot submit queries involving ID^* because otherwise impersonating ID^* would become trivial. The restrictions are all enforced by the oracles themselves.

(At the end of the first stage, ID^* is added to the set of users under attack AU and, in the case of active or concurrent attacks, removed from the set of honest users HU).

Experiment $\mathbf{Exp}^{imp-atk}_{IBI,\mathcal{A}}(t)$ //$atk \in pa, aa, ca$

$(M_{pk}, M_{sk}) \xleftarrow{R} S(1^t)$
$HU \leftarrow \emptyset, CU \leftarrow \emptyset, AU \leftarrow \emptyset$ //set of Honest, Corrupt, and Attacked users
$PS \leftarrow \emptyset$ // set of active prover sessions
If $atk = pa$ then let OR represent CONV, else let OR represent PROV
$(ID_j, St_{CP}) \leftarrow CV(1^t, M_{pk} : INIT, CORR, OR)$
$AU \leftarrow \{ID_j\}$; If $ID_j \in HU$ then return 0.
$(C, d) \xleftarrow{R} \mathbf{Run}[CP(St_{CP} : INIT, CORR, OR) \leftrightarrow V(M_{pk}, ID_j)]$
Return d.

Fig. 2. Experiment defining *imp-atk* security of IBI scheme

3.3 ID-KEM

An *ID-KEM* is described as a quadruple of PPT algorithms(**Setup, Extract, Encapsulate, Decapsulate**) [12] where, the four PPT algorithms are:

- **Setup** $G_{ID-KEM}(1^t)$: Given a security parameter t, the PPT algorithm generates system parameters, the master public key M_{pk}, and the master secret key M_{sk}.
- **Extract** $X_{ID-KEM}(M_{pk}, M_{sk}, ID_A)$: Given the system parameters M_{pk} and M_{sk} and an identity string $ID_A \in \{0,1\}^*$ for an entity A, the PPT algorithm returns the corresponding private key d_{ID_A} for A.
- **Encapsulate** $E_{ID-KEM}(M_{pk}, ID_A)$: Given the system parameters M_{pk} and an identifier ID_A, this PPT algorithm outputs a pair (e,c) where e is a random key in the key space K corresponding to the security parameter k and c is the encapsulation of e or the ciphertext of e.
- **Decapsulate** $D_{ID-KEM}(M_{pk}, d_{ID_A}, c)$: Given the system parameters and M_{pk}, the *prover* uses his private key d_{ID_A} to decapsulate the cipher text c and outputs the corresponding key e' or a reject symbol $\perp$. It is required that for an *honest prover* the decapsulated key e' matches with the original random key e encapsulated by *verifier* with probability one.

3.4 Security of ID-KEM

We describe the security of ID-KEM as given by Bentahar et al [13]. Consider the following two-stage games between an adversary $\mathcal{A}(\mathcal{A}_1, \mathcal{A}_2)$ of the ID-KEM and a challenger as depicted in Figure 3.

ID-OW Adversarial Game (one-wayness property)	ID-IND Adversarial Game (indistinguishability property)
1. $(M_{pk}, M_{sk}) \leftarrow G_{ID-KEM}(1^t)$ 2. $(s, ID^*) \leftarrow \mathcal{A}_1^{\mathcal{O}_{ID}}(M_{pk})$ 3. $(k, c^*) \leftarrow E_{ID-KEM}(ID^*, M_{pk})$ 4. $k' \leftarrow \mathcal{A}_2^{\mathcal{O}_{ID}}(M_{pk}, c^*, s, ID^*)$	1. $(M_{pk}, M_{sk}) \leftarrow G_{ID-KEM}(1^t)$ 2. $(s, ID^*) \leftarrow \mathcal{A}_1^{\mathcal{O}_{ID}}(M_{pk})$ 3. $(k_0, c^*) \leftarrow E_{ID-KEM}(ID^*, M_{pk})$ 4. $k_1 \leftarrow \mathbb{K}_{ID-KEM}(M_{pk})$ 5. $b \leftarrow \{0, 1\}$ 6. $b' \leftarrow \mathcal{A}_2^{\mathcal{O}_{ID}}(M_{pk}, c^*, s, ID^*, k_b)$

Fig. 3. Two-stage game between adversary and challenger for ID-KEM

In the above games ID-OW denotes one-wayness property in the identity-based setting, ID-IND denotes indistinguishability property in the identity-based setting, s is some state information and $\mathcal{O}_{ID}$ represents the oracles to which the adversary has access. There are two possibilities for these oracles depending on the attack model for our game. The two possibilities being:

- CPA Model - In this model the adversary only has access to a private key extraction oracle which on input of $ID_i \neq ID^*$ will output the corresponding value of d_{ID_i}.
- CCA2 Model - In this model the adversary has access to the private key extraction oracle as above, but it also has access to a decapsulation oracle with respect to any identity ID_i of the adversary's choosing. The adversary has access to this decapsulation oracle, subject to the restriction that in the second phase $\mathcal{A}$ is not allowed to call $\mathcal{O}_{ID}$ with the pair (c^*, ID^*).

For a security parameter t, the adversary's advantage in the first game is defined to be:

$$Adv_{\mathcal{A}, ID-KEM}^{ID-OW-MOD}(t) = \Pr[k' = k]$$

While the advantage in the second game is given by:

$$Adv_{\mathcal{A}, ID-KEM}^{ID-OW-MOD}(t) = |Pr[b' = b] - 1|.$$

An ID-KEM is considered to be secure, in a given goal and attack model(for example, OW-CCA2(one-way CCA2)), if for all PPT adversaries $\mathcal{A}$, the advantage in the above depicted relevant game is a negligible function of the security parameter t.

4   IBI Scheme from ID-KEM

In this section we describe our generic framework to obtain an $IBI(S, E, P, V)$ scheme which is secure against concurrent attacks from an OW-CCA2 secure $ID\text{-}KEM(G_{ID-KEM}, X_{ID-KEM}, E_{ID-KEM}, D_{ID-KEM})$ scheme, the definition of which is discussed in Section 3.3. The framework is described below:

- *Setup(S)*: PPT Master Key Generation algorithm which takes as input the security parameter(1^t) and outputs M_{pk} and M_{sk}.
- *Extract(E)*: Takes as input the public identity of a user A(ID_A), M_{sk}, M_{pk} and returns the user secret key U_{sk}.
- *Interaction Protocol(P and V)*:

  • *Verifier V*: Given ID_A, M_{pk} as input, invokes *Encapsulate* algorithm (E_{ID-KEM}) and gets (c,k), where k is a key from the Key Space and c is its corresponding cipher text.
  V sends c to *prover P*.
  • *Prover P*: Having M_{pk}, U_{sk}, c, ID_A as input, invokes *Decapsulate* algorithm (D_{ID-KEM}) and outputs $\hat{k}$.
  P sends $\hat{k}$ to V.
  • V on receiving $\hat{k}$, checks whether $k \stackrel{?}{=} \hat{k}$.
  If **YES**, then *Accept*,
  else *Reject*.

Theorem 4.1. *If an ID-KEM is OW-CCA2 secure, then the derived IBI scheme is secure against active and concurrent attacks. In other words, for an imperson-ator $\mathcal{I}$ that attacks the IBI scheme in the active and concurrent attack settings, there exists a PPT adversary $\mathcal{B}$ which can attack the ID-KEM in OW-CCA2 setting satisfying,*

$$\boldsymbol{Adv}_{\mathcal{I},IBI}^{imp-catk}(t) \leq \boldsymbol{Adv}_{\mathcal{B},ID-KEM}^{ID-OW-CCA2}(t)$$

where t is the security parameter.

Proof. Let ID-KEM* be an OW-CCA2 secure ID-KEM and let IBI* be the derived IBI scheme, derived using the construction stated above. Let $\mathcal{I}$ be an impersonator for IBI*. Using $\mathcal{I}$ as a subroutine, we can construct a *PPT* OW-CCA2 adversary $\mathcal{B}$, that attacks ID-KEM*. But as the ID-KEM* considered is already proven to be secure, no such adversary $\mathcal{B}$ can exist and hence our derived IBI* will also be secure. $\mathcal{B}$ plays a game with $\mathcal{I}$ acting as a *verifier* at one time and acting as decapsulation algorithm at the other time. The adversary $\mathcal{B}$ employs $\mathcal{I}$ to break the ID-KEM* as depicted in Figure 4.

$\mathcal{B}$ initializes its inner state after getting the inputs ID_A and M_{pk}, chooses a challenge ψ^* and invokes $\mathcal{I}$ on inputs ID_A and M_{pk}. $\mathcal{B}$ now proceeds as:

ACTING AS DECAPSULATION ALGORITHM - In case $\mathcal{I}$ sends a challenge message ψ to a *prover* clone, then $\mathcal{B}$ checks if $\psi = \psi^*$. If so, then $\mathcal{B}$ puts $k = \bot$ and the game is aborted, else $\mathcal{B}$ invokes its decapsulation oracle DEC(sk, .) for the answer of the cipher text ψ and gets as output k which it sends to $\mathcal{I}$.

ACTING AS A VERIFIER - $\mathcal{B}$ sends ψ^* to $\mathcal{I}$ as a challenge. In case $\mathcal{I}$ sends the response message $\hat{k}$ to the *verifier* V(ID_A), $\mathcal{B}$ takes it and returns $\hat{k}$ as the answer for the challenge cipher text ψ^* of ID-KEM*. Thus $\mathcal{B}$ breaks ID-KEM*.

The view of $\mathcal{I}$ in $\mathcal{B}$ is the same as its real view except for the case when $\mathcal{I}$ sends $\psi=\psi^*$ to $\mathcal{B}$. When $\mathcal{I}$ sends ψ^* to $\mathcal{B}$, it is like relaying the transcript of its interaction between $\mathcal{I}$ and *prover* $P(sk)$ to $V(pk, ID_A)$, because the *prover* is deterministic. So $\mathcal{B}$'s response of $k = \perp$ is appropriate.

The calculation for probability follows from the fact that whenever $\mathcal{I}$ wins, $\mathcal{B}$ also wins and hence the inequality holds.

Given M_{pk} and ID_A as the input, challenger $\mathcal{B}$ acts as:

Initial Setting

  - Initialize its inner state.
  - Invoke $\mathcal{I}$ on inputs ID_A, M_{pk}.

Answering $\mathcal{I}$'s Queries

  - Extraction Queries: $\mathcal{B}$ runs its extract algorithm $X_{ID-KEM^*}(M_{pk}, M_{sk}, ID_i)$ to generate the secret key for the entity ID_i, such that $i \neq I$. $\mathcal{I}$ can ask for polynomial number of extract queries.
  - In case $\mathcal{I}$ sends ψ to *prover* clone $P(d_{ID_i})$.
      • If $\psi = \psi^*$, then put $k = \perp$.
      • Else query decapsulation oracle(DEC) for the answer of ψ, i.e.
        $k \longleftarrow D_{ID-KEM^*}(M_{pk}, d_{ID_A}, c)$.
      • Send k to $\mathcal{I}$.
  - If $\mathcal{I}$ queries $V(ID_A, M_{pk})$ for the challenge message.
      • Send ψ^* to $\mathcal{I}$.
  - In case $\mathcal{I}$ sends $\hat{k}^*$ to $V(ID_A, M_{pk})$
      • Return $\hat{k}^*$ as the answer for ψ^*.

Fig. 4. An IBI scheme from an OW-CCA2 secure ID-KEM

5 Proposed IBI Scheme

We now independently propose an IBI(S,E,P,V) scheme which is derived from the ID-KEM scheme [14] after making considerable modifications. This scheme is secure against active and concurrent attacks. The construction of the scheme is outlined below:

Let t be the security parameter. The system parameters are groups $\mathbb{G}_1$, $\mathbb{G}_2$ and $\mathbb{G}_T$, which are all multiplicative cyclic groups of prime order p, where $p \approx 2^t$.

Let $\hat{e} : \mathbb{G}_1 \times \mathbb{G}_2 \longrightarrow \mathbb{G}_T$ be a bilinear map that satisfies the properties specified in Section 2.1. u_1 is generator of $\mathbb{G}_1$ and u_2 is generator of $\mathbb{G}_2$ such that $u_1 = \phi(u_2)$. The scheme uses three hash functions:

$$H_1 : \{0,1\}^* \longrightarrow \mathbb{Z}_p, \ H_2 : \mathbb{G}_T \longrightarrow \{0,1\}^n, \text{ where } \{0,1\}^n \text{ is the message space}$$
$$\text{and,}$$

$$H_3 : \{0,1\}^* \times \{0,1\}^n \longrightarrow \mathbb{Z}_p.$$

The scheme is as follows:

- $S(1^t)$
    - Select $s \in_R \mathbb{Z}_p$.
    - Calculate $R = u_1^s$.
      s is the Master Secret Key(M_{sk}).
      The system parameters along with R forms the Master Public Key(M_{pk}).

- $E(s, M_{pk}, ID_A)$
    - Compute User secret key(U_{sk}) for the identity ID_A as:
      $$D_{ID_A} = u_2^{\frac{1}{(s+H_1(ID_A))}}$$

- Interaction Protocol(P and V)
    - The *verifier* $V(ID_A, M_{pk})$ performs:
        - (a) Select $k \in_R \{0,1\}^n$ i.e. randomly select a key from KEY SPACE.
          where n is of considerable bit length $\approx t$.
        - (b) Select $r \longleftarrow H_3(ID_A, k)$.
        - (c) Compute $Q \longleftarrow R \cdot u_1^{H_1(ID_A)}$.
        - (d) Compute $U \longleftarrow Q^r$.
        - (e) Compute $V \longleftarrow k \oplus H_2(\hat{e}(u_1, u_2)^r)$.
        - (f) Set $c \longleftarrow (U, V)$.
        - (g) Send c to *Prover P*.

    - *Prover $P(M_{pk}, D_{ID_A}, ID_A, c)$.*
      The *prover* performs the following steps:
        - (a) Parse c as (U, V).
        - (b) Compute $Q \longleftarrow R \cdot u_1^{H_1(ID_A)}$.
        - (c) Compute $\alpha \longleftarrow \hat{e}(U, D_{ID_A})$.
        - (d) Compute $k' \longleftarrow H_2(\alpha) \oplus V$, and $r \longleftarrow H_3(ID_A, k')$.
        - (e) Check if $(\alpha = \hat{e}(u_1, u_2)^r)$;
          If YES, then U is CONSISTENT,
          Else ABORT.
        - (f) Send k' to *verifier*.

- *Verifier* on receiving k', checks whether $k = k'$;
  If YES, then *Accept*,
  Else *Reject*.

5.1 Security Proof

The proof of security for our scheme is explained in the Appendix A.

6   Comparison with Other Schemes

In this section, we compare our scheme with various existing IBI schemes in both standard model and random oracle model which are of Challenge-and-Response or Σ-protocol type. Our scheme, to the best of our knowledge is the first concrete IBI scheme based on the Challenge-and-Response system.

Table 1. Comparison between various IBI schemes

Schemes	Computation	Communication	Hard Problem	Model
KH-IBI [15]	$12C_M + 12C_E + 6C_P$	$5|\mathbb{Z}_p| + 4|G|$	q-SDH	Stnd
CHG-IBI [7]	$(n+4)C_M + 5C_E + 3C_P$	$|\mathbb{Z}_p| + 4|G|$	OMCDH	Stnd
BNN-IBI [6]	$4C_M + 7C_E + 2C_A$	$2|\mathbb{Z}_p| + 3|G|$	OMDL	RO
OkDL-IBI [6]	$8C_M + 9C_E + 4C_A$	$3|\mathbb{Z}_p| + 3|G|$	DL	RO
CCSR-IDKEM [14]	$2C_M + 6C_E + 3C_P$	$3|G|$	q-BDHI	RO
Our scheme	$2C_M + 3C_E + 2C_P$	$3|G|$	q-BDHI	RO

In Table 1, C_E, C_P, C_M, C_A represent the computational costs of - group exponential operation, bilinear group pairing operation, bilinear group multiplicative operation and group addition operation respectively. Also, in the table the terms q-SDH, OMCDH, OMDL, DL stand for q-Strong Diffie-Hellman [15], One-More Computational Diffie-Hellman [7], One-More Discrete Logarithm [6] and Discrete Logarithm [6] respectively. Also, the terms Stnd stands for Standard and RO stands for Random Oracle under the Model column heading. For better security we consider n(the size of the KEY SPACE) to be of considerable length $\approx$ security parameter t, hence $2n + |G| \approx 3|G|$. We have compared the efficiency of our scheme with the IBI scheme proposed in [15], the IBI scheme proposed in [7], BNN-IBI and OkDL-IBI schemes [6] and the ID-KEM scheme proposed in [14].

Moreover, our scheme requires only two pairing operations as one of the pairing operations in *prover*'s side of our scheme is needed only once. Thus our scheme is efficient in terms of both computation and communication as compared to other schemes making it suitable for mobile devices.

7   Conclusions

We presented a generic framework to construct IBI scheme from OW-CCA2 secure ID-KEM. This generic construction can be applied to any existing OW-CCA2 secure ID-KEM to get an IBI scheme. Further more, we proposed a new concrete IBI scheme based on ID-KEM [14] after making significant modifications and proved its security by directly reducing it to the q-Bilinear Diffie Hellman Inversion(q-BDHI) hard problem in the random oracle model. Our scheme is very efficient in terms of computation and communication complexity and hence can be used in mobile devices and smart cards where memory and efficient computation are of great importance. It still remains an open problem to construct an efficient IBI scheme that is provably secure against active and concurrent attacks using a weaker assumption in the standard model.

References

1. Goldwasser, S., Micali, S., Rackoff, C.: The knowledge complexity of interactive proof-systems. In: Proceedings of the Seventeenth Annual ACM Symposium on Theory of Computing, STOC 1985, pp. 291–304. ACM, New York (1985)
2. Shamir, A.: Identity-Based Cryptosystems and Signature Schemes. In: Blakely, G.R., Chaum, D. (eds.) CRYPTO 1984. LNCS, vol. 196, pp. 47–53. Springer, Heidelberg (1985)
3. Anada, H., Arita, S.: Identification schemes from key encapsulation mechanisms. In: Nitaj, A., Pointcheval, D. (eds.) AFRICACRYPT 2011. LNCS, vol. 6737, pp. 59–76. Springer, Heidelberg (2011)
4. Fiat, A., Shamir, A.: How To Prove Yourself: Practical Solutions to Identification and Signature Problems, pp. 186–194. Springer (1987)
5. Guillou, L.C., Quisquater, J.-J.: A practical zero-knowledge protocol fitted to security microprocessor minimizing both transmission and memory. In: Günther, C.G. (ed.) EUROCRYPT 1988. LNCS, vol. 330, pp. 123–128. Springer, Heidelberg (1988)
6. Bellare, M., Namprempre, C., Neven, G.: Security Proofs for Identity-Based Identification and Signature Schemes. J. Cryptol. 22(1), 1–61 (2008)
7. Chin, J.-J., Heng, S.-H., Goi, B.-M.: An Efficient and Provable Secure Identity-Based Identification Scheme in the Standard Model. In: Mjølsnes, S.F., Mauw, S., Katsikas, S.K. (eds.) EuroPKI 2008. LNCS, vol. 5057, pp. 60–73. Springer, Heidelberg (2008)
8. Boneh, D., Lynn, B., Shacham, H.: Short Signatures from the Weil Pairing. J. Cryptology 17(4), 297–319 (2004)
9. Boneh, D., Franklin, M.K.: Identity-Based Encryption from the Weil Pairing. SIAM J. Comput. 32(3), 586–615 (2003)
10. Boneh, D., Boyen, X.: Efficient Selective-ID Secure Identity Based Encryption Without Random Oracles. In: Cachin, C., Camenisch, J.L. (eds.) EUROCRYPT 2004. LNCS, vol. 3027, pp. 223–238. Springer, Heidelberg (2004)
11. Kurosawa, K., Heng, S.-H.: From Digital Signature to ID-based Identification/Signature. In: Bao, F., Deng, R., Zhou, J. (eds.) PKC 2004. LNCS, vol. 2947, pp. 248–261. Springer, Heidelberg (2004)
12. Cheng, Z.: Simple SK-ID-KEM1 (2005)
13. Bentahar, K., Farshim, P., Malone-Lee, J., Smart, N.P.: Generic Constructions of Identity-Based and Certificateless KEMs. J. Cryptol. 21(2), 178–199 (2008)
14. Chen, L., Cheng, Z., Smart, N.P., Road, F.: An Efficient ID-KEM based on the Sakai-Kasahara key construction. In: IEE Proceedings of Information Security (2006)
15. Kurosawa, K., Heng, S.-H.: Identity-Based Identification Without Random Oracles. In: Gervasi, O., Gavrilova, M.L., Kumar, V., Laganá, A., Lee, H.P., Mun, Y., Taniar, D., Tan, C.J.K. (eds.) ICCSA 2005. LNCS, vol. 3481, pp. 603–613. Springer, Heidelberg (2005)

A   Proof of Security

We follow the same approach as used by Chen et al [14] to proceed with the proof. Let q_1, q_2, q_x be the number of queries that an impersonator $\mathcal{I}$ can make to H_1, H_2 and to the key extraction oracle respectively. To prove our scheme to be secure, we show that if there exists an impersonator $\mathcal{I}$ for the IBI scheme, then we can construct another algorithm $\mathcal{B}$ to solve the q-BDHI problem, where $q = q_1 + q_x + 1$. This construction involves $\mathcal{B}$ playing the role of challenger which will simulate the protocol.

$\mathcal{B}$ takes as input $(g_1, g_2, g_2^x, g_2^{x^2}, g_2^{x^3}, \ldots\ldots, g_2^{x^q}) \in \mathbb{G}_1 \times \mathbb{G}_2^{q+1}$ with $g_1 = \phi(g_2)$ and then selects an integer $I \in \{1, \ldots\ldots, q\}$. It uses these to set up the domain parameters and keys for the IBI algorithm as described below:

Algorithm $\mathcal{B}$ selects $h_0, h_1, \ldots\ldots, h_{q-1}$ uniformly at random from $\mathbb{Z}_p$. We define the event GUESS to be that in which $h_i = -x$ for some i in $\{1, \ldots\ldots, q-1\}$.(This event can be checked by computing $g_2^{-h_i}$ for i in $\{1, \ldots\ldots, q-1\}$, and comparing these values with g_2^x).

We say that $\mathcal{I}$ wins if it outputs the correct value of the encrypted key which is randomly selected from the KEY SPACE in its attack. The advantage with which an impersonator $\mathcal{I}$ can successfully impersonate the *prover* is represented as $Adv^{IBI}(\mathcal{I})$. By definition,

$$Adv^{IBI}(\mathcal{I}) = Pr[\mathcal{I} \ wins \wedge GUESS] + Pr[\mathcal{I} \ wins \wedge \neg GUESS]$$
$$\leq Pr[GUESS] + Pr[\mathcal{I} \ wins \mid \neg GUESS]$$
$$\leq Adv^{q-BDHI}(\mathcal{B}) + Pr[\mathcal{I} \ wins \mid \neg GUESS] \qquad (1)$$

The above equation follows from the fact that in the event GUESS, the algorithm $\mathcal{B}$ itself finds x which it can use to solve the q-BDHI problem by directly computing $\hat{e}(g_1, g_2)^{1/x}$.

We now describe the non trivial part of the simulation. In the remaining part of the proof, we assume that the event $\neg$GUESS has occurred and so all the probabilities are conditioned on this event. $\mathcal{B}$ defines the following polynomial.

Let $f(z)$ be a polynomial, where $f(z) = \prod_{i=1}^{q-1}(z + h_i)$,

Rewriting f as, $f(z) = \sum_{i=0}^{q-1} c_i z^i$

The constant term c_0 is non-zero because $h_i \neq 0$ and c_i's are computable from h_i's.

$\mathcal{B}$ now computes

$$u_2 = \prod_{i=1}^{q-1}(g_2^{x^i})^{c_i} = (g_2^{f(x)}),$$

and

$$u_2' = \prod_{i=1}^{q-1} (g_2^{x^{i+1}})^{c_i} = (g_2^{x \cdot f(x)}) = u_2^x$$

Note that in the event $\neg$GUESS, we have $u_2 \neq 1$ and so u_2 is a generator of $\mathbb{G}_2$. Algorithm $\mathcal{B}$ also defines the polynomials,

$$f_i(z) = f(z)/(z + h_i) = \sum_{i=0}^{q-2} d_{i,j} z^j, \text{ for } 1 \leq i < q$$

Also,

$$u_2^{1/(x+h_i)} = g_2^{f_i(x)} = \prod_{j=1}^{q-2} (g_2^{x^j})^{d_{i,j}}$$

Let PS denote the set,

$$PS = \left\{ \left(h_j + h_0, u_2^{1/(x+h_i)} \right) \right\}_{j=1}^{q-1}$$

Algorithm $\mathcal{B}$ also sets,

$$t' = \prod_{i=1}^{q-1} (g_2^{x^{i-1}})^{c_i} = g_2^{(f(x)-c_0)/x}, \text{ and sets } \gamma_0 = \hat{e}(\phi(t'), u_2 \cdot g_2^{c_0})$$

It defines $u_1 = \phi(u_2)$ and computes the public key of the Trusted Authority(TA) as

$$R = \phi(u_2' \cdot u_2^{-h_0}) = \phi(u_2') \cdot u_1^{-h_0} = u_1^{x-h_0}$$

We need to check that R has the correct original distribution. Since we are conditioning on the event $\neg$GUESS, we know that u_2 is a generator of $\mathbb{G}_2$, which means that u_1 must be a generator of $\mathbb{G}_1$ as needed in the scheme.

Consider the following distributions associated with a generator u_1 of $\mathbb{G}_1$. Note that in the description below, $\mathcal{D}_x$ is one of a collection of distributions $\{\mathcal{D}_x\}_{x \in \mathbb{Z}_p}$ parametrized by $x \in \mathbb{Z}_p$.

$$\mathcal{D} = \{u_1^s : s \leftarrow \mathbb{Z}_p\},$$
$$\text{and, } \mathcal{D}_x = \{u_1^{x-h_0} : h_0 \leftarrow \mathbb{Z}_p\}$$

Clearly, for any $x \in \mathbb{Z}_p$, these distributions are identical. Moreover, R is chosen from $\mathcal{D}$ when the identical scheme is used in reality and R is chosen from $\mathcal{D}_x$ in our simulation(conditioned on the event $\neg$GUESS). So, we can conclude that R has the correct distribution.

Phase 1

Algorithm $\mathcal{B}$ now invokes the first stage of the algorithm for $\mathcal{I}$ with the domain parameters that it has constructed. In this phase, the impersonator $\mathcal{I}$ will play the role of a *cheating verifier*. $\mathcal{B}$ responds to the oracle calls made by $\mathcal{I}$ as follows:

- H_1 Query on ID_i : $\mathcal{B}$ maintains a list of tuples, the $\mathcal{H}_1$ list (ID_i,h_i,D_{ID_i}) indexed by ID_i. On input of ID_i, the ith distinct query, algorithm $\mathcal{B}$ acting as a challenger responds as follows:
  1. If $i = I$, then $\mathcal{B}$ responds with h_0 and adds $(ID_i,h_0,\perp)$ to the $\mathcal{H}_1$ list.
  2. Otherwise, it selects a random element $(h_i + h_0, u_2^{1/(x+h_i)})$ from PS list(without replacement). It adds $(ID_i, h_i + h_0, u_2^{1/(x+h_i)})$ to the $\mathcal{H}_1$ list, and returns $h_i + h_0$.

  If the impersonator $\mathcal{I}$ queries the same ID_i, then $\mathcal{B}$ responds with the same result that it gave the first time by looking it up on the list.

- H_2 Query on α: $\mathcal{B}$ maintains a list $\mathcal{H}_2$ of tuples(α, β). If α appears in the list $\mathcal{H}_2$, then $\mathcal{B}$ responds with β. Otherwise it chooses β at random from $\{0,1\}^n$ and it adds (α, β) to the $\mathcal{H}_2$ list before responding with β.

- H_3 Query: Algorithm $\mathcal{B}$ generates a random value $r' \in_R \mathbb{Z}_p$ for every (ID_i,k_i) and stores this value in $\mathcal{H}_3$ list. The $\mathcal{H}_3$ list is a three tuple,(ID_i,r',k_i) and is indexed by ID_i.

- *Extraction Query* for ID_i: If ID_i does not appear on the $\mathcal{H}_1$ list then $\mathcal{B}$ first makes an H_1 query. Algorithm $\mathcal{B}$ then checks whether the corresponding value of D_{ID_i} is $\perp$. If so, then it terminates (this event corresponds to challenger $\mathcal{B}$ failing to correctly guess at what point the impersonator $\mathcal{I}$ would query $\mathcal{H}_1$ with its chosen ID^*). Otherwise, it responds with D_{ID_i}, where (ID_i,h_i,D_{ID_i}) is the entry corresponding to ID_i in the $\mathcal{H}_1$ list.

- *Impersonation Queries*: $\mathcal{B}$ will respond to these queries as:
  1. When $ID_i \neq ID_I$: $\mathcal{B}$ invokes the *Extraction Query* and then uses valid private key to interact with the impersonator $\mathcal{I}$.
  2. If $ID_i = ID_I$, $\mathcal{B}$ has to find the value of r in $\mathcal{H}_3$ list for the ID_i index. $\mathcal{B}$ searches the $\mathcal{H}_3$ list with ID_i index, so as to satisfy the condition $Q^r = U$ required in the scheme. $\mathcal{B}$ then returns the corresponding k for the r, as the response to the query, from $\mathcal{H}_3$ list. If such an r is not found, then $\mathcal{B}$ returns INVALID and continues.

$\mathcal{I}$ could guess the correct or a consistent (U, V) pair even when it has not queried the H_3 oracle with probability $1/p$. We call this event as GUESS2. In GUESS2 event, the *Impersonation Queries* will be answered as invalid though they are valid, and thus $\mathcal{I}$ will come to know that he is playing with a simulated challenger, and not in a real scenario. So $\mathcal{I}$ will stop the game with probability $1/p$ which is negligibly small.

Phase 2

After some time, $\mathcal{I}$ will terminate its first phase and will return the challenge identity ID^*. If $\mathcal{I}$ has not called H_1 with input ID^*, then $\mathcal{B}$ does so for it. The corresponding value of D_{ID^*} must be $\perp$, or else $\mathcal{B}$ will have to abort.

Algorithm $\mathcal{B}$ chooses a random value of $r \in \mathbb{Z}_p$ and a random value V^* in $\{0,1\}^*$. It computes $U^* = u_1^r$ and sets the challenge cipher text as,

$$c^* = (U^*, V^*)$$

This cipher text is now passed to $\mathcal{I}$'s second stage. $\mathcal{I}$ will continue to ask *Extraction Queries* and owing to the rules of the game, $\mathcal{B}$ will not terminate unexpectedly and will continue returning appropriate values.

At some point, the algorithm $\mathcal{I}$ acting as *cheating prover* outputs the value of the underlying key k'. For a genuine key we should have

$$k' = V^* \oplus \mathcal{H}_2(\hat{e}(U^*, D_{ID^*})).$$

If H_2 is modelled as a random oracle, we know that $\mathcal{I}$ has advantage of returning the valid k' only if the list $\mathcal{H}_2$ contains an input value

$$\alpha^* = \hat{e}(U^*, D_{ID^*}).$$

Algorithm $\mathcal{B}$ selects a value α at random from the $\mathcal{H}_2$ list and we assume that it correctly selects $\alpha = \alpha^*$, thus this adds for an additional factor of $1/q_2$ to our subsequent analysis. Acting challenger $\mathcal{B}$ sets

$$\gamma = \alpha^{*1/r}$$

We have that,

$$D_{ID^*} = u_2^{1/((x-h_0)+h_0)}$$

and so

$$\gamma = \hat{e}(u_1, u_2)^{1/x}$$

The challenger's job is to compute $\hat{e}(g_1, g_2)^{1/x}$. It computes,

$$\gamma/\gamma_0 = \hat{e}(g_1, g_2)^{f(x) \cdot f(x)/x} / \hat{e}(g_1^{(f(x)-c_0)/x}, g_2^{f(x)+c_0})$$

$$= \hat{e}(g_1, g_2)^{(f(x) \cdot f(x)/x) - (f(x) \cdot f(x)/x) + (c_0^2/x)}$$

$$= \hat{e}(g_1, g_2)^{c_0^2/x}.$$

and $\mathcal{B}$ solves the q-BDHI problem by outputting $\hat{e}(g_1, g_2)^{1/x} = (\gamma/\gamma_0)^{1/c_0^2}$.

The above procedure for calculating the solution can fail if: $(1)r = 0$, $(2)c_0$ $=0$. However, this will not happen if $h_i \neq 0$ for $i=0,.....,$q-1 and $r \neq 0$. We say that the event FAIL occurs if at least one of these condition fails. We have,

$$Pr[\mathcal{I} \ wins \mid \neg GUESS] = Pr[\mathcal{I} \ wins \wedge \neg FAIL \mid \neg GUESS] +$$
$$Pr[\mathcal{I} \ wins \wedge FAIL \mid \neg GUESS]$$

$$\leq Pr[\mathcal{I} \ wins \mid \neg FAIL \wedge \neg GUESS] + \frac{q+1}{p}$$

$$\leq Pr[\mathcal{I} \ wins \mid \neg FAIL \wedge \neg GUESS] + \frac{q+1}{p} \qquad (2)$$

Let us denote the event that $\mathcal{I}$ makes the query α^* during its attack by ASK.

$$Pr[\mathcal{I} \ wins \mid \neg GUESS \wedge \neg FAIL] = Pr[\mathcal{I} \ wins \wedge ASK \mid \neg GUESS \wedge \neg FAIL] +$$
$$Pr[\mathcal{I} \ wins \wedge \neg ASK \mid \neg GUESS \wedge \neg FAIL]$$
$$= Pr[\mathcal{I} \ wins \wedge ASK \mid \neg GUESS \wedge \neg FAIL]$$
$$+ \frac{1}{2^n} \qquad (3)$$

The last inequality follows from the fact that in a random oracle model, if the event ASK does not occur, then $\mathcal{I}$ has no information about the message encrypted in the challenge ciphertext.

To conclude the proof we note that when the event ASK happens, then $\mathcal{B}$ succeeds in solving q-BDHI problem if,
(1) $\mathcal{B}$ picks the correct index I, which happens with probability $1/(q_1 + q_x + 1)$, and
(2) $\mathcal{B}$ chooses the correct entry α^* from list H_2, which happens with probability $1/q_2$,

Thus, we have,

$$Adv^{q-BDHI}(\mathcal{B}) \geq \left(\frac{1}{q_1 + q_x + 1}\right) \cdot \left(\frac{1}{q_2}\right) \cdot Pr[\mathcal{I} \ wins \wedge ASK \mid \neg GUESS \wedge \neg FAIL]$$

$$Adv^{q-BDHI}(\mathcal{B}) \geq \frac{Pr[\mathcal{I} \ wins \wedge ASK \mid \neg GUESS \wedge \neg FAIL]}{((q_1 + q_x + 1) \cdot q_2)}$$

$$Adv^{q-BDHI}(\mathcal{B}) \geq \frac{Pr[\mathcal{I} \ wins \mid \neg GUESS \wedge \neg FAIL]}{((q_1 + q_x + 1) \cdot q_2)} -$$
$$\frac{1}{(2^n \cdot ((q_1 + q_x + 1) \cdot q_2))} \qquad [Using (3)]$$

$$Adv^{q-BDHI}(\mathcal{B}) \geq \frac{Pr[\mathcal{I} \ wins \mid \neg GUESS]}{((q_1 + q_x + 1) \cdot q_2)} - \frac{1}{(2^n \cdot ((q_1 + q_x + 1) \cdot q_2))} -$$
$$\frac{(q+1)}{(p \cdot (q_1 + q_x + 1) \cdot q_2)} \qquad [Using (2)]$$

$$Adv^{q-BDHI}(\mathcal{B}) \cdot ((q_1 + q_x + 1) \cdot q_2) \geq Pr[\mathcal{I} \ wins \mid \neg GUESS] - \frac{1}{2^n} - \frac{(q+1)}{p}$$

$$Adv^{q-BDHI}(\mathcal{B}) \cdot ((q_1 + q_x + 1) \cdot q_2) + \frac{1}{2^n} + \frac{(q+1)}{p} \geq Pr[\mathcal{I} \ wins \mid \neg GUESS] \qquad (4)$$

Putting (4) in (1), we get:

$$Adv^{IBI}(\mathcal{I} \ wins) \leq Adv^{q-BDHI}(\mathcal{B}) + Adv^{q-BDHI}(\mathcal{B}) \cdot ((q_1 + q_x + 1) \cdot q_2) + \frac{q+1}{p} + \frac{1}{2^n}$$

$$Adv^{IBI}(\mathcal{I} \ wins) \leq ((q_1 + q_x + 1) \cdot q_2) + 1) \cdot Adv^{q-BDHI}(\mathcal{B}) + \frac{q+1}{p} + \frac{1}{2^n}$$

$$Adv^{IBI}(\mathcal{I} \ wins) - \left(\frac{q+1}{p} + \frac{1}{2^n}\right) \leq ((q_1 + q_x + 1) \cdot q_2 + 1) \cdot Adv^{q-BDHI}(\mathcal{B})$$

$$Adv^{q-BDHI}(\mathcal{B}) \geq \frac{Adv^{IBI}(\mathcal{I} \ wins) - (\frac{q+1}{p} + \frac{1}{2^n})}{((q_1 + q_x + 1) \cdot q_2 + 1)}$$

Since $Adv^{IBI}(\mathcal{I} \ wins)$ is a non-negligible quantity and quantities $\frac{q+1}{p}$ and $\frac{1}{2^n}$ are negligibly small, we can easily infer that $Adv^{q-BDHI}(\mathcal{B})$ is non-negligible as q_1, q_x, q_2 are polynomial quantities. Hence, the challenger solves the q-BDHI problem with non-negligible probability, which is not possible and so our scheme holds secure.

Anonymous Identity-Based Identification Scheme in Ad-Hoc Groups without Pairings

Prateek Barapatre and Chandrasekaran Pandu Rangan

Theoretical Computer Science Lab.,
Department of Computer Science and Engineering,
IIT Madras, Chennai, India
{pbarapatre.64,prangan55}@gmail.com

Abstract. Anonymous identification schemes in ad-hoc groups are cryptographic primitives that allow a participant from a set of users to prove her identity in that group, without revealing her actual identity or the group secret key. All the existing ad-hoc anonymous identification schemes in the literature make use of the bilinear pairing operation, resulting in a computational overhead. In this paper we propose a novel anonymous identity-based identification scheme for ad-hoc groups without using bilinear pairings. This scheme, to the best of our knowledge, is the first of its kind which does not use pairing operations. The proof of our scheme is based on the hardness assumption of RSA problem.

Keywords: Identity-based identification, Anonymity, Ad-hoc group, RSA assumption.

1 Introduction

An identification(ID) scheme allows an entity called a *prover*(say Alice) to securely identify herself to another entity called a *verifier*(say Bob). ID schemes enable the *prover* to convince a *verifier* that she is indeed the same entity which she claims to be, by showing that she knows some secret information without revealing her secret information. Secure identification schemes were introduced by Fiat and Shamir [1] followed by many other identification schemes [2,3,4]. Anonymous identification scheme is yet another important primitive which has wide ranging applications in the domains of e-commerce and auctions. Ad-hoc group refers to participants from a user population that can form group in an ad-hoc fashion(without the help of a group manager). An ad-hoc anonymous identification scheme is a multi-user cryptographic primitive that allows participants from a user population to form ad-hoc groups and then prove their membership in such groups anonymously. In an anonymous ad-hoc group identification scheme, a member A of a group $\mathcal{G}$ convinces another entity B outside the group, that she is one amongst those in $\mathcal{G}$ in a secure fashion without revealing any information about her own identity, thus maintaining her privacy. This is a very useful primitive which enables an entity A to control her privacy while enjoying privileges of the groups. There are many applications of such anonymous

B. Gierlichs, S. Guilley, and D. Mukhopadhyay (Eds.): SPACE 2013, LNCS 8204, pp. 130–146, 2013.

identification schemes such as providing access to a resource to only certain privileged group of users without the need for the user to reveal her actual identity, for entry in some restricted building by some group members only, etc. Anonymous authentication for dynamic group is also an indispensable component in online auctions, electronic voting and open procurement, which are becoming very popular business areas in e-commerce. Authenticating membership in a group is an important task because many privileges(such as the right to read a document, access to a hardware or application resources) are often assigned to many individuals. While the permission to exercise a privilege requires that members of the group be distinguished from non-members, members need not be distinguished from one another, just a confirmation of them belonging to the group is sufficient to authorize them to access the resource.

The concept of ad-hoc anonymous identification scheme was first introduced by Dodis et al [5] in Public-Key Infrastructure(PKI) setting and it was extended to identity-based setting by Nguyen [6]. The latter work makes use of the notions of dynamic cryptographic accumulators, which in turn are derived using bilinear pairings in their scheme. Following Nguyen's work [6], other ad-hoc anonymous identity-based identification schemes were proposed, some of which do not make use of cryptographic accumulators, but still use pairings. To the best of our knowledge, the most efficient of such schemes is the one proposed by Chunxiang Gu et al [7], which even though do not use accumulators, still make use of bilinear pairings.

Our Contribution: Many anonymous identity-based identification schemes for ad-hoc groups are available, but they all make use of the bilinear pairing operations. In this work we propose a new ad-hoc anonymous IBI scheme, which preserves the security requirements for an anonymous IBI without using bilinear maps. The proposed scheme is more efficient computationally, as the pairing operation increases the computational cost incurred. Moreover, for implementing our scheme, we do not have to be concerned for choosing appropriate bilinear maps. The security of our scheme is based on the hardness assumption of RSA problem in the composite group of integers.

Paper Organisation: The paper is organised as follows: In Section 2, we explain the preliminaries required and cover the formal definitions of ad-hoc anonymous IBI schemes along with their security requirements. In the third Section, we show the construction of our scheme followed by its security arguments in Section 4. In Section 5, we compare our scheme with various existing schemes in the literature. Finally, we conclude our work in Section 6.

2   Formal Definitions and Security Model

We first describe the hardness assumption used, then proceed to describe the canonical three-move identification protocol, followed by the formal definitions and security model for ad-hoc anonymous IBI scheme.

2.1   Hard Problem Assumption

Definition 2.1. *RSA Problem* [8]- *Let $N = pq$ be a composite integer computed from two large prime numbers p and q each k-bit long, where, k is the security parameter. Let e be a random prime number, greater than 2^l for some fixed parameter l, such that $gcd(e, \phi(N)) = 1$. Let y be a random element from $\mathbb{Z}_N^*$.*

We say that an algorithm $\mathcal{I}$ solves the RSA problem, if it receives as input the tuple (N, e, y) and outputs an element z, such that $z^e = y \bmod N$.

2.2   Canonical 3-Move Identification

A three-move protocol of the form depicted in Figure 1 is said to be *canonical* as given by Bellare et al [9]. This protocol is initiated by the *prover*. The *prover*'s first message is called commitment, then the *verifier* selects a challenge uniformly at random from a set, called challenge set $ChSet_v$, associated with its input v. After this step, the *prover* sends a response and upon receiving the response, the *verifier* applies a deterministic procedure DEC_v to arrive at a decision whether to *Accept* or *Reject*. The *prover* P has input q, a random tape R and maintains a state St. The *verifier* V has input v and returns boolean decision d of *Accept* or *Reject*.

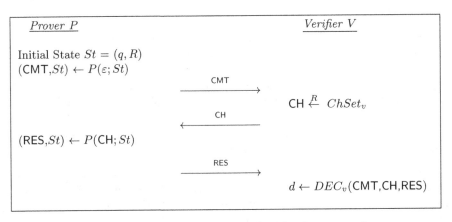

Fig. 1. A canonical three-move identification protocol

2.3   Identity-Based Ad-Hoc Anonymous Identification Schemes

The definition of anonymous identification in ad-hoc groups was originally given in the PKI setting by Dodis et al [5]. Nguyen extended the definition to the ID-based setting [6]. The changes made by Nguyen [6] to reconcile the security notions for the ID-based model are that: the *Register* algorithm is replaced by the *KeyGen* algorithm and the *Setup* algorithm is not required to maintain a database of public key of users.

We follow the same definition as given by Nguyen [6], but we also elaborate further to describe the formal games concerning the security of the ad-hoc anonymous IBI schemes.

An ad-hoc anonymous IBI scheme is defined as a five tuple, $\mathcal{IAID} = ($**Setup, KeyGen, MakeGPK, MakeGSK, IAID**$)$ of Probabilistic Polynomial Time (PPT) algorithms which are described below:

1. **Setup**: The central authority, called the Private Key Generator(PKG) runs the *Setup* algorithm. This algorithm takes as input the security parameter 1^k and outputs the public parameters param and master secret key M_{sk}. The PKG keeps the M_{sk} to itself.

2. **KeyGen**: It takes as input the public parameters param, the master secret key(M_{sk}) and the identity of the user and outputs the private key of the user. The private key of the user is then send to the user by PKG through a secure channel. The identity used is the public key of the user.

3. **MakeGPK**: This PPT algorithm takes as input the public parameters param, the set of identities and deterministically outputs the group public key, which is later used in the identification protocol $IAID$. The algorithm is *order-independent* i.e., the order in which the public keys to be aggregated are provided does not matter. The algorithm runs in linear time in the order of the number of public keys being aggregated.

4. **MakeGSK**: It takes as input param, the set of entities, an entity amongst the set of entities and its corresponding private key, and outputs the group secret key which is used in the group identification protocol. Its cost also varies linearly with the number of entities being aggregated. It should be observed that the group secret key g_{sk} must correspond to a group public key g_{pk}.

5. **IAID** $= ($IAID$_P$,IAID$_V)$ is the two party identification protocol which allows the *prover* IAID$_P$ to anonymously show her membership amongst the group of identities constructed by him. In this protocol both the IAID$_P$ and IAID$_V$ takes as input the system's parameters param and a group public key gpk. IAID$_P$ also has group secret key gsk as an additional input. At the end of an IAID protocol run, IAID$_V$ outputs a 0/1 signifying either a *Reject/Accept*.

2.4   Security Requirements for Ad-Hoc Anonymous IBI Scheme

There are three security requirements for an ad-hoc anonymous identification as proposed by Dodis et al [5]. We describe them below and specify their formal games of security in the next subsection.

1. CORRECTNESS : This property requires that during an execution of an IAID protocol, an *honest prover* will always be able to convince a *verifier*. In other words, if IAID$_P$ owns the group secret key corresponding to the common

input group public key, then the IAID$_V$ will *Accept* with an overwhelming probability, i.e. with a probability almost equal to 1.

2. SOUNDNESS : This property ensures that any dishonest entity not possessing a private key in the target ad-hoc group, will not be able to convince an *honest verifier*, and even if it does, it will be with a negligibly small probability. This requirement is modelled by a game being played between an honest dealer and an adversary and the adversary can send queries to the *Transcript Oracle*, which takes as input an identity of the user and a set of other entities and outputs a valid transcript of the IAID protocol's execution, where the user anonymously proves her membership of the group formed between him and the group of entities.

The overall game is played as follows: The honest dealer runs the *Setup* algorithm and sends the resulting public parameters to the adversary. After this the adversary is allowed to adaptively ask for the key extract queries from the *User Secret-Key-Extract Oracle* and also queries the *Transcript Oracle* during the game, or even during the execution of the IAID protocol later as a part of its training. After a certain point, the adversary who now plays the role of a *prover*, returns a target group of identities and then executes the IAID protocol with the honest dealer. Both the adversary and the honest dealer takes as inputs the public parameters and the group public key corresponding to the target group. The adversary wins the game if the honest dealer outputs *Accept* and the adversary does not have a private key corresponding to an identity in the target group. The ID-based anonymous identification scheme provides Soundness if the probability that the adversary wins this game is negligible.

3. ANONYMITY: This requirement is modelled by a game being played between an honest dealer and an adversary, where the adversary can send only one query to a *Challenge Oracle*. This oracle takes as input two 'identity-private key' pairs and a set of other identities and returns a transcript of the IAID protocol's execution, where the *prover* randomly uses one of the two private keys to prove membership of the group formed by - the set of identities along with the two identities from the pairs. The honest dealer first runs the Setup algorithm and sends the resulting public parameters to the adversary. Then, the adversary can find many pairs of 'identity-private key' during the game, even after receiving the challenge transcript from the *Challenge Oracle* later. At a point, she queries the *Challenge Oracle* and gets a challenge transcript. The adversary then can do experiments with the system before outputting an identity amongst the two identities. The adversary wins the game if the identity she outputs corresponds to the private key the *Challenge Oracle* used to generate the challenge transcript. The ID-based ad-hoc anonymous identification scheme provides anonymity if the probability that the adversary wins the game is negligibly more than a random guess. If this condition holds, even if the adversary has unlimited computing resources, the scheme is said to provide Unconditional Anonymity.

2.5 Formal Games of Security for Ad-Hoc Anonymous IBI Scheme

We formalize the security requirements in the form of games between an adversary and a challenger. The adversary will be given access to various oracles to aid him in carrying out the impersonation attacks. Let $\mathcal{PK}$ denote the domain of the user's public key and $\mathcal{SK}$ denote the domain of the corresponding user's secret key. We also assume $\mathcal{PK}'$ to be a superset of the possible user public keys i.e. $\mathcal{PK}' \supseteq \mathcal{PK}$.

User Secret-Key-Extract Oracle ($\mathcal{O}_{HReg}$)	User Corruption Oracle ($\mathcal{O}_{Cor}$)
IN: $u \in \mathcal{U}$ RUN: $d_{ID_i} \leftarrow KeyGEN(ID_i)$ OUT: d_{ID_i}	IN: $ID_i \in \mathcal{PK}'$ RUN: $d_{ID_i} \leftarrow KeyGEN(ID_i)$ OUT: d_{ID_i}

Transcript Oracle ($\mathcal{O}_{Scr}$)

IN: $S' \subseteq \mathcal{PK}', ID_i \in \mathcal{PK}'$
RUN: 1. $d_{ID_i} \leftarrow KeyGEN(ID_i)$
    KeyGEN is the key generation algorithm
2. If $d_{ID_i} = \perp$
3. then $\pi \leftarrow \perp$
4. Else $gpk \leftarrow \mathsf{MakeGPK}(\mathsf{param}, S' \cup \{ID_i\})$
5. $gsk \leftarrow \mathsf{MakeGSK}(\mathsf{param}, S', (d_{ID_i}, ID_i))$
6. $\pi \xleftarrow{R} (\mathsf{IAID}_P(\mathsf{param}, gpk, gsk) \leftrightarrow \mathsf{IAID}_V(\mathsf{param}, gpk))$
OUT: π

Challenge Oracle ($\mathcal{O}_{Ch}$)

INPUT: $S' \subseteq \mathcal{PK}', (sk_0, pk_0), (sk_1, pk_1)$
RUN: 1. $b^* \xleftarrow{R} \{0,1\}$
2. If, $sk_0 \not\leftrightharpoons pk_0$ or $sk_1 \not\leftrightharpoons pk_1$, then Abort
    where $\leftrightharpoons$ depicts a correspondence between the public key pk_i
    and the associated valid secret key sk_i
3. $G_{pk} \leftarrow MakeGSK(\mathsf{param}, S' \cup \{pk_0, pk_1\})$
4. $G_{sk}^* \leftarrow MakeGSK(\mathsf{param}, S' \cup \{pk_{1-b^*}\}, (sk_{b^*}, pk_{b^*}))$
5. $\pi^* \xleftarrow{R} (IAID_P(\mathsf{param}, gpk, gsk^*) \leftrightarrow IAID_V(\mathsf{param}, gpk)$
OUT: π^*

Fig. 2. Oracles given to adversary attacking ad-hoc IBI scheme

Game for Correctness. For correctness, we require that any honest execution of the IAID protocol shall terminate with the *verifier* outputting an *Accept* or 1, with an overwhelming probability. In this game, the IAID_P is given an additional input of group secret key gsk, related to the common input gpk.

Game for Correctness

$(\forall t \in \mathbb{N})(\forall (u_1, u_2, \ldots \ldots, u_n) \in \mathcal{U})$

$\Pr[\text{param} \xleftarrow{R} Setup(1^t);$ (where t is the security parameter)

$(sk_i, pk_i) \xleftarrow{R} KeyGEN(\text{param}, u_i),\ i = 1, \ldots \ldots, n$

$gpk \leftarrow MakeGPK(\text{param}, \{pk_1, \ldots \ldots, pk_n\});$

$gsk \leftarrow MakeGSK(\text{param}, \{pk_2, \ldots \ldots, pk_n\}, (sk_1, pk_1));$ such that,

$\quad IAID_V(\text{param}, gpk)_{IAID_P(\text{param}, gpk, gsk)} = 1] \geq 1 - \nu(t)$

(where $\nu(t)$ is a negligible function in t)

Fig. 3. Correctness *imp-atk* security of IBI scheme

Game for Soundness. The soundness guarantee can be expressed in terms of a game being played between an honest challenger and the adversary $\mathcal{A}$. In the attack game for soundness, the adversary is allowed to interact with three oracles O_{Ext}(the *honest User Secret-Key-Extract Oracle*), O_{Cor}(the *User Corruption Oracle*) and O_{Scr}(the *Transcript Oracle*) described in Figure 2.

The game begins with the honest challenger running the *Setup* algorithm with the security parameter 1^t and handing the resulting global parameters param to $\mathcal{A}$. Then, $\mathcal{A}$ arbitrarily interleaves queries to the three oracles, according to any adaptive strategy she wishes and eventually outputs a target group $S^* \subseteq \mathcal{PK}'$. After a point, $\mathcal{A}$(in the role of the *prover*) starts executing a run of the $IAID$ protocol with the challenger on common inputs param and $gpk^* = MakeGPK(\text{param}, S^*)$.

Also during this interaction, the adversary is still allowed to query the three oracles O_{Ext}, O_{Cor}, O_{Scr}. Let $\tilde{\pi}$ be the transcript resulting from such a run of the $IAID$ protocol. $\mathcal{A}$ wins the game if the following conditions hold:

1. $\forall pk^* \in S^*$, there is a valid sk^*(secret key) corresponding to the pk^*.
2. $\tilde{\pi}$ is a valid transcript i.e., the protocol run completed with the challenger outputting 1, and
3. $\forall pk^* \in S^*$, $\mathcal{A}$ never queried O_{Cor} on input pk^*.

We define $\mathsf{Succ}_{\mathcal{A}}^{\mathsf{Snd}}(t)$ to be the probability that $\mathcal{A}$ wins the above game.

Definition 2.2. *An ad-hoc anonymous IBI is sound against active chosen-ring attacks if any adversary $\mathcal{A}$ has negligible advantage to win the above game:*

$$(\forall \lambda \in N)\ (\forall\ PPT \mathcal{A})\ [\mathsf{Succ}_{\mathcal{A}}^{\mathsf{Snd}}(t) \leq \nu(t)]$$

where $\nu(t)$ is a negligible function in security parameter t.

Game for Anonymity. We formalize the anonymity requirements for an ad-hoc anonymous IBI scheme in terms of a game being played between an honest dealer and an adversary $\mathcal{A}$. In this game, the adversary is allowed to interact only once with a *Challenge Oracle* $\mathcal{O}_{Ch}$, described in Figure 2. The game begins with the honest challenger running the *Setup* algorithm for the security parameter 1^t and handing the resulting global parameters param to the adversary. Then, the adversary $\mathcal{A}$ creates as many user secret key/public key pairs as she wishes and experiments with the Make-GPK, Make-GSK, Anon-ID$_P$ and Anon-ID$_V$ algorithms as long as she deems necessary; eventually, she queries the $\mathcal{O}_{Ch}$ oracle, getting back a challenge transcript π. The adversary then continues experimenting with the algorithms of the system, trying to infer the random bit b^* used by the oracle $\mathcal{O}_{Ch}$ to construct the challenge π; finally, $\mathcal{A}$ outputs a single bit b', her best guess to the "Challenge" bit b^*. Define $\mathrm{Succ}_{\mathcal{A}}^{Anon}(t)$ to be the probability that the bit b' output by $\mathcal{A}$ at the end of the above game is equal to the random bit b^* used by the $\mathcal{O}_{Ch}$ oracle.

Definition 2.3. *An ad-hoc anonymous IBI scheme is fully anonymous if for any probabilistic polynomial-time adversary, $\mathcal{A}$ has success probability at most negligibly greater than one half:*

$$(\forall \lambda \in \mathrm{N})(\forall PPT \mathcal{A})|\mathrm{Succ}_{\mathcal{A}}^{Anon}(t)\text{-} \tfrac{1}{2}| \le \nu(t)$$

where $\nu(t)$ is a negligible function in t.

2.6   Reset Lemma

The Reset lemma was first proposed by Bellare and Palacio [9]. The Reset lemma upper bounds the probability, that a *cheating prover* $\mathcal{Q}$ can convince the *verifier* to accept as a function of the probability that a certain experiment based on resetting the *prover* yields two accepting conversation transcripts. We recall the definition of the Reset lemma as stated in [9]. Consider again the canonical three-move identification protocol between *prover* and *verifier* [10]. The *prover*'s first message is called commitment. The *verifier* selects a challenge uniformly at random from a set ChSet$_v$, associated with its input v and upon receiving a response from the *prover*, the *verifier* applies a deterministic decision predicate DEC$_v$(Cmt,Ch,Rsp) to compute a boolean decision. The *verifier* is represented by the pair (ChSet$_v$,DEC), which when given the verifier input v, defines the challenge set and decision predicate. Formally describing,

Reset Lemma: Let $\mathcal{Q}$ be a *prover* in a canonical protocol with a *verifier* represented by (ChSet,DEC), and let q and v be inputs for the *prover* and *verifier* respectively. Let $acc(q, v)$ be the probability that the *verifier* outputs *Accept* in its interaction with $\mathcal{Q}$. In other words, the probability that the following experiment returns $d = 1$.

Choose random tape R for $\mathcal{Q}$;
$St \longleftarrow (q, R);(\mathsf{CMT}, St) \longleftarrow \mathcal{Q}(\varepsilon, St);$
$\mathsf{CH} \xleftarrow{R} \mathrm{ChSet}_v;(\mathsf{RSP}, St) \leftarrow \mathcal{Q}(\mathsf{CH}, St); d \leftarrow DEC_v(\mathsf{CMT}, \mathsf{CH}, \mathsf{RSP});$
Return d.

Let $\mathsf{res}(q, v)$ be the probability that the following reset experiment returns 1.

Choose random tape R for $\mathcal{Q}; St \longleftarrow (q, R); (\mathsf{CMT}, St) \longleftarrow \mathcal{Q}(\epsilon, St)$

$CH_1 \xleftarrow{R} ChSet_v$; $(RSP_1, St_1) \leftarrow \mathcal{Q}(CH_1; St)$; $d_1 \leftarrow DEC_v(CMT, CH_1, RES_1)$

$CH_2 \xleftarrow{R} ChSet_v$; $(RSP_2, St_2) \leftarrow \mathcal{Q}(CH_2; St)$; $d_2 \leftarrow DEC_v(CMT, CH_2, RES_2)$
If($d_1 = 1$ AND $d_2 = 1$ AND $CH_1 \neq CH_2$) $return$ 1, else $return$ 0.

Then,

$$acc(q, v) \leq \tfrac{1}{|ChSet_v|} + \sqrt{res(q, v)}.$$

3   Proposed Scheme

We now present our ad-hoc anonymous IBI scheme. We build on the ideas and constructs from Guilliou-Quisquater identification scheme [11] and Herranz ring signatures scheme [8] to construct our new identification scheme for ad-hoc anonymous group. To the best of our knowledge, this is the first ad-hoc anonymous IBI scheme which does not use pairings. The various protocols involved in the scheme are described below.

- **Setup**: Based on the security parameter t, the PKG generates two random t-bit prime numbers p and q and then computes $N = pq$. For some fixed parameter l, the PKG chooses a prime number e at random, satisfying $2^l <e< 2^{l+1}$ and $gcd(e, \phi(n))=1$, and computes $d = e^{-1} \bmod \phi(n)$. Moreover, the PKG uses two hash functions $H_1 : \{0,1\}^* \longrightarrow \mathbb{Z}_N^*$, $H_2 : \{0,1\}^* \longrightarrow \{0,1\}^l$. The public output of this algorithm are the param$=(t, l, N, e, H_1, H_2)$ and the master secret key (p, q, d).
- **KeyGen**: When a user with identity $id \in \{0,1\}^*$ queries or asks for secret key, the PKG computes $SK_{id} = H_1(id)^d \bmod N$. SK_{id} is then sent to the user through a secure channel. The user can verify whether the received secret key is valid or not by checking if $SK_{id}^e = H_1(id) \bmod N$.
- **MakeGPK and MakeGSK**: From a given set of identities which are selected in an ad-hoc fashion, the ring $\mathcal{U} = \{ID_1, ID_2, ..., ID_n\}$ is formed. A user with identity $ID_s \in \mathcal{U}$ having the secret key SK_s runs the following algorithm:
  1. For all $i \in \{1, 2, ..., n\} \setminus \{s\}$, do:
     (a) Choose $\mathcal{A}_i \in \mathbb{Z}_N^*$.
     (b) Compute $R_i = \mathcal{A}_i^e \bmod N$
         and $h_i = H_2(\mathcal{U}, ID_i, R_i)$.
  2. Choose $\mathcal{A} \in_R \mathbb{Z}_N^*$
  3. Compute $R_s = \mathcal{A}^e \prod_{i \neq s} [H_1(ID_i)]^{-h_i} \bmod N$.

     If $R_s = 1 \bmod N$ or $R_s = R_i$ for some $i \neq s$; then GOTO *Step 2*, and *Repeat*.
  4. Compute $h_s = H_2(\mathcal{U}, ID_s, R_s)$.
  5. The Group Public key(GPK) is:
         $GPK = [\ \{R_i\}_{i=1}^n, \{h_i\}_{i=1}^n, \mathcal{U}\ ]$
     The Group Secret key(GSK) is:
         $GSK = SK_s^{h_s}$.

– IAID

The $IAID$ protocol is depicted in Figure 4. The various steps performed in the protocol are:

1. The *prover* P selects a message $m \in_R \mathbb{Z}_N^*$ and then computes $U = H_1(ID_s)^{h_s} \cdot m$

2. P sends U as commitment to *verifier* V.

3. V selects a random $x \in_R \mathbb{Z}_N^*$ as the challenge and sends it to P.

4. P computes $\sigma_1 = \left[(GSK)^{x+1} \cdot \mathcal{A} \cdot \prod_{i \neq s} \mathcal{A}_i \ mod \ N \right]$ and $\sigma_2 = m^x$. It then computes $W = \sigma_1^e \cdot \sigma_2$.

5. P sends W as the response to V.

6. V checks for consistency of W as:

   If $W = U^x \cdot \prod_{i=1}^{n} \left[(R_i . H_1(ID_i)^{h_i}) \right] \ mod \ N$,

   Then V Accepts, else it Rejects

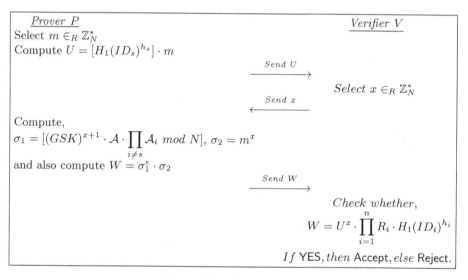

Fig. 4. The $IAID$ protocol

4   Security Proof

We depict the proof of security by showing that the three required properties of CORRECTNESS, SOUNDNESS and ANONYMITY hold true for our scheme.

1. **Correctness:** It can be easily seen that an honest entity of the ring acting as *prover* will always be able to genuinely identify herself.

$$\textbf{L.H.S.} = W = \sigma_1^e \cdot \sigma_2$$

$$= GSK^{(x+1)\cdot e} \cdot \mathcal{A}^e \cdot \left(\prod_{i \neq s} \mathcal{A}_i \bmod N\right)^e \cdot \sigma_2$$

$$= (H_1(ID_s)^{d \cdot h_s})^{(x+1)\cdot e} \cdot \left(\prod_{1 \leq i \leq n} \mathcal{A}_i \bmod N\right)^e \cdot \sigma_2$$

$$= (H_1(ID_s)^{(x+1)\cdot h_s}) \cdot \left(\prod_{1 \leq i \leq n} \mathcal{A}_i \bmod N\right)^e \cdot \sigma_2$$

$$= (H_1(ID_s)^{(x+1)\cdot h_s}) \cdot m^x \cdot \left(\prod_{1 \leq i \leq n} \mathcal{A}_i \bmod N\right)^e$$

$$\textbf{R.H.S} = U^x \cdot \prod_{1 \leq i \leq n} [R_i.H_1(ID_i)^{h_i}] \bmod N$$

$$= U^x \cdot R_s \cdot H_1(ID_s)^{h_s} \cdot \prod_{i \neq s}(R_i.H_1(ID_i)^{h_i}) \bmod N$$

$$= (H_1(ID_s)^{x \cdot h_s}) \cdot m^x \cdot \mathcal{A}^e \cdot \prod_{i \neq s}[H_1(ID_i)^{-h_i}] \cdot H_1(ID_s)^{h_s} \cdot$$

$$\prod_{i \neq s}(\mathcal{A}_i^e) \cdot H_1(ID_i)^{h_i} \bmod N$$

$$= (H_1(ID_s)^{(x+1)\cdot h_s}) \cdot m^x \cdot \left(\prod_{1 \leq i \leq n} \mathcal{A}_i \bmod N\right)^e$$

L.H.S. = R.H.S. Hence, correctness property holds.

2. **Soundness:** We show that, if an impersonator is successfully able to get herself verified as an *honest prover*, then the impersonator should have the knowledge of the GSK under the hardness assumption of RSA problem. We use Reset lemma on H_2 oracle to arrive at this result. We use the technique similar to Herranz [8] to prove the security of our scheme.

We show that the advantage of any imp-ca attacker against our scheme can be upper bounded by the advantage of a related RSA adversary and a function of the challenge length l. We first assume an instance of the RSA problem which the challenger will try to solve. Fix $t \in N$ and let (N, e, y) be an output of $\mathcal{K}_{rsa}$ running on input t, where t is the input parameter. We assume that V never repeats a request. Let (N, e, y) be the instance of RSA problem. We are going to construct a probabilistic polynomial time algorithm $\mathcal{A}$ that satisfies the condition of the Reset Lemma. This algorithm will use the impersonator $\mathcal{I}$ as a sub-routine to solve the RSA problem. Thus, the goal of $\mathcal{A}$ is to compute a value z such that $z^e = y \bmod N$. $\mathcal{A}$ will try to simulate the game, required oracles and identification transcripts to $\mathcal{I}$ perfectly.

We initialize the challenger machine $\mathcal{A}$ giving the data (N, e, y) as input to it. The machine then runs the impersonator $\mathcal{I}$ against our ad-hoc anonymous

IBI scheme. The two hash functions H_1, H_2 are modelled as random oracles, so their values will be computed and stored by $\mathcal{A}$. The RSA public key of the master entity is defined to be (N, e) and is also known to the impersonator $\mathcal{I}$. Without loss of generality, we can assume that the impersonator queries the H_1 random oracle for the value $H_1(ID)$ before asking the corresponding secret key of ID. $\mathcal{A}$ replies to the various hash oracle queries, key extract queries and impersonation queries of $\mathcal{I}$ in a manner mentioned below:

H_1 *queries*: The machine $\mathcal{A}$ constructs a table TAB_{H_1} to simulate the random oracle H_1. For this we use the technique as proposed by Coron [12]. Every time an identity ID_i is queried by $\mathcal{A}$ to the oracle H_1, the machine $\mathcal{A}$ responds as:

First, $\mathcal{A}$ checks if this input is already in TAB_{H_1}. If this is the case, then $\mathcal{A}$ sends to $\mathcal{I}$ the corresponding relation $H_1(ID_i) = PK_i$. Otherwise, $\mathcal{A}$ chooses a bit $\beta \in \{0, 1\}$, which will be $\beta_i = 0$ with probability μ, and $\beta_i = 1$ with probability $1-\mu$, where we define $\mu = (5/6)^{1/\mathcal{Q}_e}$, here, $\mathcal{Q}_e$ is the number of extraction queries. Then, $\mathcal{A}$ chooses a random element $x_i \in \mathbb{Z}_N^*$ and defines $PK_i = y^{\beta_i} \cdot x_i^e \bmod N$. The entry $(ID_i, PK_i, x_i, \beta_i)$ is stored in the table TAB_{H_1}. The relation $H_1(ID_i) = PK_i$ is sent to $\mathcal{I}$. The condition $PK_i \neq PK_j$ must be satisfied for all the different entries in TAB_{H_1}. If this is not the case, the process is repeated for one of the user.

Since we are assuming that H_1 behaves as a random function and the values PK_i are randomly chosen, the information that $\mathcal{I}$ receives is consistent.

H_2 *queries*: When $\mathcal{I}$ queries the random oracle H_2, the challenger $\mathcal{A}$ asks its own oracle for the output values of this hash function and then returns it to $\mathcal{I}$.

Key Extract Queries: Every time $\mathcal{I}$ asks for the secret key corresponding to an identity ID_i, the machine $\mathcal{A}$ looks for ID_i in the table TAB_{H_1}. If $\beta_i = 0$, then $\mathcal{A}$ sends $SK_i = x_i$ to $\mathcal{I}$ since $SK_i^e = PK_i \bmod N$ as is required. If $\beta_i = 1$, then the machine $\mathcal{A}$ cannot answer the query and halts. Note that the probability that $\mathcal{A}$ halts in this process is less than $1-\mu^{\mathcal{Q}_e} = 1/6$. So with probability greater than $5/6$, $\mathcal{A}$ will reply to the key extract queries of $\mathcal{I}$.

Identification Queries: The impersonator can ask for polynomial number of identification transcripts for the ring of identities $\mathcal{U}'$. We assume that $\mathcal{I}$ has not asked for the secret key of any of the identities in $\mathcal{U}'$, because, if this is the case, then $\mathcal{I}$ can obtain a valid identification transcript by itself. We also assume that $\mathcal{I}$ has asked for the public key of all the identities $PK_i = H_1(ID_i)$ in the ring $\mathcal{U}'$ to the random oracle H_1. To answer an identification query, the machine $\mathcal{A}$ responds as follows:

– If $\beta_i = 0$ for some $i \in \{1, \ldots, n'\}$, then $PK_i = H_1(ID_1) = (x_i)^e \bmod N$, so $\mathcal{I}$ knows the secret key for this identity and can easily compute a valid *honest prover* transcript by following the $IAID$ protocol.

- If $\beta_i = 1$ for all $i = 1, \ldots, n'$, then $\mathcal{A}$ does the following:
  (a) For all $i = \{1, \ldots, n'\}, i \neq s$, choose pairwise different $\mathcal{A}_i \in \mathbb{Z}_N^*$ uniformly at random and compute $R_i = \mathcal{A}_i^e \bmod N$.
  (b) By querying the random oracle H_2, compute $h_i = H_2(\mathcal{U}', ID_i, R_i)$, for all $i \neq s$. We can assume that $\mathcal{I}$ will later query the random oracle H_2 with these inputs.
  (c) Choose a random $h_s \in \{0,1\}^l$.
  (d) Choose at random $\sigma' \in \mathbb{Z}_N^*$.
  (e) Compute $R_s = (\sigma')^e . H_1(ID_s)^{-h_s} . \prod_{i \neq s}(R_i^{-1}.H_1(ID_i)^{-h_i}) \bmod N$. If $R_s = 1 \bmod N$ or $R_s = R_i$ for some $i \neq s$, then go back to the previous step and repeat.
  (f) At this point, the machine $\mathcal{A}$ *falsifies* the random oracle H_2 by imposing the relation $h_s = H_2(\mathcal{U}', ID_s, R_s)$. Later, when $\mathcal{I}$ asks the random oracle H_2 for this input, then $\mathcal{A}$ will answer with the same h_s.
  (g) Return the response $\theta = (\mathcal{U}', U, R_1, \ldots, R_{n'}, h_1, \ldots, h_{n'}, \sigma)$, where $U = H_1(ID_s)^{h_s} \cdot m$ is the commitment.

Since h' is a random oracle and we are considering H_2 to be a random oracle, so the information provided to $\mathcal{I}$ is indistinguishable from real execution of the identification protocol. However, some collisions may occur because of the values falsified by $\mathcal{A}$.

Note that in particular, no R_i can appear with probability greater than $1/2^k$ in the output produced. The collisions can occur in two ways:

- A tuple $(\mathcal{U}', ID_i, R_i)$ that $\mathcal{I}$ outputs inside a simulated ring identification, has been asked before to the random oracle H_2 by $\mathcal{A}$. The probability of such a collision is, however, less than $\mathcal{Q}_2 \cdot \mathcal{Q}_i \cdot (1/2^k) \leq (1/6)$, where $\mathcal{Q}_2, \mathcal{Q}_i$ are the number of H_2 and identification queries, respectively.
- The same tuple $(\mathcal{U}', ID_i, R_i)$ is output by $\mathcal{I}$ in two different simulated ring identification. The probability of this collision happening is less than $1/6$ (by birthday paradox).

Combining the above two cases, we get the probability of collision to be $\leq \frac{1}{3}$.

Summing up we have a PPT turing machine $\mathcal{A}$ that simulates the game to $\mathcal{I}$ which is trying to impersonate our scheme. Let's say the probability with which $\mathcal{I}$ can successfully impersonate is ε.

Now we use the oracle replay technique to machine $\mathcal{A}$, with respect to the hash function H_2. This means that by executing twice the machine $\mathcal{A}$ with different instantiations of the hash function H_2 we will obtain two valid transcripts $(\mathcal{U}, U, R_1, \ldots, R_n, h_1, \ldots, h_n, x, W_1)$ and $(\mathcal{U}, U, R_1, \ldots, R_n, h'_1, \ldots, h'_n, x, W_2)$ with the same commitment U, same challenge x and the same ring $\mathcal{U}$, such that $h_j \neq h'_j$ for some $j \in \{1, \ldots, n\}$ and $h_i = h'_i$ for all $i = 1, \ldots, n$ such that $i \neq j$. This is because the values $(\mathcal{U}, U, R_1, \ldots, R_n)$

have been chosen before the random oracles H_2 and H_2' differ(the oracle replay technique). We have the two transcripts as shown below:

$$W_1 = \sigma_1^e \cdot \sigma_2 = U^x \cdot \prod_{1 \leq i \leq n} \left[(R_i.H_1(ID_i)^{h_i}) \right] \ mod \ N$$

$$\text{And}, \ W_2 = (\sigma_1')^e \cdot \sigma_2 = U^x \cdot \prod_{1 \leq i \leq n} \left[(R_i.H_1(ID_i)^{h_i'}) \right] \ mod \ N$$

Dividing the above two equations we get,

$$W_1/W_2 = (\sigma_1/\sigma_1')^e = H_1(ID_j)^{h_j - h_j'}$$

We now proceed further to solve the hard problem. From above equation we have $(\sigma_1/\sigma_1')^e = H_1(ID_j)^{h_j - h_j'}$. Now we look into the table TAB_{H_1} and look for the entry $(ID_j, PK_j, x_j, \beta_j)$ corresponding to identity ID_j, since the impersonation of $\mathcal{I}$ is valid means that the secret key of user ID_j has not been queried and so, with probability $(1-\mu)$, we have $\beta_j = 1$ and $PK_j = H_1(ID_j) = y \cdot x_j^e \ mod \ N$.

The relation now becomes $(\sigma_1/\sigma_1')^e \cdot x_j^{(h_j' - h_j)e} = y^{(h_j - h_j')} \ mod \ N$. Since h_j and h_j' are outputs of the hash function $H_2 : \{0,1\}^* \rightarrow \{0,1\}^l$, we have that $| h_j - h_j' | < 2^l < e$. Furthermore, the element e is a prime number, so it holds $gcd(e, h_j - h_j') = 1$. This means that there exists two integers a and b such that $ae + b(h_j - h_j') = 1$ (by using BEZOUT's Identity). Finally we have the value,

$$z = \left((\sigma_1/\sigma_1') \cdot x_j^{(h_j' - h_j)} \right)^b \cdot y^a \ mod \ N$$

Calculating further to check the value of z^e we have,

$$z^e = \left((\sigma_1/\sigma_1') \cdot x_j^{(h_j' - h_j)} \right)^{b \cdot e} \cdot y^{a \cdot e} \ mod \ N$$

$$z^e = y^{(h_j - h_j') \cdot b} \cdot y^{a \cdot e} \ mod \ N$$

$$z^e = y^{(h_j - h_j') \cdot b + a \cdot e} = y \ mod \ N$$

and thus, we arrive at the solution of the given RSA problem.

We are now left to analyse the probability of solving the hard problem. We compute the probability with which the impersonator $\mathcal{I}$ will indeed succeed i.e. $\mathbf{Adv}_{IBI,\mathcal{I}}^{imp-ca}(t)$ as:

$\mathbf{Adv}_{IBI,\mathcal{I}}^{imp-ca}(t) = \Pr[\mathcal{I} \ succeeds \ in \ impersonation \ AND \ \mathcal{A} \ does \ not \ halt$
$AND \ no \ collisions \ occur]$
$= \Pr[\mathcal{I} \ suceeds \ in \ impersonation \ | \ \mathcal{A} \ does \ not \ halt \ AND$
$no \ collisions \ occur] \cdot (1 - \Pr[\mathcal{A} \ halts \ OR \ collisions \ occur])$
$\geq \varepsilon \left(1 - \frac{1}{6} - \frac{1}{3} \right) = \frac{\varepsilon}{2}$

Now, using the reset lemma, we calculate the probability of solving the hard problem,

$$\mathsf{acc}(St, pk) \leq 2^{-l(t)} + \sqrt{\mathsf{res}(St, pk)}$$

$$\mathbf{Adv}_{IBI,\mathcal{I}}^{imp-ca}(t) \leq 2^{-l(t)} + \sqrt{\mathbf{Adv}_{\mathcal{K}_{rsa},\mathcal{A}}^{rsa}(t)}$$

$$\mathbf{Adv}_{\mathcal{K}_{rsa},\mathcal{A}}^{rsa}(t) \geq (\mathbf{Adv}_{IBI,\mathcal{I}}^{imp-ca}(t) - 2^{-l(t)})^2$$

$$\mathbf{Adv}_{\mathcal{K}_{rsa},\mathcal{A}}^{rsa}(t) \geq \left(\frac{\varepsilon}{2} - 2^{-l(t)}\right)^2$$

which is a non-negligible quantity.

3. **Anonymity**: With respect to a given identity and a given valid transcript generated by an identity $ID_j \in \mathcal{U}$ in the ring $\mathcal{U}$, the probability that ID_j generated the response this is exactly $1/|\mathcal{U}|$. It can be easily seen that the IAID protocol transcript are uniform and independent of the user. By considering any two users i and j, the distribution of transcripts for both of them are computationally indistinguishable.

We show that the transcripts of identification for any two users is similar and is computationally indistinguishable as depicted :

Interaction Transcript by a user ID_i of the ad-hoc ring:

$$U_i = H_1(ID_i)^{h_i} \cdot m_1 \text{ and}$$

$$W_i = \sigma_{1_i}^e \cdot \sigma_{2_i} = \left[(GSK)^{x+1} \cdot A \cdot \prod_{i \neq s} \mathcal{A}_i \bmod N\right] \cdot m_1^x$$

Interaction Transcript by a user ID_j of the ad-hoc ring:

$$U_j = H_1(ID_j)^{h_j} \cdot m_2 \text{ and}$$

$$W_j = \sigma_{1_j}^e \cdot \sigma_{2_j} = \left[(GSK)^{x+1} \cdot A \cdot \prod_{i \neq s} \mathcal{A}_i \bmod N\right] \cdot m_2^x$$

It can be easily seen that the values of U_i and U_j are indistinguishable, similarly W_i and W_j are also indistinguishable. Thus, the communication transcript gives no information of the actual prover, as to who amongst the n users of the ad-hoc ring is actually involved in the identification protocol.

5   Comparison with Existing Schemes

We compare the efficiency and the communication bandwidth consumed by our scheme with the two previous schemes by Gu et al [7] and Nguyen [6]. Let C_E, C_P, C_M be the computational costs of - group exponential operation, bilinear group pairing operation and bilinear group multiplicative operation respectively. In the situation when the value $\prod_{i \neq s} \mathcal{A}_i \bmod N$ by the *prover* can be pre-computed ahead of the IAID protocol execution and the value

$\prod_{i=1}^{n} R_i \cdot H_1(ID_i)^{h_i}$ can be pre-computed by the *verifier* after it comes to know the *gpk*, our scheme requires $4C_E + 4C_M$ computations on the *prover*'s side, and $1C_E + 1C_M$ computations on the *verifier*'s side. On the other hand the existing schemes of Gu et al [7] and Nguyen [6] require $1C_E + 2C_M$ and $6C_P + 6C_E + 12C_M$ for the IAID_P algorithm respectively, and $2C_P + 3C_E + 1C_M$ and $10C_P + 10C_E + 8C_M$ for the IAID_V algorithm respectively. Moreover, the scheme prosed by Gu et al [7] assumes a maximum threshold for the ring size which is not the case with our scheme. Our scheme also has a low communication complexity in the identification protocol($IAID$). Table 1 shows the comparison with the most efficient existing schemes and our new ad-hoc anonymous IBI scheme. In this table, q represents a large prime number.

Table 1. Comparison between various ad-hoc anonymous IBI schemes in IAID protocol

Scheme	Our Scheme	Gu et al [7]	Nguyen [6]
Prover Computation	$4C_E + 4C_M$	$1C_E + 2C_M$	$6C_P + 6C_E + 12C_M$
Verifier Computation	$1C_E + 1C_M$	$2C_P + 3C_E + 1C_M$	$10C_P + 10C_E + 8C_M$
Communication	$3\mathbb{Z}_N^*$	$3\|\mathbb{G}\| + \mathbb{Z}_q^*$	$7\|\mathbb{G}\| + 8\mathbb{Z}_q^*$

6 Conclusion

In this paper we present the first IBI scheme for ad-hoc groups without pairings. Anonymous IBI in ad-hoc groups are important cryptographic primitives for access control and resource authorization services among a group of users and hence our scheme can be widely and efficiently used for such purposes. It still remains an open problem to reduce the computation overhead on *prover*'s side and provide an ad-hoc anonymous IBI scheme in standard model and also to propose a novel scheme where the group public key is independent of the ring size involved in the protocol.

References

1. Fiat, A., Shamir, A.: How to prove yourself: Practical solutions to identification and signature problems. In: Odlyzko, A.M. (ed.) CRYPTO 1986. LNCS, vol. 263, pp. 186–194. Springer, Heidelberg (1987)
2. Fiege, U., Fiat, A., Shamir, A.: Zero knowledge proofs of identity. In: Proceedings of the Nineteenth Annual ACM Symposium on Theory of Computing, pp. 210–217. ACM (1987)
3. Beth, T.: Efficient zero-knowledged identification scheme for smart cards. In: Günther, C.G. (ed.) EUROCRYPT 1988. LNCS, vol. 330, pp. 77–84. Springer, Heidelberg (1988)
4. Schnorr, C.-P.: Efficient Signature Generation by Smart Cards. J. Cryptology 4(3), 161–174 (1991)
5. Dodis, Y., Kiayias, A., Nicolosi, A., Shoup, V.: Anonymous Identification in Ad Hoc Groups. In: Cachin, C., Camenisch, J.L. (eds.) EUROCRYPT 2004. LNCS, vol. 3027, pp. 609–626. Springer, Heidelberg (2004)

6. Nguyen, L.: Accumulators from bilinear pairings and applications. In: Menezes, A. (ed.) CT-RSA 2005. LNCS, vol. 3376, pp. 275–292. Springer, Heidelberg (2005)
7. Gu, C., Zhu, Y., Ma, C.: An Efficient Identity Based Anonymous Identification Scheme for Ad-Hoc Groups from Pairings. In: 4th International Conference on Wireless Communications, Networking and Mobile Computing, WiCOM 2008, pp. 1–3 (October 2008)
8. Herranz, J.: Identity-based ring signatures from RSA. Theoretical Computer Science 389(1–2), 100–117 (2007)
9. Bellare, M., Palacio, A.: GQ and schnorr identification schemes: Proofs of security against impersonation under active and concurrent attacks. In: Yung, M. (ed.) CRYPTO 2002. LNCS, vol. 2442, pp. 162–177. Springer, Heidelberg (2002)
10. Bellare, M., Namprempre, C., Neven, G.: Security Proofs for Identity-Based Identification and Signature Schemes. J. Cryptol. 22(1), 1–61 (2008)
11. Guillou, L.C., Quisquater, J.-J.: A Practical Zero-Knowledge Protocol Fitted to Security Microprocessor Minimizing Both Transmission and Memory. In: Barstow, D., et al. (eds.) EUROCRYPT 1988. LNCS, vol. 330, pp. 123–128. Springer, Heidelberg (1988)
12. Coron, J.S.: On the Exact Security of Full Domain Hash (2000)

Dynamic Attribute Based Group Signature with Attribute Anonymity and Tracing in the Standard Model

Syed Taqi Ali and B.B. Amberker

National Institute of Technology Warangal,
Kazipet - 506004, AP, India
taqiali110@gmail.com, bba@nitw.ac.in

Abstract. Attribute Based Group Signature (ABGS) scheme is a kind of group signature scheme where the group members possessing certain privileges (attributes) only are eligible for signing the document. There are ABGS schemes proposed in the literature which do not provide *Attribute Anonymity*, a desirable feature to achieve, in the standard model. We have come up with an ABGS scheme which provides attribute anonymity along with an *Attribute Tracing* feature secure under standard model. It also achieves constant size signature.

Keywords: Group signature, attribute based, attribute anonymity, attribute tracing, standard model.

1 Introduction

A group signature (GS) scheme allows a group member to anonymously sign a message on behalf of a group later in case of any dispute a designated authority, an *opener*, can reveal the identity of the signer [9]. Bellare et al. [2] have formalized the definitions for dynamic group settings, where the number of group members are not fixed or known in the setup phase, i.e. user can join the group at any time. The basic security requirements of group signature scheme in dynamic group settings are *Anonymity*, *Traceability* and *Non-frameability* [2]. *Anonymity* means that the signature should not reveal the identity of the signer. *Traceability* means that the valid signature should always trace back to the valid identity with the help of the group secret key. *Non-frameability* means that even if two or more members collude (including group manager), they should not be able to generate a signature which trace back to a non-colluded member. Group signature schemes had several applications like company authenticating pricelist, press releases, digital contracts [7], anonymous credit cards, access control [23], e-cash [20], e-voting, e-auction [27].

Attribute Based Group Signature (ABGS) scheme is a group signature scheme where the group members possessing certain privileges, characterized by attributes, only are eligible for signing the document [22,21,12]. In ABGS scheme, each member is assigned a subset of attributes, verifier accepts the signed document only if the associated signature proves that it is signed by the member

B. Gierlichs, S. Guilley, and D. Mukhopadhyay (Eds.): SPACE 2013, LNCS 8204, pp. 147–171, 2013.

who possess sufficient attributes that satisfy the predicate, associated to document. The *predicates*, in terms of attribute relationships (the access structures), are represented by an *access tree* [22]. The first ABGS scheme was proposed by Dalia Khader in [22] and she listed *attribute anonymity* - the verifier should be able to verify whether the signer has required attributes without learning which set of attributes he used for signing, as a desirable feature to achieve. Later Dalia Khader proposed the ABGS scheme [21] with member revocation feature and does not address attribute anonymity. Emura et al. proposed an ABGS scheme [12], which is efficient when there is a frequent change in attribute's relationships but it does not provide attribute anonymity. Moreover the signature size in both the schemes depend on the number of attributes and are secure under random oracle model.

We address *attribute anonymity* issue in the standard model. We emphasize that attribute anonymity is as necessary as *anonymity* property. Consider the case where there is a unique attribute which belongs to only one group member along with other attributes. Whenever the verifier finds that attribute in the signature then he can conclude that the signature is signed by that particular group member who alone owns that attribute. Thus anonymity itself is not preserved which is the basic security requirement in any group signature scheme. For an instance, suppose

Alice wants a document to be signed by an employee in Bob's company. Alice requires that employee to have certain properties such as being part of the IT staff and at least a junior manager in the cryptography team or a senior manager in the biometrics team.

Now if group member with attributes *IT staff, biometric team, senior manager* signed the document and if there is only one senior manager in biometric team then the signature implies his identity. Many similar cases exist. Thus attribute anonymity is as important as anonymity property and we name *anonymity* property as a *user anonymity* property.

Maji et al. [25] have introduced an Attribute-Based Signatures (ABS), where a signer can sign a message with any predicate that is satisfied by his attributes. Here, the signature reveals no information about the signer's identity or the attributes he holds but guarantees that the signer possesses the required attributes. Many ABS schemes in standard model have been proposed [25,26,19,13], among which the scheme presented by Herranz et al. [19] has constant length signature but for the threshold predicates. For monotone predicates Escala et al. have given the ABS scheme whose signature size is linear in terms of the size of the predicate and with an additional property of *revocability*, which revokes the anonymity of the signer [13]. For non-monotone predicates Okamoto et al. have proposed an ABS scheme but its signature length is not constant [26]. The revocability feature of ABS is same as signer tracing feature of GS scheme which reveals the signer's identity from the signature. We note that to build an ABGS scheme with attribute anonymity in the standard model one can also combine an ABS scheme [19] with a group signature scheme [6], but it incurs cost of both the schemes.

Once we address attribute anonymity then it is also desirable to have *Attribute Tracing* feature, independent of user tracing/opening. *Attribute Tracing* feature allows a user to know with what privilege (an attribute set) the signer has signed the document regardless of who did it. With this, depending on the requirement user has choice to query to the authority either to reveal the user anonymity or the attribute anonymity of the signature, independently. Surely this will be the good feature for the applications. There is no ABGS or ABS scheme with this feature.

Our Contribution: We propose an ABGS scheme with attribute anonymity and tracing feature with constant signature size, and prove that it is secure in the standard model. For our construction we use the membership certificate format of [4,10] to achieve non-frameability in the standard model and the technique to build the access trees from [12]. We use Groth-Sahai non-interactive proof system [17] to generate the non-interactive witness indistinguishability (NIWI) proofs for the relations in the group signature under standard model. We use existing constructions [4,12] as a base to build our scheme which addresses the said issues and we prove that the build construction is secure under standard model. In contrast to other existing ABGS schemes [22,21,12], our scheme is built in the standard model with attribute anonymity and achieves a constant size signature, that is independent of the number of attributes.

In Section 2, the background is given. The proposed ABGS scheme is formally described in Section 3. In Section 4, the construction is given along with the comparison with the previous schemes. Security analysis is given in Section 5 followed by conclusion in Section 6.

2   Background

2.1   Bilinear Maps and Complexity Assumptions

Let k be the security parameter. Let $\mathbb{G}_1, \mathbb{G}_2$ and $\mathbb{G}_T$ be cyclic groups of prime order p, where $|p| = k$. Let g_1 and g_2 be generators of $\mathbb{G}_1$ and $\mathbb{G}_2$, respectively.

Definition 1 (Bilinear Maps). *Bilinear map is defined as follows:*
The bilinear map e is an efficiently computable function, $e : \mathbb{G}_1 \times \mathbb{G}_2 \to \mathbb{G}_T$ with the following properties.

- *Bilinearity : $\forall u, u' \in \mathbb{G}_1$ and $\forall v, v' \in \mathbb{G}_2$, $e(uu', v) = e(u, v)e(u', v)$ and $e(u, vv') = e(u, v)e(u, v')$.*
- *Non-degeneracy: $e(g_1, g_2) \neq 1_{\mathbb{G}_T}$ ($1_{\mathbb{G}_T}$ is the $\mathbb{G}'_T s$ identity element).*

We consider the "type-3" bilinear map, where the group isomorphism $\psi : \mathbb{G}_2 \to \mathbb{G}_1$ and its inverse $\psi^{-1} : \mathbb{G}_1 \to \mathbb{G}_2$ are not efficiently computable [15].

Definition 2 (DL Assumption). *For all PPT algorithm $\mathcal{A}$, the probability*

$$Pr[\mathcal{A}(g, g^{\xi}) = \xi]$$

is negligible function in k, where $g \in_R \mathbb{G}_1$ and $\xi \in_R \mathbb{Z}_p$.

Definition 3 (Advanced Computational Diffie-Hellman (CDH$^+$) Assumption [3]). *For all PPT algorithm $\mathcal{A}$, the probability*

$$Pr[\mathcal{A}(g_1, g_2, g_1^a, g_2^a, g_1^b) = g_1^{ab}]$$

is negligible function in k, where $a, b \in_R \mathbb{Z}_p$.

Definition 4 (Symmetric eXternal Diffie-Hellman (SXDH) Assumption [5]). *The SXDH assumption states that the DDH assumption holds in both $\mathbb{G}_1$ and $\mathbb{G}_2$.*

Definition 5 (ℓ-Decisional Diffie-Hellman Inverse (ℓ-DDHI) in $\mathbb{G}_1$). *For all PPT algorithm $\mathcal{A}$, the advantage of adversary $\mathcal{A}$*

$$|Pr[\mathcal{A}(g, g^y, ..., g^{y^\ell}, g^{1/y}) = 0] - Pr[\mathcal{A}(g, g^y, ..., g^{y^\ell}, D) = 0]|$$

is negligible function in k, where g is the generator of $\mathbb{G}_1$, $D \in_R \mathbb{G}_1$ and $y \in_R \mathbb{Z}_p^*$.

Definition 6 (q-Hybrid Hidden Strong Diffie-Hellman (q-HHSDH) Assumption in $\mathbb{G}_1, \mathbb{G}_2$ [4]). *For all PPT algorithm $\mathcal{A}$, the probability*

$$Pr[\mathcal{A}(g_1, h, g_2, g_2^\gamma, (g_1^{x_i}, g_2^{x_i}, y_i, (hg_1^{y_i})^{1/(\gamma+x_i)})_{i\in[1,q]}) = (g_1^x, g_2^x, g_1^y, g_2^y, (hg_1^y)^{1/(\gamma+x)})$$
$$\wedge (x, y) \neq (x_i, y_i)_{i\in[1,q]}]$$

is negligible, where h is a random generator of $\mathbb{G}_1$ and $\gamma, x, y, x_i, y_i \in \mathbb{Z}_p$ for $i = 1, ..., q$.

Definition 7 (Knowledge of Exponent Assumption (KEA) [18,1]). *For any adversary $\mathcal{A}$ that takes an input p, g, g^a where g is a generator of a cyclic group $\mathbb{G}_1$ and returns a pair of elements g', g'^a from $\mathbb{G}_1$, there exists an extractor $\bar{\mathcal{A}}$, which given the same inputs as $\mathcal{A}$ returns ξ such that $g^\xi = g'$.*

Definition 8 (Access Structure [16,21]). *Let $Att = \{att_1, att_2, ..., att_m\}$ be a set of attributes. For $\Gamma \subseteq 2^{Att}\backslash\{\emptyset\}$, Γ satisfies the monotone property if $\forall B, C \subseteq Att, B \in \Gamma$ and $B \subseteq C$, then $C \in \Gamma$ holds. An access structure (respectively, monotone access structure) is a collection (respectively, monotone collection) Γ of non-empty subsets of Att, i.e., $\Gamma \subseteq 2^{Att}\backslash\{\emptyset\}$.*

A *predicate* Υ is a boolean function with literals as attributes. The notation $\Upsilon(\zeta) = 1, \zeta \subset Att$ expresses the fact that a set of attributes ζ satisfies the predicate Υ. The *access structure* Γ of a predicate Υ is a collection of non-empty subset of attributes $\zeta \subset Att$ such that $\Upsilon(\zeta) = 1$.

In *threshold predicate*, atleast a threshold number of attributes are needed to satisfy the predicate. It is expressed using a Threshold gate. A *monotone predicate* is a predicate which is expressed using AND, OR and Threshold gates, an example is given in Chapter 1. It covers the threshold predicate as a special case. A *non-monotone predicate* is expressed using NOT, AND, OR and Threshold gates. It covers monotone predicate as a special case. We restrict our attention to monotone predicates.

2.2   Access Tree

An access tree T is used for expressing an access structure of a predicate Υ by using a tree structure. An access tree T consists of threshold gates as non-leaf nodes and attributes as leaves. Let l_x be the number of children of node x, and k_x $(0 < k_x \leq l_x)$ be the threshold value on the threshold gate of node x. A threshold gate represents that the number k_x of l_x children branching from the current node x need to be satisfied in order to imply that the parent node is satisfied. Note that if the number of children is equal to the threshold value it indicates an AND gate and if the threshold value is one then it indicates an OR gate. Satisfaction of a leaf is achieved by owning an attribute. The notation $\Upsilon(Leaves) = 1$ expresses the fact that a set of attributes $Leaves$ satisfies the predicate Υ.

3   ABGS with Attribute Anonymity and Tracing: Model and Security Definitions

In this section we present the model and security definitions of ABGS scheme which is similar to the one given in [12,21,2] but with the added attribute anonymity and tracing feature.

Notations: Let GM be the group manager, k the security parameter, *params* the system parameters, *Att* the universal set of attributes, Υ used to denote a predicate, $\Upsilon(\zeta) = 1$ denotes that the attribute set $\zeta \subseteq Att$ satisfies the predicate Υ, *gpk* the group public key, *ik* the issuing key used for issuing private keys to the users, ok_{user} the user opening key used to open the user identity of the group signature, tk_{att} the attribute tracing key used to trace the attributes of the group signature, $\mathcal{A}_i \subseteq Att$ the set of attributes assigned to the user U_i, sk_i denotes the private key for the member U_i and **reg** be the registration table with the group manager where the current group members information are stored.

Intuitively the user U_i can make a group signature on a document M with the predicate Υ if there exists a set of attributes $\zeta \subseteq \mathcal{A}_i$ with the user such that $\Upsilon(\zeta) = 1$.

Definition 9 (ABGS). *An ABGS scheme consists of following algorithms. Unless otherwise indicated, algorithms are randomized.*

- *params* ← Setup(1^k) : *This algorithm takes the security parameter k as an input and returns the system parameter params.*
- $(gpk, ik, ok_{user}, tk_{att})$ ← KeyGen(*params*) : *This algorithm takes the system parameter params, and returns a group public key gpk, an issuing key ik, a user opening key ok_{user} and an attribute tracing key tk_{att}.*
- sk_i ← Join($\langle params, gpk, ik, upk_i, \mathcal{A}_i \rangle$, $\langle params, gpk, upk_i, usk_i \rangle$) : *This is an interactive group joining protocol between a user U_i (using his secret key usk_i) and the GM (using the issuing key ik and the attributes $\mathcal{A}_i \subseteq Att$ for U_i). In the protocol U_i ends with a member private key sk_i and GM ends with an updated registration table **reg**.*

- $\sigma \leftarrow \texttt{Sign}(params, gpk, sk_i, \zeta, M, \Upsilon)$: *This algorithm takes params,*
  gpk, sk_i, an attribute set $\zeta \subseteq \mathcal{A}_i$, message M, and the predicate Υ as an
  input and returns a group signature σ on M.
- $0/1 \leftarrow \texttt{Verify}(params, gpk, M, \Upsilon, \sigma)$: *This is a deterministic algorithm*
  verifies the validity of the group signature σ against gpk and returns $1/0$. If
  1 then the algorithm claims that the σ is a valid group signature, otherwise,
  σ is invalid.
- $i/\bot \leftarrow \texttt{OpenUser}(params, gpk, ok_{user}, \sigma, M, \Upsilon, \textbf{reg})$: *This is a deterministic*
  algorithm which takes as input params, gpk, ok_{user}, σ, Υ, M and reg, and re-
  turns either $i \geq 1$ or $\bot$. If i, the algorithm claims that the group member with
  identity i has produced σ, and if $\bot$, then no group member produced σ.
- $\zeta/\bot \leftarrow \texttt{TraceAtt}(params, gpk, tk_{att}, \sigma, M, \Upsilon)$: *This is a deterministic al-*
  gorithm which takes as input params, gpk, tk_{Att}, σ, M and Υ, and outputs
  either the attribute set $\zeta \subseteq Att$ or $\bot$. Here it claims that ζ is the attribute
  set that is used to satisfy Υ in producing σ. If $\bot$, then the algorithm claims
  that no attribute set is used to produce σ.

Entities. There are several entities in ABGS scheme:

- The group manager GM, also known as *Issuer*, has issuing key ik using
  which he enrolls a users into the group by allotting some privileges (in terms
  of attributes) say $\mathcal{A}_i \subseteq Att$ and issuing a user's private key sk_i, by running
  interactive Join algorithm with the user.
- The *Opener* has user opening key ok_{user} by which he is able to open the
  signature and reveal the user identity through OpenUser algorithm.
- The *Attribute Tracer* has the attribute tracing key tk_{att} by which he can
  trace the attribute set ζ from the group signature, which is used to satisfy
  the predicate Υ, by running the TraceAtt algorithm.
- Group members, or signers, who are having their private keys sk_i. They run
  Sign algorithm to produce a group signature on a document M with predi-
  cate Υ; if they possess valid attribute set $\mathcal{A}_i$ which satisfies the predicate.
- Outsider, or verifier, who can only verify the group signature using the group
  public key, gpk.

Note. Normally the Setup and KeyGen algorithm is run by some trusted party
and he will distribute the appropriate keys to concern entities. Opener and attribute tracer are trusted entities as far as signer's anonymity is concerned.

Definition 10 (Correctness). *Correctness requires that for all params $\leftarrow$*
$\texttt{Setup}(1^k)$, *all $(gpk, ik, ok_{user}, tk_{att}) \leftarrow \texttt{KeyGen}(params)$, $sk_i \leftarrow \texttt{Join}(\langle$*
params, $gpk, ik, upk_i, \mathcal{A}_i \rangle, \langle params, gpk, upk_i, usk_i \rangle)$, all Υ, all $\zeta \subseteq Att$ and all
$M \in \{0,1\}^*$,
  if $U_i \in \textbf{reg}$, $\zeta \subseteq \mathcal{A}_i, \Upsilon(\zeta) = 1$ and $\sigma = \texttt{Sign}(params, gpk, sk_i, \zeta, M, \Upsilon)$ then

$$1 \leftarrow \texttt{Verify}(params, gpk, M, \Upsilon, \sigma)$$

$$\bigwedge i \leftarrow \texttt{OpenUser}(params, gpk, ok_{user}, \sigma, M, \Upsilon, \textbf{reg})$$

$$\bigwedge \zeta \leftarrow \texttt{TraceAtt}(params, gpk, tk_{att}, \sigma, M, \Upsilon)$$

holds.

In the following definitions the adversary can run the Join protocol (similar to [4]):

- either through the joinP-oracle (passive join), which means that it creates an honest user for whom it does not know the private keys: the index i is added to the HU (Honest Users) list;
- or through the joinA-oracle (active join), which means that it interacts with the group manager to create a user it will control: the index i is added to the CU (Corrupted Users) list.

Note that when the adversary is given the issuing key (the group manager is corrupted) then the adversary does not need access to the joinA oracle since it can simulate it by itself, to create corrupted users (that are not necessarily in CU). After a user is created, the adversary plays the role of corrupted users, and can interact with honest users, granted some oracles:

- corrupt(i), if $i \in$ HU, provides the specific private key of this user. The adversary can now control it during the whole simulation. Therefore i is moved from HU to CU;
- sign(i, M, Υ), if $i \in$ HU, plays as the honest user i would do in the signature process to generate a signature on message M with predicate Υ;
- openusr(M, σ, Υ), if (M, Υ, σ) is valid, returns the identity i of the signer;
- tratt(M, σ, Υ), if (M, Υ, σ) is valid, returns the attribute set ζ which used to satisfy Υ in producing σ.

Definition 11 (Attribute Anonymity). *We say that the ABGS scheme preserves attribute anonymity if for all PPT $\mathcal{A}$, the probability that $\mathcal{A}$ wins the following game is negligible.*

- ***Setup:*** *The challenger $\mathcal{C}$ runs $(gpk, ik, ok_{user}, tk_{att}) \leftarrow$ KeyGen($params$). $\mathcal{C}$ gives gpk, ik, ok_{user} to $\mathcal{A}$.*
- **Phase1** : *$\mathcal{A}$ is given access to the oracles:* joinP, corrupt, sign *and* tratt.
- **Challenge** : *$\mathcal{A}$ outputs M^*, Υ^*, and an uncorrupted users U_i (i.e. $i \notin$ CU) such that $\exists \zeta_{i_0}, \zeta_{i_1} \subseteq A_i$ and $\Upsilon(\zeta_{i_0}) = 1, \Upsilon(\zeta_{i_1}) = 1$ holds. $\mathcal{C}$ randomly selects $\kappa \in_R \{0, 1\}$ and responds with a group signature $\sigma^* \leftarrow$ Sign($params, gpk, sk_i, \zeta_{i_\kappa}, M, \Upsilon$).*
- **Phase 2** : *$\mathcal{A}$ can make queries similar to Phase 1. However $\mathcal{A}$ cannot make query to* corrupt *on i.*

Output: *Finally, $\mathcal{A}$ outputs a bit κ', and wins if $\kappa' = \kappa$.*
The advantage of $\mathcal{A}$ is defined as $Adv^{att-anon}(\mathcal{A}) = |Pr(\kappa = \kappa') - \frac{1}{2}|$.

Thus there should not exists any PPT adversary to link a group signature to a set of attributes used to generate it.

Definition 12 (User Anonymity). *We say that the ABGS scheme preserves user anonymity if for all PPT $\mathcal{A}$, the probability that $\mathcal{A}$ wins the following game is negligible.*

- **Setup:** *The challenger* $\mathcal{C}$ *runs* $(gpk, ik, ok_{user}, tk_{att}) \leftarrow$ KeyGen$(params)$. $\mathcal{C}$ *gives* gpk, ik, tk_{att} *to* $\mathcal{A}$.
- Phase1 : $\mathcal{A}$ *is given access to the oracles:* joinP, corrupt, sign *and* openusr.
- Challenge : $\mathcal{A}$ *outputs* M^*, Υ^*, *and an uncorrupted users* U_{i_0}, U_{i_1} *(i.e.* $i_0, i_1 \notin$ CU*) and,* $\zeta : \zeta \subseteq \mathcal{A}_{i_0}, \zeta \subseteq \mathcal{A}_{i_1}$ *and* $\Upsilon(\zeta^1) = 1$. $\mathcal{C}$ *randomly selects* $\kappa \in_R \{0, 1\}$ *and responds with a group signature* $\sigma^* \leftarrow$ Sign$($ $params, gpk, sk_{i_\kappa}, \zeta, M, \Upsilon)$.
- Phase 2 : $\mathcal{A}$ *can make queries similar to Phase 1. However* $\mathcal{A}$ *cannot make query to* corrupt *on* i_0 *and* i_1 *at any time.*

Output: *Finally,* $\mathcal{A}$ *outputs a bit* κ', *and wins if* $\kappa' = \kappa$.
The advantage of $\mathcal{A}$ *is defined as* $Adv^{user-anon}(\mathcal{A}) = |Pr(\kappa = \kappa') - \frac{1}{2}|$.

Thus there should not exists any PPT adversary to link a group signature to a signer with non negligible probability.

Definition 13 (Traceability). *We say that the ABGS scheme preserves* traceability *if for all PPT* $\mathcal{A}$, *the probability that* $\mathcal{A}$ *wins the following game is negligible.*

- **Setup:** *The challenger* $\mathcal{C}$ *runs* $(gpk, ik, ok_{user}, tk_{att}) \leftarrow$ KeyGen$(params)$. $\mathcal{C}$ *gives* gpk, ok_{user} *and* tk_{att} *to* $\mathcal{A}$.
- **Queries:** $\mathcal{A}$ *is given access to the oracles:* joinP, joinA, corrupt *and* sign.
- **Output:** $\mathcal{A}$ *outputs a message* M^*, *a predicate* Υ^* *and a group signature* σ^*.

$\mathcal{A}$ *wins if*
(1) Verify$(params, gpk, M^*, \Upsilon^*, \sigma^*) = 1$ *and*
(2) OpenUser$(params, gpk, ok_{user}, \sigma^*, M^*, \Upsilon^*, \mathbf{reg}) = \bot$.
The advantage of $\mathcal{A}$ *is defined as the probability that* $\mathcal{A}$ *wins.*

Thus it should be impossible to produce an untraceable valid group signature by any PPT adversary.

Definition 14 (Non-frameability). *We say that the ABGS scheme preserves* non-frameability *if for all PPT* $\mathcal{A}$, *the probability that* $\mathcal{A}$ *wins the following game is negligible.*

- **Setup:** *The challenger* $\mathcal{C}$ *runs* $(gpk, ik, ok_{user}, tk_{att}) \leftarrow$ KeyGen$(params)$. $\mathcal{C}$ *gives* gpk, ik, ok_{user} *and* tk_{att} *to* $\mathcal{A}$.
- **Queries:** $\mathcal{A}$ *is given access to the oracles:* joinP, corrupt *and* sign.
- **Output:** *Finally,* $\mathcal{A}$ *outputs a message* M^*, *a predicate* Υ^* *and a group signature* σ^*.

$\mathcal{A}$ *wins if*
(1) Verify$(params, gpk, M^*, \Upsilon^*, \sigma^*) = 1$,
(2) OpenUser$(params, gpk, ok_{user}, \sigma^*, M^*, \Upsilon^*, \mathbf{reg}) = i^*$,
(3) $i \in$ HU.
The advantage of $\mathcal{A}$ *is defined as the probability that* $\mathcal{A}$ *wins.*

---

[1] Here ζ can be different for U_{i_0}, U_{i_1} but we are concerned about user anonymity rather than attribute anonymity

Thus even the group manager should not be able to forge a group signature which trace back to a honest member.

Definition 15 (Attribute Unforgeability). *We say that the ABGS scheme preserves* attribute unforgeability *if for all PPT $\mathcal{A}$, the probability that $\mathcal{A}$ wins the following game is negligible.*

- **Setup:** *The challenger $\mathcal{C}$ runs $(gpk, ik, ok_{user}, tk_{att}) \leftarrow$ KeyGen$(params)$. $\mathcal{C}$ gives gpk, ok_{user} and tk_{att} to $\mathcal{A}$.*
- **Queries:** *$\mathcal{A}$ is given access to the oracles:* joinP, joinA, corrupt *and* sign.
- **Output:** *$\mathcal{A}$ outputs a message M^*, a predicate Υ^* and a group signature σ^*.*

$\mathcal{A}$ wins if
(1) Verify$(params, gpk, M^*, \Upsilon^*, \sigma^*) = 1$,
(2) OpenUser$(params, gpk, ok_{user}, \sigma^*, M^*, \Upsilon^*, \mathbf{reg}) = i^*$ *and*
(3) $\nexists \zeta \in \mathcal{A}_{i^*} : \Upsilon(\zeta) = 1$.
The advantage of $\mathcal{A}$ is defined as the probability that $\mathcal{A}$ wins.

Thus it should be impossible for any PPT adversary to satisfy the predicate with invalid set of attributes.

Definition 16 (Collusion resistance of Attributes). *We say that the ABGS scheme preserves* collusion resistance of attributes *if for all PPT $\mathcal{A}$, the probability that $\mathcal{A}$ wins the following game is negligible.*

- **Setup:** *The challenger $\mathcal{C}$ runs $(gpk, ik, ok_{user}, tk_{att}) \leftarrow$ KeyGen$(params)$. $\mathcal{C}$ gives gpk, ok_{user} and tk_{att} to $\mathcal{A}$.*
- **Queries:** *$\mathcal{A}$ is given access to the oracles:* joinP, joinA, corrupt *and* sign.
- **Output:** *$\mathcal{A}$ outputs a message M^*, a predicate Υ^* and a group signature σ^*.*

$\mathcal{A}$ wins if
(1) Verify$(params, gpk, M^*, \Upsilon^*, \sigma^*) = 1$, *and*
(2) $\mathcal{A}$ has obtained $sk_{i_1}, ..., sk_{i_k} : \Upsilon^*(\cup_{j=1}^{k} \mathcal{A}_{i_j}) = 1$ and $\Upsilon^*(\mathcal{A}_{i_j}) \neq 1$ for $j = 1, ..., k$.
The advantage of $\mathcal{A}$ is defined as the probability that $\mathcal{A}$ wins.

Thus the users with invalid set of attributes each, cannot collude with each other to pool a valid attribute set for producing a valid group signature.

3.1 Cryptographic Tools

Assignment of Secret Values to Access Trees. We use the *Bottom-up Approach* for the construction of access tree of the predicate given by Emura et al. [12]. This includes the following three functions:

1. AddDummyNode(T): This algorithm takes as input an access tree T, adds dummy nodes to it and returns the *extended access tree T^{ext}*.
   Let D_T be a set of dummy nodes added.

2. `AssignedValue`(S, T^{ext}): This algorithm takes as input a prime p, an attribute secret values $S = \{s_j\}_{att_j \in Att} \in \mathbb{Z}_p^*$ and T^{ext}, and returns a secret value for each dummy node $\{s_{d_j}\}_{d_j \in D_T} \in \mathbb{Z}_p^*$, where p is prime, and a root secret $s_T \in \mathbb{Z}_p^*$.

3. `MakeSimplifiedTree`$(Leaves, T^{ext})$: This algorithm takes as input the attribute set $Leaves \subseteq Att$ satisfying the tree T, and returns the product of Lagranges coefficients $\Delta_{leaf}(\forall lcaf \in Leaves \cup D_T^{Leaves})$, Such that

$$\sum_{att_j \in Leaves} \Delta_{att_j} s_j + \sum_{d_j \in D_T^{Leaves}} \Delta_{d_j} s_{d_j} = s_T \qquad (1)$$

holds, where $D_T^{Leaves} \subseteq D_T$ is the set of dummy nodes related to $Leaves$.

The details of these algorithms are given in [12]. For completeness it is quoted in appendix A.

Waters Signature. We use a slight variant of Waters signature [28,3], in the SXDH setting: Given three generators $(g_1, h, g_2) \in \mathbb{G}_1^2 \times \mathbb{G}_2$, a public key $pk = (g_1^t, g_2^t)$, the secret key t to sign a message M, a user simply needs to pick a random scalar s and compute $\sigma = (h^t . \mathcal{F}(M)^s, g_2^s)$. Here, $\mathcal{F}$ is the waters function defined as $\mathcal{F}(M) = v' \Pi v_j^{m_i}$, where (v', v_j) are independent generators of $\mathbb{G}_1$ and $M = (m_i)$. The verification simply consists in checking if $e(\sigma_1, g_2) = e(h, pk_2).e(\mathcal{F}(M), \sigma_2)$. This scheme is proven to be existentially unforgeable under CDH$^+$ assumption.

Groth-Sahai Proof Systems. We use the Groth-Sahai proof system [17] under SXDH settings to commit the signature elements. The commitment key consists of $u = (u_1, u_2 = u_1^t) \in \mathbb{G}_1^{2 \times 2}$ and $v = (v_1, v_2 = v_1^{t'}) \in \mathbb{G}_2^{2 \times 2}$, where $u_1 = (g_1, g_1^\alpha)$ and $v_1 = (g_2, g_2^{\alpha'})$ for some $g_1 \in \mathbb{G}_1, g_2 \in \mathbb{G}_2$ and $t, t', \alpha, \alpha' \in \mathbb{Z}_p^*$. There exist two initializations of the parameters either in the perfectly binding setting, or in the perfectly hiding one. And these initializations are indistinguishable under SXDH assumption which will be used in the simulation. We note that for equal dimension vectors or matrices A and B containing group elements, $A \odot B$ denotes their entry-wise product. We note $\mathcal{C}(X) = (1, X) \odot u_1^r \odot u_2^s \in \mathbb{G}_1^2$ is a commitment of a group element $X \in \mathbb{G}_1$ with a random $r, s \in \mathbb{Z}_p^*$. Similarly a group element of $\mathbb{G}_2$ is committed using v_1 and v_2 with $r', s' \in_R \mathbb{Z}_p^*$. An element is always committed in the group ($\mathbb{G}_1$ or $\mathbb{G}_2$) it belongs to. If one knows the commitment key in the perfectly binding setting, one can extract the value of X, else it is perfectly hidden. We note $\mathcal{C}^{(1)}(x) = \varphi^x \odot u_1^r \in \mathbb{G}_1^2$ is a commitment of a scalar embedded in $\mathbb{G}_1$ as g_1^x, where $\varphi = u_2 \odot (1, g_1)$ and $r \in_R \mathbb{Z}_p^*$. If one knows the commitment key in the perfectly binding setting, one can extract the value of g_1^x else x is perfectly hidden. The same things can be done in $\mathbb{G}_2$, if we want to commit a scalar, embedding it in $\mathbb{G}_2$, we denote it as $\mathcal{C}^{(2)}(x)$ and $\varphi' = v_2 \odot (1, g_2)$.

Using Groth-Sahai technique one can have non-interactive witness-indistinguishable (NIWI) proofs for the committed variables that satisfy the set of equations (either pairing-product equation or quadratic equation). The whole proof consists of one commitment per variable and two proof elements $\Theta = (\pi, \theta)$ (each contains a constant number of group elements) per equation.

For the variables $\mathcal{X}_1, ..., \mathcal{X}_m \in \mathbb{G}_1, \mathcal{Y}_1, ..., \mathcal{Y}_n \in \mathbb{G}_2, x_1, ..., x_{m'}, y_1, ..., y_{n'} \in \mathbb{Z}_p$.

- The pairing-product equations are of the form

$$\prod_{i=1}^{n} e(\mathcal{A}_i, \mathcal{Y}_i) \prod_{i=1}^{m} e(\mathcal{X}_i, \mathcal{B}_i) \prod_{i=1}^{n} \prod_{j=1}^{m} e(\mathcal{X}_i, \mathcal{Y}_j)^{\gamma_{ij}} = t_T, \qquad (2)$$

for the constants $\mathcal{A}_i \in \mathbb{G}_1, \mathcal{B}_i \in \mathbb{G}_2, t_T \in \mathbb{G}_T$ and $\gamma_{ij} \in \mathbb{Z}_p$. The proof cost 4 elements in each group. Linear pairing-product equation (when $\gamma_{ij} = 0$ for all i, j) proof cost 2 elements of respective group.

- And the quadratic equations in $\mathbb{Z}_p$ are of the form

$$\sum_{i=1}^{n'} a_i y_i + \sum_{i=1}^{m'} x_i b_i + \sum_{i=1}^{m'} \sum_{j=1}^{n'} \gamma_{ij} x_i y_i = t \bmod p, \qquad (3)$$

for the constants $a_i, b_i, \gamma_{ij}, t \in \mathbb{Z}_p$. The proof requires 2 elements in each group. Linear equation proof requires 1 element in $\mathbb{Z}_p$.

The details of verification process of the proofs is given in [17].

4   Construction

A construction of the ABGS scheme with *attribute anonymity* and *attribute tracing* features is presented in this section.

4.1   ABGS Scheme with Attribute Anonymity and Tracing

For a polynomial number of scalars $z_i \in \mathbb{Z}_p^*$, and a pair $(g, g^y) \in \mathbb{G}_1^2$, the values $g^{1/(y+z_i)}$ looks to be random and independent [11]. This is used to build our identifier, $\mathrm{ID}(y, z_i) = g^{1/(y+z_i)}$, in the group signature. In the proof of user anonymity, the simulator will be able to choose a z_i prior to any interaction with the adversary and we depend on q-DDHI assumption [11]. Let T_Υ be an access tree representing the predicate Υ, $\mathcal{T}_\Upsilon$ the public values associated with T_Υ, (upk_i, usk_i) the verification/signing key of a signature scheme $DSig$ for user U_i, A_i the membership certificate for U_i, $\{T_{i,j}\}_{\mathrm{att}_j \in \mathcal{A}_i}$ denotes the attribute certificates of U_i and the $T_{i,j}$ is the attribute certificate of the attribute $att_j \in Att$ of user U_i.

- Setup(1^k): It generates the system parameters, $params = (p, \mathbb{G}_1, \mathbb{G}_2, \mathbb{G}_T, e, g_1, g_2, Att)$; where
  1. $\mathbb{G}_1, \mathbb{G}_2, \mathbb{G}_T$ are the cyclic groups of prime order p, where $2^{k-1} < p < 2^k$.
  2. $e : \mathbb{G}_1 \times \mathbb{G}_2 \to \mathbb{G}_T$ is a bilinear map.

3. g_1 and g_2 are the generators of the groups $\mathbb{G}_1$ and $\mathbb{G}_2$, respectively.
4. $Att = \{att_1, ..., att_m\}$, for $m = O(k)$ is the universal set of attributes[2].

- KeyGen($params$): It takes an input system parameters $params$ and outputs a group public key gpk, an issuing key ik, a user opening key ok_{user} and an attribute tracing key tk_{att}.
    1. Select the generators $h, v', v_1, ..., v_{m'} \in \mathbb{G}_1$ and define the Waters function, $\mathcal{F} : \{0,1\}^{m'} \to \mathbb{G}_1$, for $M = (\mu_1, ..., \mu_{m'}) \in \{0,1\}^{m'} \mathcal{F}(M) = v' \Pi_{j=1}^{m'} v_j^{\mu_j}$, where $m' = O(k)$.
    2. Select $\gamma \in_R \mathbb{Z}_p^*$, and computes $\omega = g_2^{\gamma}$.
    3. For each $att_j \in Att$, choose a secret $s_j \in_R \mathbb{Z}_p^*$, sets $S = \{s_j\}_{att_j \in Att}$, and computes $g_{att_j} = g_1^{s_j}, \forall att_j \in Att$.
    4. For the Groth-Sahai proof under the instantiation based on SXDH assumption, choose a vectors $\boldsymbol{u} = (\boldsymbol{u}_1, \boldsymbol{u}_2 = \boldsymbol{u}_1^{t_1}), \boldsymbol{u'} = (\boldsymbol{u'}_1, \boldsymbol{u'}_2 = \boldsymbol{u'}_1^{t_1})$ and $\boldsymbol{v} = (\boldsymbol{v}_1, \boldsymbol{v}_2 = \boldsymbol{v}_1^{t_2})$, where $\boldsymbol{u}_1 = (g_1, g_1^{\alpha_1}) \in \mathbb{G}_1^2, \boldsymbol{u'}_1 = (g_1, g_1^{\alpha'_1}) \in \mathbb{G}_1^2$ and $\boldsymbol{v}_1 = (g_2, g_2^{\alpha_2}) \in \mathbb{G}_2^2$ for $t_1, t_2, \alpha_1, \alpha'_1, \alpha_2 \in_R \mathbb{Z}_p^*$. α_1 and α_2 are commitment keys.
    5. Outputs,

$$gpk = (h, \omega, \mathcal{F}, \{g_{att_j}\}_{att_j \in Att}, \boldsymbol{u}, \boldsymbol{u'}, \boldsymbol{v}),$$
$$ik = (\gamma, S), ok_{user} = \alpha_1, tk_{att} = \alpha'_1.$$

The description of $\mathcal{F}$ includes the generators $v', v_1, ..., v_{m'}$. If both the authorities, opener and attribute tracer, are same we can remove $\boldsymbol{u'}$ from the gpk and has common key for ok_{user} and tk_{att}.

- Join($< params, gpk, ik, upk_i, \mathcal{A}_i >, < params, gpk, upk_i, usk_i >$): A user U_i with the pair of keys (upk_i, usk_i) in the PKI, interacts with the group manager, with the issuing ik and the set of attributes $\mathcal{A}_i$, to join the group. This is similar to the Join protocol in [4,10]. As a result of this protocol, U_i gets private key $sk_i = ((A_i, X_i, y_i), \{T_{i,j}\}_{att_j \in \mathcal{A}_i})$, where (A_i, X_i, y_i) is a *membership certificate*, $\{T_{i,j}\}_{att_j \in \mathcal{A}_i}$ is the set of *attribute certificates* and $\mathcal{A}_i \subseteq Att$ is the set of U_i 's attributes. And GM ends with the updated **reg**. The protocol begins as follows,
    1. U_i picks $y'_i \in_R \mathbb{Z}_p^*$, computes and sends $Y'_i = g_1^{y'_i}$, an extractable commitment of y'_i, the trapdoor of the commitment will not be known to anybody except to the simulator in the security proof to be able to extract y'_i.
    2. GM selects new $x_i \in \mathbb{Z}_p^*$ and a random $y''_i \in_R \mathbb{Z}_p^*$, computes $A_i = (hY'_iY''_i)^{1/(\gamma+x_i)}, X_{i,2} = g_2^{x_i}$ and $T_{i,j} = h^{\frac{s_j}{\gamma+x_i}} (\forall att_j \in \mathcal{A}_i)$, where $Y''_i = g_1^{y''_i}$ and sends $y''_i, A_i, X_{i,2}, \{T_{i,j}\}_{\forall att_j \in \mathcal{A}_i}$.
    3. U_i checks whether $e(A_i, \omega g_2^{x_i}) = e(h, g_2)e(g_1, g_2)^{y'_i+y''_i}$. Then U_i computes $y_i = y'_i + y''_i$ and makes a signature $\sigma_i = DSig_{usk_i}(A_i, X_{i,2}, Y_i = g_1^{y_i})$.

---

[2] For $m = 1$ it becomes group signature scheme.

4. GM verifies σ_i under upk_i and appends the tuple $(i, upk_i, A_i, X_i = (X_{i,1} = g_1^{x_i}, X_{i,2}), Y_i, \sigma_i)$ to reg. Then GM sends $X_{i,1}$.

5. U_i checks the relation $e(X_{i,1}, g_2) = e(g_1, X_{i,2})$. U_i owns an valid membership certificate (A_i, X_i, y_i) and attribute certificates $\{T_{i,j}\}_{\forall att_j \in \mathcal{A}_i}$, where y_i is known to him only. Thus, $sk_i = (A_i, X_i, y_i, \{T_{i,j}\}_{att_j \in \mathcal{A}_i}) \in \mathbb{G}_1^2 \times \mathbb{G}_2 \times \mathbb{Z}_p^* \times \mathbb{G}_1^{|\mathcal{A}_i|}$.

GM chooses $s_{m+1} \in \mathbb{Z}_p^*$, and computes $g_{att_{m+1}} = g_1^{s_{m+1}}$ when a new attribute att_{m+1} is added. Let U_i be issued $T_{i,m+1}$. Then GM computes and sends $T_{i,m+1} = h^{\frac{s_{m+1}}{\gamma + x_i}}$ to U_i and also opens $g_{att_{m+1}}$ into gpk.

- BuildTree$(params, S, \Upsilon)$:
  1. Let T_Υ be the tree that represents the predicate Υ.
  2. Get extension tree $T^{ext} \leftarrow$ AddDummyNode(T_Υ).
  3. Get secret value for each dummy node and the secret value of the root of T^{ext} using $(\{s_{d_j}\}_{d_j \in D_T}, s_T) \leftarrow$ AssignedValue(S, T^{ext}).
  4. Output the public values of Υ,

$$\mathcal{T}_\Upsilon = (\{s_{d_j}\}_{d_j \in D_{T_\Upsilon}}, v_T = g_2^{s_T}, T^{ext}).$$

Normally the verifier with his own predicate approaches the GM for a group signature request and GM runs BuildTree algorithm to generate the public values of the predicate Υ and stores it in a public repository. Then anyone among the group members who are eligible will generate a group signature by using the predicate public value. And in order to verify whether the published values of the predicate are correct one (specially the verifier) can use the BuildTree-Validity algorithm. This allows us to remove the trust of GM towards outsiders (verifier) in producing predicate public values.

- BuildTree-Validity$(params, gpk, \mathcal{T}_\Upsilon)$:
  1. Randomly choose an attribute set, $Leaves \subseteq Att : \Upsilon(Leaves) = 1$ And gets the corresponding $\Delta_{att_j}(\forall att_j \in Leaves)$, and $\Delta_{d_j}(\forall d_j \in D_{T_\Upsilon}^{Leaves})$ by running MakeSimplified-Tree$(Leaves, T^{ext})$.
  2. Compute $g_{root} = \prod_{att_j \in Leaves} g_{att_j}^{\Delta_{att_j}} \times \prod_{d_j \in D_{T_\Upsilon}^{Leaves}} g_1^{s_{d_j} \Delta_{d_j}}$

  $= \prod_{att_j \in Leaves} g_1^{s_j \Delta_{att_j}} \times \prod_{d_j \in D_{T_\Upsilon}^{Leaves}} g_2^{s_{d_j} \Delta_{d_j}}$

  $= g_1^{\sum_{att_j \in Leaves} \Delta_{att_j} s_j + \sum_{d_j \in D_{T_\Upsilon}^{Leaves}} \Delta_{d_j} s_{d_j}} \qquad = g_1^{s_T}$ from (1).

  3. Verify whether $e(g_{root}, g_2) \overset{?}{=} e(g_1, v_T)$. If not then $\mathcal{T}_\Upsilon$ is the invalid public values of the predicate Υ.

- Sign$(params, gpk, sk_i, \zeta, M, \Upsilon)$: It generates a group signature σ on message $M \in \{0,1\}^{m'}$ with the user private key sk_i who satisfy the predicate Υ with his subset of attributes $\zeta \subseteq \mathcal{A}_i : \Upsilon(\zeta) = 1$.

1. Get the public values of Υ, $\mathcal{T}_\Upsilon = (\{s_{d_j}\}_{d_j \in D_{T_\Upsilon}}, v_T, T^{ext})$, from the public repository.
2. Let $s_{T_1} = \Sigma_{att_j \in \zeta} \Delta_{att_j} s_j$ and $s_{T_2} = \Sigma_{d_j \in D_T^\zeta} \Delta_{d_j} s_{d_j}$. Then from (1), $s_{T_1} + s_{T_2} = s_T$.
3. Get $(\{\Delta_{att_j}\}_{(\forall att_j \in \zeta)}, \{\Delta_{d_j}\}_{(\forall d_j \in D_{T_\Upsilon}^\zeta)}) \leftarrow \texttt{MakeSimplifiedTree}(\zeta, T^{ext})$ and compute s_{T_2}.
4. Creates an ephemeral ID, $\text{ID}(y_i, z) = g_1^{1/(z+y_i)}$, with a random $z \in \mathbb{Z}_p^*$.
5. Select $r \in_R \mathbb{Z}_p^*$ and set $\rho_1 = A_i, \rho_2 = y_i, \rho_3 = X_i = (g_1^{x_i}, g_2^{x_i}), \rho_4 = \Pi_{att_j \in \zeta} T_{i,j}^{\Delta_{att_j}} = h^{\frac{s_{T_1}}{\gamma + x_i}}, \rho_5 = h^{s_{T_2}}, \rho_6 = \text{ID}(y_i, z), \rho_7 = (g_1^z, g_2^z), \rho_8 = h^z \mathcal{F}(M)^r$ and $\rho_9 = g_2^r$.
6. Commit the group elements $\sigma_i = \mathcal{C}(\rho_i)$, for $i = \{1,3,4,5\}$ and $\sigma_2 = (\mathcal{C}^{(1)}(\rho_2), \mathcal{C}^{(2)}(\rho_2))$. Note that for committing the ρ_4 and ρ_5 one has to use u'. This is to separate the opening of user with the tracing of attributes.
7. Compute the NIWI Groth-Sahai proofs for the committed variables $\rho_1, \rho_2, \rho_3, \rho_4, \rho_5$ satisfy the following equations

$$e(\rho_1, \omega \rho_{3,2}) = e(h, g_2) \times e(g_1, g_2^{\rho_2}) \tag{4}$$

$$e(\rho_4, \omega \rho_{3,2}) \times e(\rho_5, g_2) = e(h, v_T) \tag{5}$$

$$e(\rho_6, g_2^{\rho_2} \rho_{7,2}) = e(g_1, g_2) \tag{6}$$

$$e(\rho_8, g_2) = e(h, \rho_{7,2}) \times e(\mathcal{F}(M), \rho_9) \tag{7}$$

$$e(g_1^{\rho_2}, g_2) = e(g_1, g_2^{\rho_2}) \tag{8}$$

$$e(\rho_{3,1}, g_2) = e(g_1, \rho_{3,2}) \tag{9}$$

$$e(\rho_{7,1}, g_2) = e(g_1, \rho_{7,2}) \tag{10}$$

8. Output the signature $\sigma = (\{\sigma_i\}_{i=1}^5, \{\rho\}_{i=6}^9) \in \mathbb{G}_1^{13} \times \mathbb{G}_2^6$

We add the corresponding Groth-Sahai proofs to the signature to prove the validity of the above pairing equations. Equation (4) is a pairing product equation, establishes that the signer has a valid membership certificate issued through the Join algorithm (i.e. A_i is well-formed), and the Groth-Sahai proof requires 4 elements in each group. Equation (5) is a paring product equation, establishes that the signer possess a required attributes (an attribute certificates) that satisfy the predicate Υ and also proves the association of the membership certificate with attribute certificates, and the proof requires 4 elements in each group. Equation (6) is a linear pairing product, establishes that ρ_6 is a well formed ID, and the proof requires only 2 extra elements in $\mathbb{G}_1$. Equation (7) does not use any committed data so it can be directly checked, it establishes that (ρ_8, ρ_9) is a Waters signature of M under the key ρ_7. Equation (8) is a quadratic equation, establishes that same y_i is committed in both groups which is needed for Traceability adversary modeling, and it can proof with 2 elements in each group. Equation (9) is a pairing product equation, establishes that X_i is well-formed which is needed for Traceability adversary modeling, and the proof requires 4 elements in each group. Equation (10) does not use any committed data so it can be checked directly and this equation is needed for non-frameability

Table 1. Comparison with other schemes

	Dalia Khader [21]	Emura et al. [12]	Herranz et al. [19] +Boyen et al. [6]	Our Scheme
Non-frameability	no	yes	no	yes
CCA-Anonymity	no	yes	no	yes
Attribute Anonymity	no	no	yes	yes
Attribute Revocation	yes	no	no	no
Predicate	general	general	threshold	general
Signature Length	$O(\phi)$	$O(\phi)$	$15|\mathbb{G}_p|+6|\mathbb{G}_n|=O(1)$	$29|\mathbb{G}_1|+20|\mathbb{G}_2|=O(1)$
User's Key Length	$(\hat{m}+1)|\mathbb{G}_1|+|\mathbb{Z}_p^*|$	$(\hat{m}+1)|\mathbb{G}_1|+2|\mathbb{Z}_p^*|$	$(m+\hat{m})|\mathbb{G}_p|+3|\mathbb{G}_n|$	$(2+\hat{m})|\mathbb{G}_1|+|\mathbb{G}_2|+|\mathbb{Z}_p^*|$
Assumption	DLIN, q-SDH	DL,DDH, q-SDH	DLin,(ℓ,m,t)-aMSE-CDH, q-HSDH,SGD	DL,q-HSDH, SXDH,q-HHSDH, ℓ-DDHI,CDH+, KEA
Model	Random Oracle	Random Oracle	Standard	Standard
Verification cost	$(6+2r)\mathbb{G}_1+(8+2\phi)\mathbb{G}_T=O(\phi+r)$ $+(\phi+2r+1)e$	$(11+2\phi)\mathbb{G}_1+(\phi+1)\mathbb{G}_2=O(\phi)$ $+14\mathbb{G}_T+6e$	$((4m+6m')\mathbb{G}_p+21\mathbb{G}_T+33e)$ $+((m'+1)\mathbb{G}_p+5\mathbb{G}_T+6e)=O(m)$	$O(1)$

adversary modeling. Overall we will need 29 group elements in $\mathbb{G}_1$ and 20 in $\mathbb{G}_2$. Note that the signature is independent of the number of attributes $|\zeta|$.

- Verify$(params, gpk, M, \sigma, \Upsilon)$: It verifies to see whether all the paring equations hold according to Groth-Sahai proof verification.

- OpenUser$(params, gpk, ok_{user}, \sigma, M, \Upsilon, \mathbf{reg})$: For the valid group signature the Opener just opens the commitment of A_i in σ_1, and outputs the corresponding identity i from the $\mathbf{reg}$ wrt A_i, if it presents, otherwise outputs $\perp$.

- TraceAtt$(params, gpk, tk_{att}, \sigma, M, \Upsilon)$: For the valid group signature the Attribute Tracer opens the commitment of $\rho_5 = h^{s_{T_2}}$ from σ_5. Then for all $\zeta_k : \Upsilon(\zeta_k) = 1$, it checks $\rho_5 \stackrel{?}{=} h^{s^k_{T_2}}$, where $s^k_{T_2} = \Sigma_{d_j \in D^{\zeta_k}_{T_\Upsilon}} \Delta_{d_j} s_{d_j}$. If any such ζ_k exists then outputs it else outputs $\perp$. We note that for each unique ζ there is unique s_{T_2} value, it is from Lagranges interpolation.

4.2   Comparison

Let $\phi = |\zeta|$, where ζ be the set of attributes which is associated with a signature and $m = |Att|$. Let $\hat{m}$ be the average number of attributes assigned to any user and m' is the length of the message, a constant. e represents the paring operation and r represents the number of revoked members. In Table 1, we compare the efficiency of our scheme with other schemes. Note that the verification cost of the proposed scheme is independent of the number of attributes, where as in other schemes the verification cost is linear in terms of the number of attributes. From the table it can be noticed that non-frameability is not achieved by combined scheme of Herranz et al. [19] and Boyen et al. [6]. Further, the combined scheme has verification cost that is not independent of the number of attributes and also the key lengths are large.

5   Security Analysis

Theorem 1. *The proposed ABGS scheme is correct.*

Proof. The correctness follows from the Groth-Sahai proof system.   □

Theorem 2. *The proposed ABGS scheme preserves attribute anonymity under SXDH assumption.*

Proof. The proof follows from the Groth-Sahai proof system. Namely the attribute details are hidden in the components ρ_4 and ρ_5 which are committed with Groth-Sahai proof technique to σ_4 and σ_5, therefore under SXDH assumption it is perfectly hiding.   □

Theorem 3. *If there exists an adversary $\mathcal{A}$ that can break the user anonymity of the scheme, then there exists an adversary $\mathcal{B}$ that can break the ℓ-DDHI problem* *in* $\mathbb{G}_1$ *or the SXDH assumption, where ℓ is the maximal number of signing queries for a user. And we have*

$$Adv^{\text{user}-\text{anon}} \leq 1/n.(2.Adv^{\text{SXDH}} + Adv^{\ell-\text{DDHI}}) \qquad (11)$$

where n is the maximal number of join queries and ℓ is the maximal number of signing queries for a user.

Theorem 4. *The proposed scheme preserves the attribute unforgeability under KEA and DL assumptions.*

Theorem 5. *The proposed scheme preserves the collusion resistance of attribute under KEA and DL assumptions.*

Theorem 6. *If there exists an adversary $\mathcal{A}$ that breaks the traceability of the scheme, then we can build an adversary $\mathcal{B}$ that can break the q-HHSDH assumption, where q is the maximal number of users.*

Theorem 7. *If there exists an adversary $\mathcal{A}$ that breaks the non-frameability of the scheme, then we can build an adversary $\mathcal{B}$ that can either break the q-HSDH or the CDH^+ computational problems, or the 1-DDHI or the SXDH decisional problems, where q is the maximal number of signing queries for a user.*

Proofs are given in Appendix B.

6   Conclusion

We have proposed an ABGS scheme which achieves attribute anonymity and provides attribute tracing feature with constant signature size, and proven that it is secure under the standard model. We have given independent user opening and attribute tracing method. Our scheme is dynamic w.r.t. user and attribute i.e. anytime the user can join and attributes can be added without changing the keys. We note that our scheme is efficient than the other ABGS schemes in terms of verification cost and signature length. The attribute revocation is taken as future work.

Acknowledgments. This work was supported by Ministry of Human Resource Development (MHRD), Government of INDIA.

References

1. Bellare, M., Palacio, A.: The knowledge-of-exponent assumptions and 3-round zero-knowledge protocols. In: Franklin (ed.) [14], pp. 273–289
2. Bellare, M., Shi, H., Zhang, C.: Foundations of group signatures: The case of dynamic groups. In: Menezes, A. (ed.) CT-RSA 2005. LNCS, vol. 3376, pp. 136–153. Springer, Heidelberg (2005)

3. Blazy, O., Fuchsbauer, G., Pointcheval, D., Vergnaud, D.: Signatures on random-izable ciphertexts. In: Catalano, et al. (eds.) [8], pp. 403–422
4. Blazy, O., Pointcheval, D.: Traceable signature with stepping capabilities. In: Nac-cache, D. (ed.) Quisquater Festschrift. LNCS, vol. 6805, pp. 108–131. Springer, Heidelberg (2012)
5. Boneh, D., Boyen, X., Shacham, H.: Short group signatures. In: Franklin (ed.) [14], pp. 41–55
6. Boyen, X., Waters, B.: Full-domain subgroup hiding and constant-size group sig-natures. In: Okamoto, T., Wang, X. (eds.) PKC 2007. LNCS, vol. 4450, pp. 1–15. Springer, Heidelberg (2007)
7. Camenisch, J., Stadler, M.: Efficient group signature schemes for large groups. In: Kaliski Jr., B.S. (ed.) CRYPTO 1997. LNCS, vol. 1294, pp. 410–424. Springer, Heidelberg (1997)
8. Catalano, D., Fazio, N., Gennaro, R., Nicolosi, A. (eds.): PKC 2011. LNCS, vol. 6571. Springer, Heidelberg (2011)
9. Chaum, D., van Heyst, E.: Group signatures. In: EUROCRYPT, pp. 257–265 (1991)
10. Delerablée, C., Pointcheval, D.: Dynamic fully anonymous short group signatures. In: Nguyên, P.Q. (ed.) VIETCRYPT 2006. LNCS, vol. 4341, pp. 193–210. Springer, Heidelberg (2006)
11. Dodis, Y., Yampolskiy, A.: A verifiable random function with short proofs and keys. In: Vaudenay, S. (ed.) PKC 2005. LNCS, vol. 3386, pp. 416–431. Springer, Heidelberg (2005)
12. Emura, K., Miyaji, A., Omote, K.: A dynamic attribute-based group signature scheme and its application in an anonymous survey for the collection of attribute statistics. JIP 17(1), 216–231 (2009)
13. Escala, A., Herranz, J., Morillo, P.: Revocable attribute-based signatures with adaptive security in the standard model. In: Nitaj, A., Pointcheval, D. (eds.) AFRICACRYPT 2011. LNCS, vol. 6737, pp. 224–241. Springer, Heidelberg (2011)
14. Franklin, M. (ed.): CRYPTO 2004. LNCS, vol. 3152. Springer, Heidelberg (2004)
15. Galbraith, S.D., Paterson, K.G., Smart, N.P.: Pairings for cryptographers. Discrete Applied Mathematics 156(16), 3113–3121 (2008)
16. Goyal, V., Pandey, O., Sahai, A., Waters, B.: Attribute-based encryption for fine-grained access control of encrypted data. In: ACM Conference on Computer and Communications Security, pp. 89–98. ACM (2006)
17. Groth, J., Sahai, A.: Efficient non-interactive proof systems for bilinear groups. In: Smart, N.P. (ed.) EUROCRYPT 2008. LNCS, vol. 4965, pp. 415–432. Springer, Heidelberg (2008)
18. Hada, S., Tanaka, T.: On the existence of 3-round zero-knowledge protocols. In: Krawczyk (ed.) [24], pp. 408–423
19. Herranz, J., Laguillaumie, F., Libert, B., Ràfols, C.: Short attribute-based sig-natures for threshold predicates. In: Dunkelman, O. (ed.) CT-RSA 2012. LNCS, vol. 7178, pp. 51–67. Springer, Heidelberg (2012)
20. Hirschfeld, R. (ed.): FC 1998. LNCS, vol. 1465. Springer, Heidelberg (1998)
21. Khader, D.: Attribute based group signature with revocation. IACR Cryptology ePrint Archive 2007, 241 (2007)
22. Khader, D.: Attribute based group signatures. IACR Cryptology ePrint Archive 2007, 159 (2007)
23. Kilian, J., Petrank, E.: Identity escrow. In: Krawczyk (ed.) [24], pp. 169–185
24. Krawczyk, H. (ed.): CRYPTO 1998. LNCS, vol. 1462. Springer, Heidelberg (1998)

25. Maji, H.K., Prabhakaran, M., Rosulek, M.: Attribute-based signatures. In: Kiayias, A. (ed.) CT-RSA 2011. LNCS, vol. 6558, pp. 376–392. Springer, Heidelberg (2011)
26. Okamoto, T., Takashima, K.: Efficient attribute-based signatures for non-monotone predicates in the standard model. In: Catalano, et al. (eds.) [8], pp. 35–52
27. Song, D.X.: Practical forward secure group signature schemes. In: ACM Conference on Computer and Communications Security, pp. 225–234 (2001)
28. Waters, B.: Efficient identity-based encryption without random oracles. In: Cramer, R. (ed.) EUROCRYPT 2005. LNCS, vol. 3494, pp. 114–127. Springer, Heidelberg (2005)

A   Assignment of Secret Values to Access Trees

This is from [12]. Let $index(x)$ be the function which returns a unique integer value for the node x, and p be a prime number. Let l_x represents the number of children of a node x and k_x denotes the threshold value of a node $x, 0 \leq k_x \leq l_x$. We assume that the tree T represents a subset of Att.

AddDummyNode(T): This algorithm takes as input an access tree T, and returns the *extended access tree* T^{ext} with dummy nodes on T.

1. For an interior node x of T, the number of dummy nodes $l_x - k_x$ is added to x's children.
2. Change the threshold value of x from k_x to l_x.
3. All nodes are assigned unique index numbers from $\mathbb{Z}_q^*$.
4. The resulting tree, called T^{ext}, is output.

Let D_T be a set of dummy nodes determined by AddDummyNode. Let $s_j \in \mathbb{Z}_p^*$ be a secret value for an attribute att$_j \in Att$. Let $S = \{s_j\}_{\mathrm{att}_j \in Att}$.

AssignedValue(S, T^{ext}): This algorithm takes as input S and T^{ext} and returns a secret value $s_x \in \mathbb{Z}_p^*$ for each node x of T^{ext}. Let $\{child\}_x$ be the set of node x's children except the dummy nodes, and $\{d\}_x$ be the set of node x's dummy nodes.

1. For the interior node x of T^{ext}, a polynomial q_x of degree $l_x - 1$ is assigned as follows:
   (a) q_x passes through $(index(x'), s_{x'})$ for each $x' \in \{child\}_x$. Note that $|\{child\}_x| = l_x$, so we can construct the unique polynomial.
   (b) For a dummy node $d_j \in \{d\}_x$, the secret value $s_{d_j} = q_x(index(d_j))$ is assigned.
   (c) For $x, s_x = q_x(0)$ is assigned.
2. Repeat the above procedure up to the root node, $s_T = q_{root}(0)$ is the secret value of T.
3. Output $\{s_{d_j}\}_{d_j \in D_T}$ and s_T.

`MakeSimplifiedTree`($Leaves, T^{ext}$): This algorithm takes as input the set $Leaves \subseteq Att$ satisfying $Leaves \models T$, and returns the product of Lagranges coefficients Δ_{leaf}.

1. The set of attributes $\{att_j\}_{att_j \in Att \backslash Leaves}$ are deleted from T^{ext}.
2. Interior nodes x having children less than the threshold value (namely, l_x) are deleted from T^{ext} along with x's descendants.
3. Let D_T^{Leaves} be the set of dummy nodes which have remained after the steps 1 and 2, and T^{Leaves} be the access tree after 1 and 2.
4. We assume that the leaves are at depth 0. For each node x of T^{Leaves} except root, define L_x as follows:
   (a) For x, define the depth 1 subtree of T^{Leaves} with x as leaf node. Let c_x be the set of indices of leaves of the subtree.
   (b) Compute $L_x = \prod_{k \in c_x \backslash \{index(x)\}} \frac{-k}{index(x)-k}$.
5. Let $leaf \in Leaves \cup D_T^{Leaves}$ be a leaf node of T^{Leaves}.
   For $leaf$, we define Δ_{leaf} as follows:
   (a) Let $Path_{leaf} = \{leaf, parent_1, ..., parent_{n_{leaf}} = root\}$ be the set of nodes that appears in the path from $leaf$ to root node.
   (b) Compute $\Delta_{leaf} = \prod_{node \in Path_{leaf} \backslash \{root\}} L_{node}$.
   Output $\Delta_{leaf} (\forall leaf \in Leaves \cup D_T^{Leaves})$.

Clearly, $\sum_{att_j \in Leaves} \Delta_{att_j} s_j + \sum_{d_j \in D_T^{Leaves}} \Delta_{d_j} s_{d_j} = s_T$ holds.

B Security Proofs

B.1 User Anonymity

Proof of Theorem 3. The proof follows the approach of anonymity adversary in [4]. The proof is organized in a sequence of games such that adversary has no advantage in final game where as the first game is the real attack game as given in definition (12). Let S_i denotes the event that the adversary wins in the game G_i with advantage $Adv_i = |Pr[S_i] - 1/2|$.

G_1: This is the real game as define in the definition (12). Challenger $\mathcal{B}$ sets up the scheme and defines the parameters as in the real scheme,

$$params = (p, \mathbb{G}_1, \mathbb{G}_2, \mathbb{G}_T, e, g_1, g_2, Att)$$
$$gpk = (h, \omega, \mathcal{F}, \{g_{att_j}\}_{att_j \in Att}, \boldsymbol{u}, \boldsymbol{u'}, \boldsymbol{v})$$
$$ik = (\gamma, S), ok_{user} = \alpha_1, tk_{att} = \alpha_1'$$

$\mathcal{B}$ gives gpk, ik and tr_{att} to $\mathcal{A}$. With this $\mathcal{B}$ answers all the queries made by adversary. At challenge phase $\mathcal{A}$ chooses 2 unrevoked and uncorrupted users U_{i_0}, U_{i_1} and is given a challenge signature σ^* on behalf of U_{i_κ}, $\kappa \in_R \{0,1\}$. In the output phase, adversary outputs her guess $\kappa' \in \{0,1\}$ and the advantage is $Adv_1 = |Pr[S_1] - 1/2|$.

G_2: Let n be the total number of passive join queries, joinP queries. In this game we modify the simulation G_1, $\mathcal{B}$ picks a challenge user id i^*. In the challenge phase, $\mathcal{B}$ aborts if $i_\kappa \neq i^*$. $\mathcal{B}$ also aborts if i^* is queried to corrupt or revoke oracle before or during challenge phase period. The probability that $\mathcal{B}$ succeed in picking correct i^* is $1/n$. Therefore, $Adv_2 \overset{\bullet}{=} Adv_1/n$.

G_3: We modify the simulation of G_2. $\mathcal{B}$ chooses $y \in_R \mathbb{Z}_p^*$ and define the ℓ–DDHI like tuple $A = (g, g^y, ..., g^{y^\ell}) \in \mathbb{G}_1^{\ell+1}, D = g^{1/y} \in \mathbb{G}_1$. $\mathcal{B}$ chooses different random values $z^*, z_1, ..., z_{\ell-1} \in \mathbb{Z}_p^\ell$, and define the polynomial $f(X) = \Pi_{i=1}^{\ell-1}(X - z_i)$, of degree $\ell - 1$. From the above tuple, $\mathcal{B}$ can compute $g_1 = g^{f(X)}$. The future challenge user i^* will virtually have $y_{i^*} = y - z^*$ and $x_{i^*} \in_R \mathbb{Z}_p^*$. $\mathcal{B}$ compute $g^{y_{i^*}} = g^y/g_1^{z^*}$ from the above tuple. The membership certificate for the challenge user is $(g_1^{x_{i^*}}, g_2^{x_{i^*}}, g_1^y/g_1^{z^*}, A_{i^*} = (hg_1^y/g_1^{z^*})^{\beta/(\gamma+x_{i^*})}, \{T_{i^*,j} = h^{\frac{s_j}{\gamma+x_{i^*}}}\}_{att_j \in \mathcal{A}_{i^*}})$. The setup is indistinguishable from G_2, since all keys are having same distribution.

$\mathcal{B}$ answers all queries according to definition (12) and for the challenge user U_{i^*}, the j-th signing queries, he computes $\rho_6 = g_1^{1/(y_{i^*}+z_j)} = g^{\Pi_{i \neq j}(y+z_i)}$, that can be done from the defined tuple, the rest is done as in the real scheme using z_j as random. $\mathcal{B}$ can also answer any corruption query, that should not happen for the challenge user, even if we know y in this game.

For the challenge signing query, he does the same as above with the ephemeral value z^*, and the expected ID, $\rho_6 = g_1^{1/(y_{i^*}+z^*)} = g^{f(y)/y} = g^{f'(y)}g^{\Pi(z_i)/y}$, where $f'(X) = (\Pi_{i=1}^\ell(X + z_i) - \Pi(z_i))/X$ is a polynomial of degree $\ell - 1$ and thus $g^{f'(y)}$ can be computable from the tuple. $\mathcal{B}$ thus compute $\rho_6 = g^{f'(y)}.D^{\Pi(z_i)}$ and returns the challenge signature σ^*. Therefore, $Adv_3 = Adv_2$.

G_4: We modify the game G_3. Here we initialize Groth-Sahai commitment keys in a perfectly hiding setting with the trapdoor, to allow the simulator to cheat in the proofs. Then all the proofs are simulated. This game is indistinguishable from the previous one under the SXDH. Thus $|Pr[S_4] - Pr[S_3]| = 2.Adv^{\text{SXDH}}$.

G_5: In this game, we do not know anymore y, that we did not use anymore anyway, and thus this game is perfectly indistinguishable from previous one. Thus $Pr[S_5] = Pr[S_4]$.

G_6: In this game, we replaces the defined ℓ–DDHI tuple with the actual ℓ–DDHI challenge instance, where y is unknown to $\mathcal{B}$ and D is a random value. Thus this game is indistinguishable from the previous one under the ℓ–DDHI assumption. Therefore, $|Pr[S_6] - Pr[S_5]| \leq Adv^{\ell-\text{DDHI}}$.

Note the challenger signature does not depend anymore on the challenge user. When we combine all the probabilities we obtain the upper bound (11) on $\mathcal{A}$'s advantage in game G_1.   □

B.2   Attribute Unforgeability

Proof of Theorem 4. Lemma 1 implies the Theorem 4.

Lemma 1. *Under the DL and KEA assumptions there exists no PPT adversary $\mathcal{A}$ which passes verification with forged attributes with non negligible probability.*

Proof. The input to the simulator $\mathcal{B}$ is an instance of the DL problem, $(g, g') \in \mathbb{G}_1^2$. Let $\xi = log_g g'$.

Setup: According to the ABGS scheme setup $\mathcal{B}$ generates the system parameters, *params*. $\mathcal{B}$ sets $g_1 = g$ and $h = g'$, and generate the remaining parameters, $gpk, ik, ok_{user}, tk_{att}$. $\mathcal{B}$ gives gpk, ok_{user} and tk_{att} to $\mathcal{A}$.

Queries: As $\mathcal{B}$ knows all the keys, it can answer all the queries generated by an adversary $\mathcal{A}$ according to the definition of *attribute unforgeability*.

Output: Finally, $\mathcal{A}$ outputs a signature σ^* with forged attribute certificates on message M^*, a predicate Υ^* whose public values are $\mathcal{T}_{\Upsilon^*} = (\{s_{d_j}\}_{d_j \in D_{T_{\Upsilon^*}}}, v_T = g_2^{s_T}, T^{\text{ext}})$, and signer's secret key sk_{i^*} such that $\Upsilon(\mathcal{A}_{i^*}) \neq 1$ and $\Upsilon(\mathcal{A}_{i^*} \cup att_j) = 1$. As it is a valid signature which passes verification algorithm and from (5) $\rho_4^* = h^{\frac{s_{T_1}}{\gamma + x_{i^*}}}$ and $\rho_5^* = h^{s_{T_2}}$ such that $s_{T_1} + s_{T_2} = s_T$. This can be viewed as $\rho_4^* = h^{\frac{s'_{T_1}}{\gamma + x_{i^*}}} h^{\frac{s_j}{\gamma + x_{i^*}}}$, where $s_{T_1} = s'_{T_1} + s_j$ and $h^{\frac{s_j}{\gamma + x_{i^*}}}$ is unknown to $\mathcal{A}$ but she is producing it in signature.

It is like $\mathcal{B}$ is giving input $(g_1 = g, g_1^{s_j} = g_{att_j} = g^{s_j})$ to $\mathcal{A}$ and $\mathcal{A}$ implicitly returns $(h = g', h^{s_j} = g'^{s_j})$. Then by KEA assumption, $\mathcal{B}$ can utilize the extractor $\bar{A}$ to extract a value ξ. Under DL assumption it can be done with negligible probability. Thus the signature produced by the forged attribute certificates can pass verification with negligible probability. Note that the $\mathcal{A}$ can also produce the missing attribute in the value ρ_5^* to satisfy the relation (5) but similarly its probability is negligible under KEA and DL assumption. □

B.3   Collusion Resistance of Attributes

Proof of Theorem 5. Lemma 2 implies the Theorem 5.

Lemma 2. *Even if some malicious participants $U_{i_1}, ..., U_{i_k}(k > 1)$ with the set of attributes $\zeta_{i_1}, ..., \zeta_{i_k}$ collude, they cannot make a valid signature associated with a predicate Υ, where $(\cup_{j=1}^{k} \Upsilon(\zeta_{i_j}) = 1)$ and $\Upsilon(\zeta_{i_j}) \neq 1$ for $j = 1, ..., k$ with non-negligible probability under KEA and DL assumptions.*

Proof. There are two cases possible, in case 1 adversary tries produce the signature by combining the attribute certificates of different users and in case 2 adversary tries to produce the signature by forging the required attribute certificates for one user with the knowledge of attributes public key and attribute certificates of other users. Without loss of generality, we assume that U_{i_1} with ζ_{i_1}

and U_{i_2} with ζ_{i_2} represent malicious participants. U_{i_1} and U_{i_2} attempt to make a valid signature associated with Υ which satisfies $\Upsilon(\zeta_{i_1} \cup \zeta_{i_2}) = 1, \Upsilon(\zeta_{i_1}) \neq 1$ and $\Upsilon(\zeta_{i_2}) \neq 1$. They can satisfy the relations (4) and (5) because they have a valid membership certificate (A_{i_1}, X, y_{i_1}). We assume that $T_{i_1,j}^t = T_{i_2,j}$, where $t \in \mathbb{Z}_p^*$. Note that the probability of $t = 1$ is negligible.

Case 1: The malicious participants tries to compute

$$\rho_6 = h^{\frac{1}{\gamma+x_{i_1}}(\Sigma_{\mathrm{att}_j \in \mathcal{A}_{i_1}} \Delta_{\mathrm{att}_j} s_j)} \times h^{\frac{1}{\gamma+x_{i_2}}(\Sigma_{\mathrm{att}_j \in \mathcal{A}_{i_2}} \Delta_{\mathrm{att}_j} s_j)}$$

$$= h^{\frac{1}{\gamma+x_{i_1}}(\Sigma_{\mathrm{att}_j \in \mathcal{A}_{i_1}} \Delta_{\mathrm{att}_j} s_j + t\Sigma_{\mathrm{att}_j \in \mathcal{A}_{i_2}} \Delta_{\mathrm{att}_j} s_j)}$$

Then from (1) $\Sigma_{\mathrm{att}_j \in \mathcal{A}_{i_1}} \Delta_{\mathrm{att}_j} s_j + t\Sigma_{\mathrm{att}_j \in \mathcal{A}_{i_2}} \Delta_{\mathrm{att}_j} s_j + \Sigma_{d_j \in D_T^\varsigma} \Delta_{d_j} s_{d_j} \neq s_T$ holds. Since $t \neq 1$. This means that they cannot collude the attribute certificates.

Case 2: The malicious participants tries to produce the signature by forging the attribute certificates for U_{i_1} using the knowledge of attributes public key and attribute certificates of U_{i_2}. Then similar to the proof of attribute unforgeability under KEA and DL assumptions it is negligible.   □

B.4   Traceability

Proof of Theorem 6. Since the membership certificate format is similar to the one proposed in [10,4], the proof directly reduces to the q-HHSDH assumption. The simulator $\mathcal{B}$ receives q-HHSDH challenge $(g_1, h, g_2, \omega = g_2^\gamma, (g_1^{x_i}, g_2^{x_i}, y_i, A_i = (hg_1^{y_i})^{1/(\gamma+x_i)})_{i \in [1,q]})$ and tries to solve it, from $\mathcal{A}$ that breaks the traceability of our scheme.

Setup: $\mathcal{B}$ generates the commitment keys, attribute secret and public values, and other parameters as in the ABGS scheme by using the q-HHSDH challenge values. $\mathcal{B}$ gives gpk, ok_{user} and tk_{att} to $\mathcal{A}$.

Queries: To answer the i-th join queries, if this is an active join, $\mathcal{B}$ extracts y_i' chooses his y_i'' so that $y_i' + y_i'' = y_i$, if it is a passive join, $\mathcal{B}$ directly chooses y_i. Thus $\mathcal{B}$ can answer all the queries according to traceability definition.

Output: After atmost q join quires, $\mathcal{A}$ outputs a new signature with a new certificate tuple with non-negligible probability. As $\mathcal{B}$ knows the trapdoor of the commitment scheme, he can obtain $(g_1^x, g_2^x, g_1^y, g_2^y, A = (hg_1^y)^{1/(\gamma+x)})$. Thus $\mathcal{B}$ answers the challenge q-HHSDH instance with the same advantage of $\mathcal{A}$.   □

B.5   Non-frameability

Proof of Theorem 7. The proof is similar to the proof of non-frameability in the Blazy and Pointcheval [4] traceable signature. There exists two types of adversary, one breaks the non-frameability by forging the new ID, ρ_6, on an uncorrupted user and another breaks the non-frameability by reusing an existing

ID with the corresponding certificate but on a new message. With $1/2$ probability $\mathcal{B}$ decides which type of adversary it is.

Type I: The simulator $\mathcal{B}$ receives q-HSDH challenge $((g_1, g_2, g_1^y, g_2^y), (g_1^{t_i}, g_2^{t_i}, g_1^{1/(y+t_i)})_{i \in [1,q]})$ and tries to solve it, from an adversary $\mathcal{A}$ that breaks the non-frameability of our scheme by forging a new ID, ρ_6, on an uncorrupted user.

Setup: $\mathcal{B}$ generates the gpk, ik, ok_{user} and tk_{att} as the real settings and gives it to $\mathcal{A}$. $\mathcal{B}$ selects the target user on which he expect the attack and set his membership certificate corresponding to one with y as a secret key.

Queries: $\mathcal{B}$ can answer any joinP query as he knows ik, as well as corrupt query on any user except the target user, otherwise the simulation fails. $\mathcal{B}$ can answer the sign queries and can answer to atmost q sign queries for the target user with the help of challenge q-HSDH tuple.

Output: After all the queries and the atmost q signing queries for target user, $\mathcal{A}$ succeed in breaking the non-frameability with non negligible probability by generating a new tuple $(\rho_6 = g_1^{1/(y+t)}, \rho_7 = (g_1^t, g_2^t))$, on an uncorrupted user. Thus $\mathcal{B}$ solves the q-HSDH challenge.

Type 2: The simulator $\mathcal{B}$ is given an asymmetric Waters public key ($pk = (g_1^t, g_2^t)$ for the global parameters $(g_1, g_2, h, \mathcal{F})$). $\mathcal{B}$ tries to break this signature, and thus the CDH$^+$ problem, from an adversary $\mathcal{A}$ breaking the non-frameability of our scheme by reusing an existing tuple ρ_6, ρ_7 on a new message.

In the first game, G_1, $\mathcal{B}$ knows the discrete logarithm value t, generates a new ik, ok_{user}, tk_{att} and gives ik, ok_{user}, tk_{att} to $\mathcal{A}$ together with the public key $gpk = (h, \omega, \mathcal{F}, \{g_{att_j}\}_{att_j \in Att})$. $\mathcal{B}$ can answer any joinP query as he knows ik and extract the secret keys from the extraction key of the commitment scheme, one of those uncorrupted user is expected to be a challenge user, with the secret key y, the one $\mathcal{A}$ has to frame.

$\mathcal{B}$ can answer any signing queries. On one of them for the challenge user, say on M, he will use the above ξ as ephemeral Waters public key (for the z), and thus computes a $\rho_6 = g_1^{1/(y+t)}$ with the corresponding Groth-Sahai proof. This way $\mathcal{A}$ possesses a valid signature on M, with $\rho_7 = (g_1^t, g_2^t), \rho_8 = h^t \mathcal{F}(\mathcal{M})^s, \rho_9 = g_2^s$. With non-negligible probability $\mathcal{A}$ breaks the non-frameability of our scheme, by hypothesis $\mathcal{A}$ does it by reusing an existing $\rho_1, ..., \rho_7$, as uncorrupted users are indistinguishable, $\mathcal{A}$ frames our challenge user with non-negligible probability, and as the signing queries are finite, he will use $\rho_7 = (g_1^t, g_2^t)$ with non-negligible probability. Therefore, with non-negligible probability $\mathcal{A}$ outputs a new valid signature on M' with $\rho_7 = (g_1^t, g_2^t)$, this means we have (ρ_7, ρ_8, ρ_9) such that $e(\rho_{7,1}, g_2) = e(g_1, \rho_{7,2}), e(\rho_8, g_2) = e(h, \rho_{7,2}) \times e(\mathcal{F}(\mathcal{M}'), \rho_9)$, and thus $\mathcal{B}$ can output a valid forgery on the Waters challenge for the public key (g_1^t, g_2^t). But in this game, we know t.

In a second game, G_2, the Groth-Sahai setup is used as hiding one, so that the proofs can be simulated, and namely without using t. This is indistinguishable from the previous game under the SXDH assumption.

In the third game, G_3, replace ρ_6 by a random value, still simulating the proofs. A random ρ_6 is indistinguishable from the real one under the DDHI problem as seen in user anonymity proof. Furthermore, here there is only one elements, hence the $1-$DDHI assumption. In the last game, one does not need to know t anymore, and thus the signature forgery reduces to breaking the asymmetric CDH^+. $\qquad\square$

From Selective-ID to Full-ID IBS without Random Oracles

Sanjit Chatterjee and Chethan Kamath

Dept. of Computer Science and Automation,
Indian Institute of Science,
Bangalore
{sanjit,chethan0510}@csa.iisc.ernet.in

Abstract. Since its induction, the selective-identity (sID) model for identity-based cryptosystems and its relationship with various other notions of security has been extensively studied. As a result, it is a general consensus that the sID model is much weaker than the full-identity (ID) model. In this paper, we study the sID model for the particular case of identity-based signatures (IBS). The main focus is on the problem of constructing an ID-secure IBS given an sID-secure IBS without using *random oracles*–the so-called *standard* model–and with reasonable security degradation. We accomplish this by devising a generic construction which uses as black-box: *i*) a *chameleon* hash function and *ii*) a *weakly-secure* public-key signature. We argue that the resulting IBS is ID-secure but with a tightness gap of $\mathcal{O}(q_s)$, where q_s is the upper bound on the number of signature queries that the adversary is allowed to make. To the best of our knowledge, this is the first attempt at such a generic construction.

Keywords: Identity-Based Signatures, Security Models, Selective-Identity Security, Generic Chosen-Message Attack, Chameleon Hash Function.

1 Introduction

The concept of identity-based cryptosystems (IBC) was introduced by Shamir in 1984 [19]. In IBC, any arbitrary string such as an e-mail address can act as the public key. In traditional public-key cryptosystems (PKC), users have to exchange public-key certificates before being able to communicate securely. These certificates provide the external binding between the public key and the identity of a user. In some scenarios certificates can prove to be cumbersome. Using IBC one can avoid the complicated certificate management–this was Shamir's foresight.

Identity-based signatures. The notion of identity-based signatures (IBS) is an extension of the idea of digital signatures to the identity-based setting. As in traditional public-key signature (PKS) schemes, the signer uses her secret key

B. Gierlichs, S. Guilley, and D. Mukhopadhyay (Eds.): SPACE 2013, LNCS 8204, pp. 172–190, 2013.

to sign a message. However, the signature can be verified by anyone using the signer's identity and the master public key of the private-key generator[1] (PKG). IBS–or more generally, IBC–does not require any certificates to be exchanged and hence can be advantageous over the traditional PKI based systems in certain scenarios. IBS, in particular, turns out to be quite practical in wireless sensor-networks, BGP protocol, MANET routing *etc.*. Therefore, the question of designing efficient and secure IBS is an important problem in the context of applied cryptography. With the advent of pairings [4], the interest in IBS–and, of course, identity-based encryption (IBE) schemes–mushroomed, resulting in numerous efficient schemes [8,14,15].

The selective-identity model. The selective-identity (`sID`) model for identity-based cryptographic schemes was introduced in [9]. The distinguishing feature of this model is that the adversary has to commit, beforehand, to a "target" identity–*i.e.*, the identity which it eventually forges on. Since its induction, the relationship of the `sID` notion with various other notions of security has been extensively studied [10,7,11,12]. One of the interesting results is the separation between the `sID` models and `ID` models for IBE in the standard model [11]. Therefore, it is a general consensus that the `sID` model is much weaker than the full-identity (`ID`) model. However, it is *easier* to design efficient schemes, based on weaker assumptions, that are secure in the `sID` model compared to the `ID` model. This is, in particular, highlighted by the disparity in the construction of IBE schemes given in [1] and [21]. The former is simple and efficient, whereas the latter, involved. Therefore, a generic transformation from an `sID` scheme to `ID` scheme would be a problem worth pursuing. We could design efficient `sID`-secure schemes and then just bootstrap it to `ID`-security using the transformation. In fact, this is a long-standing open problem.

Existing techniques for constructing IBS. The task of constructing IBS is generally considered to be a much easier task than that of constructing IBE. [5] contains a comprehensive list of such techniques, along with the security arguments. The "folklore" construction of IBS using two applications of PKS (certificate) is one of the well-known techniques. A PKS, on the other hand, can be derived from a *weakly*-secure PKS [13] using a *chameleon* hash function (CHF) [17]. This approach was used implicitly in [20] and, later, formalised in [16]. The (existence of) two aforementioned techniques implies one can construct an IBS from a weakly-secure PKS and a CHF.

There exist techniques to construct (`ID`-secure) IBS from `sID`-secure IBS as well. An efficient (comparatively) black-box method to convert an `sID`-secure IBE scheme to `ID` security was suggested in [4]. But the method relies on *random oracles* [6]. This was followed by [1], in which the problem is solved without using random oracles–in the so-called *standard* model–albeit with an *exponential* loss of tightness. Both these methods can be adapted to IBS.

---

[1] The PKG is a trusted third party whose duty is to create and then communicate the secret keys to the users in the system through a secure channel.

Our Contribution. The primary focus of this paper is on the question of constructing an ID-secure IBS, given an sID-secure IBS, in the standard model, and with reasonable security degradation. We accomplish this through a generic transformation which uses a CHF and a *weakly*-secure PKS as black-box. We go one step further by applying the same construction technique to a *relaxed* notion of IBS security which we call the *weak* selective-identity (wID) model. The distinguishing feature of the wID model is that the adversary, apart from committing to the target identity, has to commit to a set of "query" identities— the set of identities which it wishes to query the signature and extract oracle with (see §4 for the definition of the security model). Thus, we reduce the problem of constructing an ID-secure IBS to that of constructing wID-secure IBS, an EU-GCMA-secure PKS and a CHF. Our approach can be considered to be an alternative paradigm to the aforementioned folklore construction of IBS.

The security argument constitutes the main hurdle–the construction itself is quite straightforward. The line of argument, roughly, is: given an adversary that breaks the ID-IBS, we construct algorithms to break either the sID/wID-IBS, the PKS or the CHF. It leads to a tightness gap of $\mathcal{O}(q_s)$, where q_s is the upper bound on the number of signature queries that the adversary is allowed to make.

Organisation. We start with the formal definitions in §2. The generic transformation, along with its security argument and analysis, is given in §3. In §4 we show that our construction can be used to construct an ID-secure IBS from a wID-secure IBS. Finally, we conclude with some remarks in §5.

2   Definitions

2.1   Public-Key Signatures

Definition 1 (Public-Key Signature). *A public-key signature (PKS) consists of three polynomial-time non-deterministic algorithms* $\{\mathcal{K}, \mathcal{S}, \mathcal{V}\}$.

> **Key Generation,** $\mathcal{K}(\kappa)$: It takes as input the security parameter κ and outputs the public key pk and the secret key sk.
> **Signing,** $\mathcal{S}(m, \text{sk})$: It takes as input a message m and the secret key of the user sk to generate a signature σ.
> **Verification,** $\mathcal{V}(\sigma, m, \text{pk})$: It takes as input the signature σ, the message m and the public key of the user pk. It outputs the b which is 1 if σ is valid signature on m or 0 if the signature is invalid.

The standard *correctness* condition: $1 \leftarrow \mathcal{V}(\mathcal{S}(m, \text{sk}), m, \text{pk})$, should be satisfied for all m and $(\text{pk}, \text{sk}) \xleftarrow{\$} \mathcal{K}(\kappa)$.

Security Notions. The standard security notion for PKS schemes is *existential unforgeability under chosen-message attack* (EU-CMA) [13].

Definition 2 (EU-CMA Game). *The security of a PKS scheme in the* EU-CMA *model is argued in terms of the following game between a challenger* $\mathcal{C}$ *and an adversary* $\mathcal{A}$.

Set-up: $\mathcal{C}$ invokes $\mathcal{K}$ to obtain the public key $\mathbf{pk}$ and the secret key $\mathbf{sk}$. $\mathcal{A}$ is given the public key but the secret key is kept by $\mathcal{C}$.

Signature queries: $\mathcal{A}$ can adaptively make signature queries to an oracle $\mathcal{O}_s$. For a query on a message m, $\mathcal{C}$ responds by running $\mathcal{S}$ on m to obtain a signature σ, which is forwarded to $\mathcal{A}$.

Forgery: $\mathcal{A}$ outputs a signature $\hat{\sigma}$ on a message $\hat{m}$ and wins the game if
1. $\hat{\sigma}$ is a valid signature on $\hat{m}$.
2. $\mathcal{A}$ has not made a signature query on $\hat{m}$.

The advantage $\mathcal{A}$ has in the above game, denoted by $\mathrm{Adv}_{\mathcal{A}}^{\mathtt{EU-CMA}}$, is defined as the probability with which it wins the above game, *i.e.*

$$\Pr\left[1 \leftarrow \mathcal{V}(\hat{\sigma}, \hat{m}, \mathbf{pk}) \mid (\mathbf{sk}, \mathbf{pk}) \xleftarrow{\$} \mathcal{K}(\kappa); (\hat{\sigma}, \hat{m}) \xleftarrow{\$} \mathcal{A}^{\mathcal{O}_s}(\mathbf{pk})\right]$$

provided $\hat{\sigma}$ is a valid forgery. An adversary $\mathcal{A}$ is said to be an (ϵ, t, q_s)-forger of a PKS scheme if it has advantage of at least ϵ in the above game, runs in time at most t and makes at most q_s signature queries.

A weaker notion of security for PKS is *existential forgery under generic chosen-message attack* (`EU-GCMA`) [13]. In the `EU-GCMA` model, the adversary initially commits to a set of messages $m_1, \ldots, m_{q_s}$ to the challenger. Next, it is given the signatures correspond to the committed messages along with the public key to be attacked. The adversary finally outputs a forgery on a message that was not part of the committed set. A more formal definition follows.

Definition 3 (`EU-GCMA` Game). *The security of a PKS scheme in the `EU-GCMA` model is argued in terms of the following game between a challenger $\mathcal{C}$ and an adversary $\mathcal{A}$.*

Commitment: $\mathcal{A}$ commits to a set of messages $\tilde{\mathbb{M}} := \{m_1, \ldots, m_{q_s}\}$.

Set-up: $\mathcal{C}$ invokes $\mathcal{G}$ to obtain the public key $\mathbf{pk}$ and the secret key $\mathbf{sk}$. $\mathcal{A}$ is given the public key but the secret key is kept by $\mathcal{C}$.

Signing: $\mathcal{C}$ invokes the signing algorithm $\mathcal{S}$ on each $m_i \in \tilde{\mathbb{M}}$ to generate signatures $\sigma_1, \ldots, \sigma_{q_s}$ and passes them on to $\mathcal{A}$.

Forgery: $\mathcal{A}$ outputs a signature $\hat{\sigma}$ on a message $\hat{m}$ and wins the game if
1. $\hat{\sigma}$ is a valid signature on $\hat{m}$.
2. $\hat{m}$ was not a part of the committed set $\tilde{\mathbb{M}}$.

The advantage $\mathcal{A}$ has in the above game, denoted by $\mathrm{Adv}_{\mathcal{A}}^{\mathtt{EU-GCMA}}$, is defined as the probability with which it wins the above game, *i.e.*

$$\Pr\left[1 \leftarrow \mathcal{V}(\hat{\sigma}, \hat{m}, \mathbf{pk}) \wedge \hat{m} \notin \tilde{\mathbb{M}} \mid \tilde{\mathbb{M}} \xleftarrow{\$} \mathcal{A}(q_s); (\mathbf{sk}, \mathbf{pk}) \xleftarrow{\$} \mathcal{K}(\kappa);\right.$$
$$\left.(\hat{\sigma}, \hat{m}) \xleftarrow{\$} \mathcal{A}(\mathbf{pk}, \sigma_1, \ldots, \sigma_{q_s})\right]$$

An adversary $\mathcal{A}$ is said to be an (ϵ, t, q_s)-forger of a PKS scheme if it has advantage of at least ϵ in the above game, runs in time at most t, after initially committing to a set of q_s messages.

2.2 Identity-Based Signatures

Definition 4 (Identity-Based Signature). *An IBS scheme consists of four polynomial-time non-deterministic algorithms* $\{\mathcal{G}, \mathcal{E}, \mathcal{S}, \mathcal{V}\}$ *described below.*

> **Set-up,** $\mathcal{G}(\kappa)$: It takes as input the security parameter κ. It outputs the master secret key msk and the master public key mpk.
>
> **Key Extraction,** $\mathcal{E}(\mathrm{id}, \mathrm{msk})$: It takes as input the user's identity id, the master secret key msk to generate the secret key usk of a user.
>
> **Signing,** $\mathcal{S}(\mathrm{id}, m, \mathrm{usk})$: It takes as input the user's identity id, a message m and the user's secret key usk to generate a signature σ.
>
> **Verification,** $\mathcal{V}(\sigma, \mathrm{id}, m, \mathrm{mpk})$: It takes as input a signature σ, a message m, an identity id and master public key mpk. It outputs the result bit b which is 1 if σ is a valid signature on (id, m) or 0 if the signature is invalid.

The standard *correctness* condition: $1 \leftarrow \mathcal{V}(\mathcal{S}(\mathrm{id}, m, \mathrm{usk}), \mathrm{id}, m, \mathrm{mpk})$, should be satisfied for all id, m, $(\mathrm{msk}, \mathrm{mpk}) \xleftarrow{\$} \mathcal{G}(\kappa)$ and $\mathrm{usk} \xleftarrow{\$} \mathcal{E}(\mathrm{id}, \mathrm{msk})$.

Security Notions. We use the standard security notion for IBS schemes given in [5]. In addition, we also describe the weaker selective-identity notion of IBS security.

Definition 5 (EU-ID-CMA Game[2]). *The security of an IBS scheme in the EU-ID-CMA model is argued in terms of the following game between a challenger* $\mathcal{C}$ *and an adversary* $\mathcal{A}$.

> **Set-up:** $\mathcal{C}$ invokes $\mathcal{G}$ to obtain master public key mpk and the master secret key msk. $\mathcal{A}$ is given master public key but the master secret key is kept by $\mathcal{C}$.
>
> **Queries:** $\mathcal{A}$ can adaptively make extract queries to an oracle $\mathcal{O}_{\varepsilon}$ and signature queries to an oracle $\mathcal{O}_s$. These queries are handled as follows.
>
> > **Extract query,** $\mathcal{O}_{\varepsilon}(\mathrm{id})$: $\mathcal{A}$ asks for the secret key of a user with identity id. If there has already been an extract query on id, $\mathcal{C}$ returns the user secret key that was generated during the earlier query. Otherwise, $\mathcal{C}$ uses the knowledge of msk to run $\mathcal{E}$ and generate the user secret key usk, which is passed on to $\mathcal{A}$.
> >
> > **Signature query,** $\mathcal{O}_s(\mathrm{id}, m)$: $\mathcal{A}$ asks for the signature of a user with identity id on a message m. $\mathcal{C}$ first generates a user secret key for id, as in the extract query. Next, it uses the knowledge of usk to run $\mathcal{S}$ and generate a signature σ, which is passed to $\mathcal{A}$.
>
> **Forgery:** $\mathcal{A}$ outputs a signature $\hat{\sigma}$ on an identity $\hat{\mathrm{id}}$ and a message $\hat{m}$, and wins the game if
> 1. $\hat{\sigma}$ is a valid signature on $\hat{m}$ by $\hat{\mathrm{id}}$.
> 2. $\mathcal{A}$ has not made an extract query on $\hat{\mathrm{id}}$.
> 3. $\mathcal{A}$ has not made a signature query on $(\hat{\mathrm{id}}, \hat{m})$.

---

[2] The security game in [5], *i.e.* $\mathrm{Exp}_{\mathrm{IBS}, \hat{\mathbb{F}}}^{\mathrm{uf\text{-}cma}}$, is explained in terms of the three oracles: INIT, CORR and SIGN. But we use a slightly simpler, but equivalent, formulation using the two oracles: $\mathcal{O}_{\varepsilon}$ and $\mathcal{O}_s$.

The advantage $\mathcal{A}$ has in the above game, denoted by $\mathrm{Adv}_{\mathcal{A}}^{\mathrm{EU-ID-CMA}}$, is defined as the probability with which it wins the above game, *i.e.*

$$\Pr\left[1 \leftarrow \mathcal{V}(\hat{\sigma}, \hat{\mathrm{id}}, \hat{m}, \mathrm{mpk}) \mid (\mathrm{msk}, \mathrm{mpk}) \overset{\$}{\leftarrow} \mathcal{G}(\kappa); (\hat{\sigma}, \hat{\mathrm{id}}, \hat{m}) \overset{\$}{\leftarrow} \mathcal{A}^{\mathcal{O}_\varepsilon, \mathcal{O}_s}(\mathrm{mpk})\right]$$

provided $\hat{\sigma}$ is a valid forgery on $(\hat{\mathrm{id}}, \hat{m})$. An adversary $\mathcal{A}$ is said to be an $(\epsilon, t, q_\varepsilon, q_s)$-forger of an IBS scheme if it has advantage of at least ϵ in the above game, runs in time at most t and makes at most q_ε and q_s extract and signature queries respectively. If the security argument uses the random oracle methodology [6], the adversary is also allowed to make queries to the random oracle(s).

Definition 6 (EU-sID-CMA Game). *The security of an IBS scheme in the* `EU-sID-CMA` *model is argued in terms of the following game between a challenger* $\mathcal{C}$ *and an adversary* $\mathcal{A}$.

> **Commitment**: $\mathcal{A}$ commits to a target identity $\tilde{\mathrm{id}}$.
> **Set-up**: $\mathcal{C}$ runs the set-up algorithm $\mathcal{G}$ to obtain the master keys (mpk,msk). It passes mpk as the challenge master public key to $\mathcal{A}$.
> **Queries**: $\mathcal{A}$ can adaptively make extract queries to an oracle $\mathcal{O}_\varepsilon$ and signature queries to an oracle $\mathcal{O}_s$. It is restricted though from making extract query on the target identity $\tilde{\mathrm{id}}$. These queries are handled as follows.
>
> > **Extract query, $\mathcal{O}_\varepsilon(\mathrm{id})$:** $\mathcal{A}$ asks for the secret key of a user with identity id. $\mathcal{C}$ responds by running $\mathcal{E}$ and passes the secret key usk to $\mathcal{A}$.
> > **Signature query, $\mathcal{O}_s(\mathrm{id}, m)$:** $\mathcal{A}$ asks for the signature of a user with identity id on a message m. $\mathcal{C}$ responds by first running $\mathcal{E}$ on id to obtain the secret key usk of the user and then running $\mathcal{S}$ to obtain a signature σ, which is forwarded to $\mathcal{A}$.
> **Forgery**: $\mathcal{A}$ outputs a signature $\hat{\sigma}$ on a message $\hat{m}$ by identity $\tilde{\mathrm{id}}$, and wins the game if
> 1. $\hat{\sigma}$ is a valid signature on $\hat{m}$ by $\tilde{\mathrm{id}}$.
> 2. $\mathcal{A}$ has not made a signature query on $(\tilde{\mathrm{id}}, \hat{m})$.

The advantage $\mathcal{A}$ has in the above game, denoted by $\mathrm{Adv}_{\mathcal{A}}^{\mathrm{EU-sID-CMA}}$, is defined as the probability with which it wins the game, *i.e.*

$$\Pr\left[1 \leftarrow \mathcal{V}(\hat{\sigma}, \tilde{\mathrm{id}}, \hat{m}, \mathrm{mpk}) \mid \tilde{\mathrm{id}} \overset{\$}{\leftarrow} \mathcal{A}; (\mathrm{msk}, \mathrm{mpk}) \overset{\$}{\leftarrow} \mathcal{G}(\kappa);\right.$$
$$\left.(\hat{\sigma}, \tilde{\mathrm{id}}, \hat{m}) \overset{\$}{\leftarrow} \mathcal{A}^{\mathcal{O}_\varepsilon, \mathcal{O}_s}(\mathrm{mpk})\right]$$

An adversary $\mathcal{A}$ is said to be an $(\epsilon, t, q_\varepsilon, q_s)$-forger of an IBS scheme in the `EU-sID-CMA` model if it has advantage of at least ϵ in the above game, runs in time at most t and makes at most q_ε and q_s extract and signature queries respectively.

2.3   Chameleon Hash Function

A chameleon hash function (CHF) is a randomised trapdoor hash function. Apart from the *collision resistance* property, it has an additional "chameleon" property which enables anyone with the trapdoor information to efficiently generate collisions.

Definition 7 (Chameleon Hash Function [3,17,18]). *A family of CHF $\mathfrak{H}$ consists of three* polynomial-time *algorithms* $\{\mathcal{G}, h, h^{-1}\}$ *described below.*

> **Key Generation,** $\mathcal{G}(\kappa)$: It takes as input the security parameter κ. It outputs the evaluation key ek and the trapdoor key td.
> **Hash Evaluation,** $h(ek, m, r)$: It takes as input the evaluation key ek, a message m from the message-space $\mathbb{M}$ and a randomiser r from the domain $\mathbb{R}$. It outputs the hash value y from the range $\mathbb{Y}$.
> **Collision Generation,** $h^{-1}(td, m, r, m')$: It takes as input the trapdoor key td, two messages $m, m' \in \mathbb{M}$ and $r \in \mathbb{R}$. It outputs $r' \in \mathbb{R}$ such that $h(ek, m, r) = h(ek, m', r')$; in other words, (m, r) and (m', r') is a collision.

Any CHF should satisfy the following two properties.

(i) *Uniformity.* The distribution induced by $h(ek, m, r)$ for all messages m and a randomly chosen r should be the same. In other words, the distributions $(ek, h(ek, m, r))$ and (ek, y) should be computationally indistinguishable, where $(ek, td) \xleftarrow{\$} \mathcal{G}(\kappa), r \in_R \mathbb{R}$ and $y \in_R \mathbb{Y}$.

(ii) *Collision Resistance.* Given the evaluation key ek, it should be hard to compute a pair $(m, r) \neq (m', r')$ such that $h(ek, m, r) = h(ek, m', r')$, *i.e.* the probability given below should be negligible for all *polynomial-time non-deterministic* adversaries $\mathcal{A}$.

$$\Pr\left[h(ek, m, r) = h(ek, m', r') \wedge (m, r) \neq (m', r') \mid \right.$$
$$\left. (ek, td) \xleftarrow{\$} \mathcal{G}(\kappa); (m, r, m', r') \xleftarrow{\$} \mathcal{A}(ek)\right]$$

3   The Generic Transformation

The transformation takes as input: *i)* an sID-secure IBS $\mathfrak{I}_s := \{\mathcal{G}_s, \mathcal{E}_s, \mathcal{S}_s, \mathcal{V}_s\}$; *ii)* an EU-GCMA-secure PKS $\mathfrak{P} := \{\mathcal{K}, \mathcal{S}_p, \mathcal{V}_p\}$; and *iii)* a CHF $\mathfrak{H} := \{\mathcal{G}_h, h, h^{-1}\}$, to output an ID-secure IBS $\mathfrak{I} := \{\mathcal{G}, \mathcal{E}, \mathcal{S}, \mathcal{V}\}$. The basic idea is to *map* an identity id in $\mathfrak{I}$ to an identity id_s in $\mathfrak{I}_s$ using the CHF. These two identities are then *bound* by using the PKS. A formal description follows.

Assumptions. We denote the identity-space of $\mathfrak{I}_s$ (and that of resulting $\mathfrak{I}$) by $\mathbb{I}$ and its message-space by $\mathbb{M}$. For simplicity, we assume that *i)* the message-space of $\mathfrak{P}$ *ii)* the message-space of $\mathfrak{H}$ (denoted by $\mathbb{M}_h$) and *iii)* the range of $\mathfrak{H}$ (denoted by $\mathbb{Y}$) *are all* the same set $\mathbb{I}$, *i.e.*, $\mathbb{M}_h = \mathbb{Y} = \mathbb{I}$.[3] In addition, the randomness space of $\mathfrak{H}$ is denoted by $\mathbb{R}$. Therefore, for a particular evaluation key $\mathbf{ek}$, the hash evaluation algorithm can be considered as a function $h : \mathbb{I} \times \mathbb{R} \to \mathbb{I}$. The description of the transformation is given in **Figure 1**. It is followed by the argument that the resultant IBS $\mathfrak{I}$ is secure in the ID model.

$\mathfrak{I} \leftarrow \mathfrak{T}(\mathfrak{I}_s, \mathfrak{P}, \mathfrak{H})$

Set-up, $\mathcal{G}(\kappa)$: Invoke the algorithms $\mathcal{G}_s$, $\mathcal{K}$ and $\mathcal{G}_h$ (all) on κ to obtain $(\mathbf{msk}_s, \mathbf{mpk}_s)$, $(\mathbf{sk}, \mathbf{pk})$ and $(\mathbf{ek}, \mathbf{td})$ respectively. Return $\mathbf{msk} := (\mathbf{msk}_s, \mathbf{sk})$ as the master secret key and $\mathbf{mpk} := (\mathbf{mpk}_s, \mathbf{pk}, \mathbf{ek})$ as the master public key.

Key Extraction, $\mathcal{E}(\mathbf{id}, \mathbf{msk})$: Select $r \in_R \mathbb{R}$ and compute $\mathbf{id}_s \leftarrow h(\mathbf{ek}, \mathbf{id}, r)$. Next, run $\mathcal{E}_s(\mathbf{id}_s, \mathbf{msk}_s)$ and $\mathcal{S}_p(\mathbf{id}_s, \mathbf{sk})$ to obtain $\mathbf{usk}_s$ and σ_p respectively. Finally, return $\mathbf{usk} := (\mathbf{usk}_s, r, \sigma_p)$ as the user secret key.

Signing, $\mathcal{S}(\mathbf{id}, m, \mathbf{usk})$: Parse the user secret key $\mathbf{usk}$ as $(\mathbf{usk}_s, r, \sigma_p)$ and compute $\mathbf{id}_s \leftarrow h(\mathbf{ek}, \mathbf{id}, r)$. Next, run $\mathcal{S}_s(\mathbf{id}_s, m, \mathbf{usk}_s)$ to obtain σ_s. Finally, return $\sigma := (\sigma_s, r, \sigma_p)$ as the signature.

Verification, $\mathcal{V}(\sigma, \mathbf{id}, m, \mathbf{mpk})$: Parse σ as (σ_s, r, σ_p) and compute $\mathbf{id}_s \leftarrow h(\mathbf{ek}, \mathbf{id}, r)$. Return 1 only if σ_p is a valid signature on $\mathbf{id}_s$ and σ_s is a valid signature on $(\mathbf{id}_s, m)$. In other words, if $\mathbf{b}_p \leftarrow \mathcal{V}_p(\sigma_p, \mathbf{id}_s, \mathbf{pk})$ and $\mathbf{b}_s \leftarrow \mathcal{V}_s(\sigma_s, \mathbf{id}_s, m, \mathbf{mpk})$, return $(\mathbf{b}_p \wedge \mathbf{b}_s)$.

Fig. 1. Constructing ID-secure IBS from an sID-secure IBS

The **Hash Evaluation** function h is used to map an identity $\mathbf{id}$ in $\mathfrak{I}$ on to an identity $\mathbf{id}_s$ in $\mathfrak{I}_s$. The mapped identities are then bound using σ_p. This is reflected in the structure of the user secret key for $\mathbf{id}$ which is of the form $(\mathbf{usk}_s, r, \sigma_p)$.

Remark 1. Note that we have omitted $\mathbf{td}$ from the master secret key. The trapdoor key $\mathbf{td}$–hence the collision generation function h^{-1}–is not used *per se* in the transformation. However, it *does* play a crucial role in its security argument.

---

[3] This assumption can be relaxed–to accommodate a CHF with $\mathbb{M}_h \neq \mathbb{Y} \neq \mathbb{I}$–using two collision resistant hash functions H and G defined as follows:

$$H : \mathbb{I} \to \mathbb{M}_h \quad \text{and} \quad G : \mathbb{Y} \to \mathbb{I}$$

These hash functions can be used in the protocol, and also in the security argument, to couple the CHF with the IBS.

3.1   Security Argument

For simplicity, we consider the security of the specific case of EU-sID-CMA model; we argue that the resulting IBS is EU-ID-CMA-secure. The details of both the security models is given in §2.2. The line of argument can be easily extended to other models as well[4].

Theorem 1. *Given an $(\epsilon, t, q_\varepsilon, q_s)$-adversary $\mathcal{A}$, in the EU-ID-CMA model, against the IBS $\mathfrak{I}$, we can construct either*

(i) *Algorithm $\mathcal{B}_s$ which $(\epsilon_s, t_s, q_\varepsilon, q_s)$-breaks $\mathfrak{I}_s$ in the EU-sID-CMA model, where*

$$\epsilon_s \geq \frac{1}{3q_s}\epsilon \quad and \quad t_s \leq t + (q_\varepsilon + q_s)\tau_1, \quad or$$

(ii) *Algorithm $\mathcal{B}_p$ which $(\epsilon_p, t_p, q_\varepsilon + q_s)$-breaks $\mathfrak{P}$ in the EU-GCMA model, where*

$$\epsilon_p = \frac{1}{3}\epsilon \quad and \quad t_p \leq t + (q_\varepsilon\tau_2 + q_s\tau_3), \quad or$$

(iii) *Algorithm $\mathcal{B}_h$ which (ϵ_h, t_h)-breaks $\mathfrak{H}$, where*

$$\epsilon_h = \frac{1}{3}\epsilon \quad and \quad t_h \leq t + (q_\varepsilon + q_s)\tau_1 + (q_\varepsilon\tau_2 + q_s\tau_3).$$

Here, q_ε (resp. q_s) denotes the upper bound on the number of extract (resp. signature) queries that $\mathcal{A}$ can make. τ_1 is the time taken for generating a signature in $\mathfrak{P}$; τ_2 (resp. τ_3) denotes the time taken to generate a user secret key (resp. signature) in $\mathfrak{I}_s$.

Proof. We classify the forgeries (mutually-exclusively and exhaustively) into three: *Type 1, Type 2* and *Type 3*. A forgery qualifies as *Type 1* if the adversary makes *at least* one signature query on the "target" identity–the identity which $\mathcal{A}$ eventually forges on–and produces a forgery with the binding (provided by the simulator) *intact*. In both *Type 2* and *Type 3* forgeries, the binding is violated by the adversary by some means. The strategy adopted in each of the three cases is different; we give a reduction $\mathcal{B}_s$ for *Type 1*, $\mathcal{B}_p$ for *Type 2* and $\mathcal{B}_h$ for *Type 3* adversary. The details follow.

Classifying the forgery. Consider an adversary $\mathcal{A}$ in the EU-ID-CMA model. At the beginning of the security game, $\mathcal{A}$ is given the challenge master public key mpk by (its challenger) $\mathcal{C}$. $\mathcal{A}$ produces a forgery after making a series of queries–extract and signature–adaptively with $\mathcal{C}$. Let id_i denote the ith extract query made by $\mathcal{A}$, which is responded to with $\text{usk}_i = (\text{usk}_{s,i}, \dot{r}_i, \dot{\sigma}_{p,i})$ by $\mathcal{C}$. Similarly,

---

[4] *e.g.*, consider the sM-sID-CMA model–the *selective-message, selective-identity chosen-message attack* model. It is similar to the EU-sID-CMA model, except that the adversary–in addition to committing to the target identity–has to commit to the target message too. If we start from sM-sID-CMA-secure IBS, we end up with an sM-ID-CMA-secure IBS.

$(\mathtt{id}_i, m_i)$ denotes the ith signature query by $\mathcal{A}$, which is responded to with $\sigma_i = (\sigma_{s,i}, r_i, \sigma_{p,i})$ by $\mathcal{C}$. Note that the number of extract (*resp.* signature) queries is bounded by q_ε (*resp.* q_s). Finally, let $\hat{\sigma} = (\hat{\sigma}_s, \hat{r}, \hat{\sigma}_p)$ be the forgery produced by $\mathcal{A}$ on $(\hat{\mathtt{id}}, \hat{m})$. The identity $\hat{\mathtt{id}}$ is the so-called target identity. The forgeries can be partitioned into three types,*viz.*:

(i) *Type 1* forgery. $\mathcal{A}$ produces the forgery with $(\hat{\mathtt{id}}, \hat{r}) = (\mathtt{id}_i, r_i)$ for some $i \in \{1, \ldots, q_s\}$.

(ii) *Type 2* forgery. $\mathcal{A}$ produces the forgery with $(\hat{\mathtt{id}}, \hat{r}) \neq (\mathtt{id}_i, r_i)$ for all $i \in \{1, \ldots, q_s\}$, and with
   (a) $\mathrm{h}(\mathtt{ek}, \hat{\mathtt{id}}, \hat{r}) \neq \mathrm{h}(\mathtt{ek}, \dot{\mathtt{id}}_i, \dot{r}_i)$ for all $i \in \{1, \ldots, q_\varepsilon\}$, and
   (b) $\mathrm{h}(\mathtt{ek}, \hat{\mathtt{id}}, \hat{r}) \neq \mathrm{h}(\mathtt{ek}, \mathtt{id}_i, r_i)$ for all $i \in \{1, \ldots, q_s\}$.

(iii) *Type 3* forgery. $\mathcal{A}$ produces the forgery with $(\hat{\mathtt{id}}, \hat{r}) \neq (\mathtt{id}_i, r_i)$ for all $i \in \{1, \ldots, q_s\}$, but with
   (a) $\mathrm{h}(\mathtt{ek}, \hat{\mathtt{id}}, \hat{r}) = \mathrm{h}(\mathtt{ek}, \dot{\mathtt{id}}_i, \dot{r}_i)$ for some $i \in \{1, \ldots, q_\varepsilon\}$, or
   (b) $\mathrm{h}(\mathtt{ek}, \hat{\mathtt{id}}, \hat{r}) = \mathrm{h}(\mathtt{ek}, \mathtt{id}_i, r_i)$ for some $i \in \{1, \ldots, q_s\}$.

If $\mathcal{A}$ produces a forgery of *Type 1*, we construct an algorithm $\mathcal{B}_s$ which breaks the IBS scheme $\mathfrak{I}_s$; whereas, in case of *Type 2* forgery, we construct an algorithm $\mathcal{B}_p$ which breaks the PKS scheme $\mathfrak{P}$; and finally, in case of *Type 3* forgery, we construct an algorithm $\mathcal{B}_h$ that breaks collision resistance property of the CHF $\mathfrak{H}$. We describe these reductions in the subsequent sections.

3.1.1 Reduction $\mathcal{B}_s$

Recall that in *Type 1* forgeries, $\mathcal{A}$ makes at least one signature query on the target identity $\hat{\mathtt{id}}$. The strategy is to guess the index of this identity and map it to the identity that $\mathcal{B}_s$ *commits* to (initially) in the `EU-sID-CMA` game. This leads to a degradation of $\mathcal{O}(q_s)$.

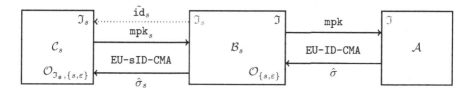

Fig. 2. Reduction $\mathcal{B}_s$

Let $\mathcal{C}_s$ be the challenger in the `EU-sID-CMA` game. $\mathcal{B}_s$ plays the role of the adversary in the `EU-sID-CMA` game and, at the same time, the role of the challenger to $\mathcal{A}$ in the `EU-ID-CMA` game (see **Figure 2**). $\mathcal{B}_s$ starts by running the **Key Generation** algorithms $\mathcal{K}$ and $\mathcal{G}_h$ to obtain $(\mathtt{pk}, \mathtt{sk})$ and $(\mathtt{ek}, \mathtt{td})$ respectively. In order to initiate the `EU-sID-CMA` game, $\mathcal{B}_s$ has to commit to a target identity. It does so by selecting an identity $\tilde{\mathtt{id}} \in_R \mathbb{I}$ and a randomiser $\tilde{r} \in_R \mathbb{R}$, and committing $\tilde{\mathtt{id}}_s \leftarrow \mathrm{h}(\mathtt{ek}, \tilde{\mathtt{id}}, \tilde{r})$ to $\mathcal{C}_s$. As a result, $\mathcal{C}_s$ releases the challenge master public key $\mathtt{mpk}_s$ to $\mathcal{B}_s$. $\mathcal{B}_s$ is also allowed access to a signature oracle $\mathcal{O}_{\mathfrak{I}_s, s}$. Now, $\mathcal{B}_s$ passes $\mathtt{mpk} := (\mathtt{mpk}_s, \mathtt{pk}, \mathtt{ek})$ as its own challenge master public key to $\mathcal{A}$. Next, $\mathcal{B}_s$ guesses $1 \leq \tilde{\ell} \leq q_s$ as the index of the target identity.

Mapping the identities. In order to track the mapping between the identities in $\mathfrak{I}$ and $\mathfrak{I}_s$, $\mathcal{B}_s$ maintains a table $\mathfrak{L}$. It also maintains a counter ℓ (initially 1) to track the index of these identities. $\mathfrak{L}$ contains tuples of the form $\langle \text{id}, \text{id}_s, \ell, \text{usk} \rangle$. Here, id and id_s are the related identities from $\mathfrak{I}$ and $\mathfrak{I}_s$ respectively; ℓ is the index of the identity id. The usk-field stores the user secret key for id and hence contains elements of the form $(\text{usk}_s, r, \sigma_p)$. If any component of the usk-field is yet to be generated, it is indicated by a '$\perp$'.

An identity id has already been mapped if there exists $\langle \text{id}_i, \text{id}_{s,i}, \ell_i, \text{usk} \rangle$ in $\mathfrak{L}$ such that $\text{id}_i = \text{id}$. For mapping a *fresh* identity id, $\mathcal{B}_s$ chooses $r \in_R \mathbb{R}$ and sets $\text{id}_s \leftarrow \text{h}(\text{ek}, \text{id}, r)$.[5] Finally, it adds $\langle \text{id}, \text{id}_s, \ell, (\perp, r, \perp) \rangle$ to $\mathfrak{L}$ and increments ℓ by one. A more formal description of the mapping function is given below.

$\text{M}_s(\text{id})$:

if $\exists$ a tuple $\langle \text{id}_i, \text{id}_{s,i}, \ell_i, \text{usk}_i \rangle \in \mathfrak{L}$ such that $(\text{id}_i = \text{id})$ **then**

  Set $\tau := (\text{id}_{s,i}, \ell_i, \text{usk}_i)$

else

  if $(\ell = \tilde{\ell})$ **then** set $r \leftarrow \text{h}^{-1}(\text{td}, \tilde{\text{id}}, \tilde{r}, \text{id})$ **else** choose $r \in_R \mathbb{R}$

  Compute $\text{id}_s \leftarrow \text{h}(\text{ek}, \text{id}, r)$ and set $\tau := (\text{id}_s, \ell, (\perp, r, \perp))$

  Add $\langle \text{id}, \text{id}_s, \ell, (\perp, r, \perp) \rangle$ to $\mathfrak{L}$ and increment ℓ by one

end if

return τ

Queries. The extract and signature queries by $\mathcal{A}$ are answered as per the following specifications.

Extract query, $\mathcal{O}_{\mathfrak{I}, \varepsilon}(\text{id})$: Invoke $\text{M}_s(\text{id})$ to obtain $(\text{id}_s, \ell, (\text{usk}_s, r, \sigma_p))$.

  (i) If $(\ell = \tilde{\ell})$ then $\mathcal{B}_s$ *aborts* (abort_1).

  (ii) Otherwise, if $(\text{usk}_s \neq \perp)$ then return $\text{usk} := (\text{usk}_s, r, \sigma_p)$ as the user secret key.

  (iii) Otherwise, $\mathcal{B}_s$ makes an extract query with $\mathcal{O}_{\mathfrak{I}_s, \varepsilon}$ on id_s to obtain usk_s. Next, it uses the knowledge of sk to compute $\sigma_p := \mathcal{S}_p(\text{id}_s, \text{sk})$. Finally, it returns $\text{usk} := (\text{usk}_s, r, \sigma_p)$ as the user secret key and updates the usk-field of the tuple corresponding to id in $\mathfrak{L}$.

Signature query, $\mathcal{O}_{\mathfrak{I}, s}(\text{id}, m)$: Invoke $\text{M}_s(\text{id})$ to get $(\text{id}_s, \ell, (\text{usk}_s, r, \sigma_p))$.

  (i) If $((\ell = \tilde{\ell}) \vee (\text{usk}_s = \perp))$ then $\mathcal{B}_s$ makes a signature query with $\mathcal{O}_{\mathfrak{I}_s, s}$ on (id_s, m) to obtain σ_s. It uses the knowledge of sk to compute $\sigma_p := \mathcal{S}_p(\text{id}_s, \text{sk})$. Finally, it returns $\sigma := (\sigma_s, r, \sigma_p)$ as the signature.

  (ii) Otherwise, $\mathcal{B}_s$ uses the knowledge of the user secret key usk to generate the signature, *i.e.* it returns $\sigma := \mathcal{S}(\text{id}, m, \text{usk})$.

---

[5] If there already exists a tuple $\langle \text{id}_i, r_i, \text{id}_{s,i}, \ell_i, \text{usk}_i \rangle$ such that $\text{id}_{s,i} = \text{id}_s$, to maintain injection in the mapping, $\mathcal{B}_s$ repeats the process with a fresh r.

Forgery. At the end of the simulation, $\mathcal{A}$ produces a *Type 1* forgery $\hat{\sigma} = (\hat{\sigma}_s, \hat{r}, \hat{\sigma}_p)$ on $(\hat{\text{id}}, \hat{m})$. Let $\langle \text{id}_{\hat{i}}, \text{id}_{s,\hat{i}}, l_{\hat{i}}, \text{usk}_{\hat{i}} \rangle$ be the tuple in $\mathfrak{L}$ such that $\text{id}_{\hat{i}} = \hat{\text{id}}$. If $l_{\hat{i}}$ matches $\mathcal{B}_s$'s initial guess for the target index (*i.e.* $l_{\hat{i}} = \tilde{l}$), it wins the `EU-sID-CMA` game with $\mathcal{C}_s$ by passing $\hat{\sigma}_s$ as a forgery on $(\hat{\text{id}}_s, \hat{m})$ to $\mathcal{C}_s$; otherwise it *aborts* (abort_2).

Analysis. The probability of success of the reduction $\mathcal{B}_s$ is governed by the two events abort_1 and abort_2. To be precise,

$$\epsilon_s = \Pr\left[\neg\text{abort}_1 \wedge \neg\text{abort}_2\right] \epsilon$$
$$= \Pr\left[\neg\text{abort}_1 \mid \neg\text{abort}_2\right] \Pr\left[\neg\text{abort}_2\right] \epsilon.$$

Since $\tilde{l}$ is hidden from the adversary, it is easy to see that

$$\Pr\left[\neg\text{abort}_2\right] = \Pr\left[l_{\hat{i}} = \tilde{l}\right] = 1/q_s.$$

On the other hand, $\Pr\left[\neg\text{abort}_1 \mid \neg\text{abort}_2\right] = 1$. This follows from the fact that if the simulator's guess of the target index was indeed correct ($\neg\text{abort}_2$), then the adversary *would not* have made an extract query on that identity (which causes abort_1). Thus, $\epsilon_s = \epsilon/q_s$. As for the time complexity, if τ_1 is the time taken for generating a signature in $\mathfrak{P}$, then the time taken by $\mathcal{B}_s$ can be easily seen as $t_s \leq t + (q_\varepsilon + q_s)\tau_1$.

3.1.2 Reduction $\mathcal{B}_p$

The strategy adopted in $\mathcal{B}_p$ is similar to that in security arguments of [16,20]. It is also, on a high level, related to the technique used in [2] for proving the security of the `EU-CMA`-secure PKS scheme constructed from `EU-GCMA`-secure PKS scheme (using CHF implicitly). The details follow.

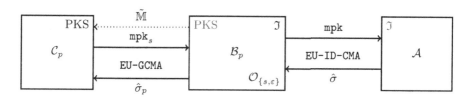

Fig. 3. Reduction $\mathcal{B}_p$

Let $\mathcal{C}_p$ be the challenger in the `EU-GCMA` game. $\mathcal{B}_p$ plays the role of the adversary in the `EU-GCMA` game and, at the same time, the role of the challenger to $\mathcal{A}$ in the `EU-ID-CMA` game (see **Figure 3**). It starts by running the **Key Generation** algorithms $\mathcal{G}_s$ and $\mathcal{G}_h$ to obtain $(\text{mpk}_s, \text{msk}_s)$ and (ek, td) respectively. In order to initiate the `EU-GCMA` game, $\mathcal{B}_p$ has to commit to a set of q_s messages to $\mathcal{C}_p$. On the other hand, it also has to answer the adaptive queries by $\mathcal{A}$. Let's see how this is accomplished using the CHF. $\mathcal{B}_p$ first selects pairs $(\tilde{\text{id}}_1, \tilde{r}_1), \ldots, (\tilde{\text{id}}_{q_s}, \tilde{r}_{q_s})$ independently and uniformly at random from $\mathbb{I} \times \mathbb{R}$.

Next, it commits $\tilde{\mathbb{M}} := \{\tilde{id}_{s,1}, \ldots, \tilde{id}_{s,q_s}\}$ to $\mathcal{C}_p$, where $\tilde{id}_{s,i} \leftarrow h(ek, \tilde{id}_i, \tilde{r}_i)$. As a result, $\mathcal{C}_p$ releases the challenge public key pk to $\mathcal{B}_p$ along with the set of signatures $\{\sigma_{p,1}, \ldots, \sigma_{p,q_s}\}$ on the (respective) committed messages. All this information is stored in a table $\mathfrak{C}$ as tuples $\langle \tilde{id}_i, \tilde{r}_i, \tilde{id}_{s,i}, \sigma_{p,i} \rangle$. Now, $\mathcal{B}_p$ initiates the EU-ID-CMA game by passing $mpk := (mpk_s, pk, ek)$ as the challenge master public key to $\mathcal{A}$.

Mapping the identities. $\mathcal{B}_p$ too maintains the table $\mathfrak{L}$; but, it's structure is slightly different from that in $\mathcal{B}_s$. $\mathfrak{L}$ contains tuples of the form $\langle id, \tilde{id}_s, usk \rangle$. Here, id and id_s are the related identities from $\mathfrak{I}$ and $\mathfrak{I}_s$ respectively. The usk-field stores the user secret key for id and hence contains elements of the form (usk_s, r, σ_p). If any component of the usk-field is yet to be generated, it is indicated by a '$\perp$'.

The way in which the mapping is maintained between the identities is somewhat different from that in $\mathcal{B}_s$. For mapping a *fresh* identity id, $\mathcal{B}_p$ first picks a tuple $t = \langle \tilde{id}_s, \tilde{id}, \tilde{r}, \sigma_p \rangle$ randomly from $\mathfrak{C}$. It then computes $r \leftarrow h^{-1}(td, \tilde{id}, \tilde{r}, id)$, and adds the tuple $\langle id, \tilde{id}_s, (\perp, r, \sigma_p) \rangle$ to $\mathfrak{L}$. Finally it removes the tuple t from $\mathfrak{C}$. As a result of these actions, id is effectively mapped to $\tilde{id}_s$ since $h(ek, id, r) = h(ek, \tilde{id}, \tilde{r}) = \tilde{id}_s$. A more formal description follows.

$M_p(id)$:
if $\exists$ a tuple $\langle id_i, id_{s,i}, usk_i \rangle \in \mathfrak{L}$ such that $(id_i = id)$ **then**
    Set $\tau := (id_{s,i}, usk_i)$
else
    Pick $t \xleftarrow{\$} \mathfrak{C}$ and parse it as $\langle \tilde{id}, \tilde{r}, \tilde{id}_s, \sigma_p \rangle$
    Compute $r \leftarrow h^{-1}(td, \tilde{id}, \tilde{r}, id)$ and set $\tau := (id_s, (\perp, r, \sigma_p))$
    Add $\langle id, id_s, (\perp, r, \sigma_p) \rangle$ to $\mathfrak{L}$ and remove t from $\mathfrak{C}$
end if
return τ

Queries: The extract and signature queries by $\mathcal{A}$ are answered as follows.

Extract query, $\mathcal{O}_{\mathfrak{I},\varepsilon}(id)$: Invoke $M_p(id)$ to obtain $(\tilde{id}_s, \ell, (usk_s, r, \sigma_p))$.
  (i) If $(usk_s \neq \perp)$ then return $usk := (usk_s, r, \sigma_p)$ as the user secret key.
  (ii) Otherwise, $\mathcal{B}_s$ uses the knowledge of the master secret key msk_s to generate the user secret key $usk_s := \mathcal{E}_s(\tilde{id}_s, msk_s)$ for $\tilde{id}_s$. It returns $usk := (usk_s, r, \sigma_p)$ as the user secret key for id and updates the usk_s-field of the tuple corresponding to id in $\mathfrak{L}$.

Signature query, $\mathcal{O}_{\mathfrak{I},s}(id, m)$: Invoke $M_p(id)$ to get $(\tilde{id}_s, \ell, (usk_s, r, \sigma_p))$.
  (i) If $(usk_s \neq \perp)$ then $\mathcal{B}_p$ uses the knowledge of usk to return the signature $\sigma := \mathcal{S}(id, m, usk)$
  (ii) Otherwise, $\mathcal{B}_s$ uses step (ii) of **Extract query** to generate a user secret key usk for id and then uses this usk to return a signature $\sigma := \mathcal{S}(id, m, usk)$.

Forgery. Finally, $\mathcal{A}$ produces a forgery $\hat{\sigma} = (\hat{\sigma}_s, \hat{r}, \hat{\sigma}_p)$ on $(\hat{\mathrm{id}}, \hat{m})$. As the forgery is of *Type 2*, it implies $\hat{\mathrm{id}}_s := \mathrm{h}(\mathrm{ek}, \hat{\mathrm{id}}, \hat{r}) \notin \tilde{\mathbb{M}}$. Therefore $\hat{\sigma}_p$ is a valid forgery in the EU-GCMA game and $\mathcal{B}_p$ passes it to $\mathcal{C}_s$ to win the game.

Analysis. Since no abort is involved in $\mathcal{S}_p$, there is no degradation involved either. Thus, its advantage in attacking $\mathfrak{P}$ is $\epsilon_p = \epsilon$. If τ_2 and τ_3 denote the time taken for generating a secret key and a signature respectively in $\mathfrak{I}_s$, then the time taken by $\mathcal{B}_p$ is $t_p \leq t + (q_\varepsilon \tau_2 + q_s \tau_3)$.

3.1.3   Reduction $\mathcal{B}_h$

$\mathcal{B}_h$ first obtains the challenge evaluation key ek for $\mathfrak{H}$ from its challenger $\mathcal{C}_h$. Then it invokes the algorithms $\mathcal{G}_s$ and $\mathcal{K}$ to generate $(\mathrm{msk}_s, \mathrm{mpk}_s)$ and $(\mathrm{sk}, \mathrm{pk})$ respectively. Finally, it passes $(\mathrm{mpk}_s, \mathrm{pk}, \mathrm{ek})$ as the challenge master public key to $\mathcal{A}$ (see **Figure 4**).

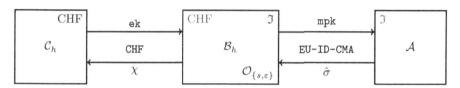

Fig. 4. Reduction $\mathcal{B}_h$

Mapping the identities. The table used for maintaining the mapping has the same structure as in $\mathcal{B}_p$. However, the actual method used for mapping identities is far simpler than in $\mathcal{B}_p$ as shown below.

$\mathrm{M}_h(\mathrm{id})$:
if $\exists$ a tuple $\langle \mathrm{id}_i, \mathrm{id}_{s,i}, \mathrm{usk}_i \rangle \in \mathfrak{L}$ such that $(\mathrm{id}_i = \mathrm{id})$ **then**
    Set $\tau := (\mathrm{id}_{s,i}, \mathrm{usk}_i)$
else
    Pick $r \in_R \mathbb{R}$ and compute $\mathrm{id}_s := \mathrm{h}(\mathrm{ek}, \mathrm{id}, r)$
    Set $\tau := (\mathrm{id}_s, (\bot, r, \sigma_p))$ add $\langle \mathrm{id}, \mathrm{id}_s, (\bot, r, \bot) \rangle$ to $\mathfrak{L}$
end if
return τ

Queries: The extract and signature queries by $\mathcal{A}$ are answered as follows.

Extract query, $\mathcal{O}_{\mathfrak{I}_\varepsilon}(\mathrm{id})$: Invoke $\mathrm{M}_h(\mathrm{id})$ to obtain $(\mathrm{id}_s, (\mathrm{usk}_s, r, \sigma_p))$.
  (i) If $(\mathrm{usk}_s \neq \bot)$ then return $\mathrm{usk} := (\mathrm{usk}_s, r, \sigma_p)$ as the user secret key.
  (ii) Otherwise, $\mathcal{B}_h$ uses the knowledge of the master secret key msk_s to generate the user secret key $\mathrm{usk}_s := \mathcal{E}_s(\mathrm{id}_s, \mathrm{msk}_s)$ for id_s. It also uses sk to generate $\sigma_p := \mathcal{S}_p(\mathrm{id}_s)$. Finally, $\mathcal{B}_h$ returns $\mathrm{usk} := (\mathrm{usk}_s, r, \sigma_p)$ as the user secret key for id and updates the usk_s-field and σ_p-field of the tuple corresponding to id in $\mathfrak{L}$.

Signature query, $\mathcal{O}_{\mathfrak{I},s}(\text{id}, m)$: Invoke $M_h(\text{id})$ to obtain $(\text{id}_s, (\text{usk}_s, r, \sigma_p))$.
  (i) If $(\text{usk}_s \neq \perp)$ then $\mathcal{B}_h$ uses the knowledge of usk to return the signature
        $\sigma := \mathcal{S}(\text{id}, m, \text{usk})$.
  (ii) Otherwise, $\mathcal{B}_h$ uses step (ii) of **Extract query** to generate a user
        secret key usk for id and then use this usk to return a signature
        $\sigma := \mathcal{S}(\text{id}, m, \text{usk})$.

Forgery. Finally, $\mathcal{A}$ produces a *Type 3* forgery $\hat{\sigma} = (\hat{\sigma}_s, \hat{r}, \hat{\sigma}_p)$ on $(\hat{\text{id}}, \hat{m})$. Recall that this implies $\mathcal{A}$ produces the forgery with $(\hat{\text{id}}, \hat{r}) \neq (\text{id}_i, r_i)$ for all $i \in \{1, \ldots, q_s\}$, but with

  (a) $h(\text{ek}, \hat{\text{id}}, \hat{r}) = h(\text{ek}, \dot{\text{id}}_i, \dot{r}_i)$ for some $i \in \{1, \ldots, q_\varepsilon\}$, or
  (b) $h(\text{ek}, \hat{\text{id}}, \hat{r}) = h(\text{ek}, \text{id}_i, r_i)$ for some $i \in \{1, \ldots, q_s\}$.

Both the cases tantamount to breaking the collision resistance property of $\mathfrak{H}$. In case (a) (*resp.* case (b)) $\mathcal{B}_h$ passes $((\hat{\text{id}}, \hat{r}), (\dot{\text{id}}_i, \dot{r}_i))$ (*resp.* $((\hat{\text{id}}, \hat{r}), (\text{id}_i, r_i))$) as a collision to the challenger $\mathcal{C}_h$ to win the game.

Analysis. As in $\mathcal{B}_p$, there is no abort involved in $\mathcal{B}_h$. Therefore, its advantage in attacking $\mathfrak{H}$ is $\epsilon_p = \epsilon$. Again, if τ_2 and τ_3 denote the time taken for generating a secret key and a signature respectively in $\mathfrak{I}_s$, then the time taken by $\mathcal{B}_h$ is $t_p \leq t + (q_\varepsilon \tau_2 + q_s \tau_3)$.

4   Transforming from the EU-wID-CMA Model

The construction technique described in the previous section can as well be used with a *relaxed* version of the selective-identity model which we call the *weak selective-identity* (wID) model. In this model the adversary, apart from committing to the "target" identity $\tilde{\text{id}}$, has to commit a set of "query" identities $\tilde{\mathbb{I}}$. The adversary is allowed to query the extract oracle only on identities belonging to $\tilde{\mathbb{I}}$; whereas, it is allowed to query the signature oracle with identities from $\tilde{\mathbb{I}}$ *as well as* the target identity. Finally, as in the sID model, the adversary has to produce a forgery on $\tilde{\text{id}}$. One may see the analogy between the EU-GCMA model for PKS and the wID model–both involve the adversary committing, beforehand, to the identities/messages that it wants to query. The only change involved is in the security argument–the way in which mapping is handled by the simulator. We elaborate on this later. But first, let's formally define the EU-wID-CMA model for IBS.

Definition 8 (EU-wID-CMA Game). *The security of an IBS scheme in the EU-wID-CMA model is argued in terms of the following game between a challenger $\mathcal{C}$ and an adversary $\mathcal{A}$.*

  Commitment: $\mathcal{A}$ commits to a target identity $\tilde{\text{id}}$ and a set of query identities $\tilde{\mathbb{I}} := \{\tilde{\text{id}}_1, \ldots, \tilde{\text{id}}_{\tilde{q}}\} \subset \mathbb{I} \setminus \{\tilde{\text{id}}\}$.
  Set-up: $\mathcal{C}$ runs the set-up algorithm $\mathcal{G}$ to obtain the master keys (mpk,msk). It passes mpk as the challenge master public key to $\mathcal{A}$.

Queries: $\mathcal{A}$ can adaptively make extract queries on identities from $\tilde{\mathbb{I}}$ to an oracle $\mathcal{O}_\varepsilon$ and signature queries involving identities from $\tilde{\mathbb{I}} \cup \{\tilde{\text{id}}\}$ to an oracle $\mathcal{O}_s$. These queries are handled as follows.

Extract query, $\mathcal{O}_\varepsilon(\text{id})$: $\mathcal{A}$ asks for the secret key of a user with identity $\text{id} \in \tilde{\mathbb{I}}$. $\mathcal{C}$ computes $\text{usk} := \mathcal{E}(\text{id})$ and passes it to $\mathcal{A}$.

Signature query, $\mathcal{O}_s(\text{id}, m)$: $\mathcal{A}$ asks for the signature of a user with identity $\text{id} \in \tilde{\mathbb{I}} \cup \{\tilde{\text{id}}\}$ on a message m. $\mathcal{C}$ first runs $\mathcal{E}$ on id to obtain the user secret key usk. Next, it computes $\sigma := \mathcal{S}(\text{id}, m, \text{usk})$ and forwards it to $\mathcal{A}$.

Forgery: $\mathcal{A}$ outputs a signature $\hat{\sigma}$ on a message $\hat{m}$ and the target identity $\tilde{\text{id}}$. $\mathcal{A}$ wins the game if:

1. $\hat{\sigma}$ is a valid signature on $\hat{m}$ by $\tilde{\text{id}}$.
2. $\mathcal{A}$ has not made a signature query on $(\tilde{\text{id}}, \hat{m})$.

The advantage $\mathcal{A}$ has in the above game, denoted by $\text{Adv}_{\mathcal{A}}^{\text{EU}-\text{wID}-\text{CMA}}$, is defined as the probability with which it wins the game, *i.e.*

$$\Pr\left[1 \leftarrow \mathcal{V}(\hat{\sigma}, \tilde{\text{id}}, \hat{m}, \text{mpk}) \mid (\tilde{\text{id}}, \tilde{\mathbb{I}}) \xleftarrow{\$} \mathcal{A}; (\text{msk}, \text{mpk}) \xleftarrow{\$} \mathcal{G}(\kappa);\right.$$
$$\left.(\hat{\sigma}, \tilde{\text{id}}, \hat{m}) \xleftarrow{\$} \mathcal{A}^{\mathcal{O}_\varepsilon, \mathcal{O}_s}(\text{mpk})\right]$$

where the oracles $\mathcal{O}_\varepsilon$ and $\mathcal{O}_s$ are restricted to answering queries involving identities from $\tilde{\mathbb{I}}$ and $\tilde{\mathbb{I}} \cup \{\tilde{\text{id}}\}$ respectively. An adversary is said to be an $(\epsilon, t, q_\varepsilon, q_s, \tilde{q})$-forger of an IBS scheme in the EU-wID-CMA model if it has advantage of at least ϵ in the above game, runs in time at most t and makes at most q_ε and q_s extract and signature queries respectively, provided the number of identities involved in the signature and extract queries, excluding the target identity, is at most $\tilde{q}$. It is easy to see that $\tilde{q} \leq q_\varepsilon + q_s$. As we pointed out, the same transformation technique applies; the only change is in the security argument.

Theorem 2. *Given an $(\epsilon, t, q_\varepsilon, q_s)$-adversary $\mathcal{A}$, in the EU-ID-CMA model, against the IBS $\mathfrak{I}$, we can construct either*

(i) *Algorithm $\mathcal{B}_w$ which $(\epsilon_w, t_w, q_\varepsilon, q_s, q_\varepsilon + q_s)$-breaks $\mathfrak{I}_w$ in the EU-wID-CMA model, where*

$$\epsilon_w \geq \frac{1}{3q_s}\epsilon \quad \text{and} \quad t_w \leq t + (q_\varepsilon + q_s)\tau_1, \quad \text{or}$$

(ii) *Algorithm $\mathcal{B}_p$ which $(\epsilon_p, t_p, q_\varepsilon + q_s)$-breaks $\mathfrak{P}$ in the EU-GCMA model, where*

$$\epsilon_p = \frac{1}{3}\epsilon \quad \text{and} \quad t_p \leq t + (q_\varepsilon\tau_2 + q_s\tau_3), \quad \text{or}$$

(iii) *Algorithm $\mathcal{B}_h$ which (ϵ_h, t_h)-breaks $\mathfrak{H}$, where*

$$\epsilon_h = \frac{1}{3}\epsilon \quad \text{and} \quad t_h \leq t + (q_\varepsilon + q_s)\tau_1 + (q_\varepsilon\tau_2 + q_s\tau_3).$$

Here, q_ε (resp. q_s) denotes the upper bound on the number of extract (resp. signature) queries that $\mathcal{A}$ can make. τ_1 is the time taken for generating a signature in $\mathfrak{P}$; τ_2 (resp. τ_3) denotes the time taken to generate a user secret key (resp. signature) in $\mathfrak{J}_s$.

Proof. The security argument is similar to the one discussed in §3.1. The only difference lies in the way in which the mapping of identities is handled in $\mathcal{B}_w$ as described below. Let $\mathcal{C}_w$ be the challenger in the EU-wID-CMA game. $\mathcal{B}_w$ plays the role of the adversary in the EU-wID-CMA game and, at the same time, the role of the challenger to $\mathcal{A}$ in the EU-ID-CMA game. In order to initiate the EU-wID-CMA game, $\mathcal{B}_w$ has to commit to a target identity and a target set. It selects an identity $\tilde{\mathrm{id}} \in_R \mathbb{I}$ and a randomiser $\tilde{r} \in_R \mathbb{R}$, and commits $\tilde{\mathrm{id}}_w \leftarrow \mathrm{h}(\mathrm{ek}, \tilde{\mathrm{id}}, \tilde{r})$ as the target identity to $\mathcal{C}_w$. Similarly, it selects $\{\tilde{\mathrm{id}}_i, \ldots, \tilde{\mathrm{id}}_{\tilde{q}}\} \xleftarrow{\$} \mathbb{I}$, $\{\tilde{r}_1, \ldots, \tilde{r}_{\tilde{q}}\} \xleftarrow{\$} \mathbb{R}$ and commits $\hat{\mathbb{I}} := \{\tilde{\mathrm{id}}_{1,w}, \ldots, \tilde{\mathrm{id}}_{\tilde{q},w}\}$, where $\tilde{\mathrm{id}}_{i,w} \leftarrow \mathrm{h}(\mathrm{ek}, \tilde{\mathrm{id}}_i, \tilde{r}_i)$, as the target set to $\mathcal{C}_w$. As a result, $\mathcal{C}_w$ releases the challenge master public key mpk_w to $\mathcal{B}_s$. All this information is stored in a table, denoted by $\mathfrak{D}$, as tuples $\langle \tilde{\mathrm{id}}_i, \tilde{r}_i, \tilde{\mathrm{id}}_{w,i} \rangle$.

Mapping. $\mathcal{B}_w$ maintains a table $\mathfrak{L}$ with structure the same as that in reduction $\mathcal{B}_p$. For mapping a *fresh* identity id, $\mathcal{B}_w$ chooses a tuple $\mathrm{t} = \langle \tilde{\mathrm{id}}, \tilde{r}, \tilde{\mathrm{id}}_w \rangle$ randomly from $\mathfrak{D}$. Next, it computes $r := \mathrm{h}^{-1}(\mathrm{td}, \tilde{\mathrm{id}}, \tilde{r}, \mathrm{id})$ and adds $\langle \mathrm{id}, \tilde{\mathrm{id}}_w, (\bot, r, \bot) \rangle$ to $\mathfrak{L}$. Finally, it removes the tuple t from $\mathfrak{D}$. As a result of these actions, id is effectively mapped to $\tilde{\mathrm{id}}_w$ as $\mathrm{h}(\mathrm{ek}, \mathrm{id}, r) = \mathrm{h}(\mathrm{ek}, \tilde{\mathrm{id}}, \tilde{r}) = \tilde{\mathrm{id}}_w$. A more formal description follows.

$\mathrm{M}_w(\mathrm{id})$:
if $\exists$ a tuple $\langle \mathrm{id}_i, \mathrm{id}_{w,i}, \mathrm{usk}_i \rangle \in \mathfrak{L}$ such that $(\mathrm{id}_i = \mathrm{id})$ **then**
    Set $\tau := (\mathrm{id}_{w,i}, \mathrm{usk}_i)$
else
    Pick $\mathrm{t} \xleftarrow{\$} \mathfrak{C}$ and parse it as $\langle \tilde{\mathrm{id}}, \tilde{r}, \tilde{\mathrm{id}}_w \rangle$
    Compute $r \leftarrow \mathrm{h}^{-1}(\mathrm{td}, \tilde{\mathrm{id}}, \tilde{r}, \mathrm{id})$ and set $\tau := (\mathrm{id}_w, (\bot, r, \bot))$
    Add $\langle \mathrm{id}, \mathrm{id}_w, (\bot, r, \bot) \rangle$ to $\mathfrak{L}$ and remove t from $\mathfrak{C}$
end if
return τ

Remark 2 (Comparison with the folklore paradigm). The (identities-based) signature of an IBS scheme constructed using the folklore technique consists of *two* (public-key) signatures and *one* public key of the underlying (fully-secure) PKS. In contrast, the signature of an IBS scheme using our approach consists of *one* signature each of the underlying (wID-secure) IBS and (weakly-secure) PKS and *one* randomiser from the CHF. The time taken for signing and verification is comparable, bar the time taken to compute the hash value.

5   Conclusion

In this paper, we described a generic transformation from sID/wID IBS to full-identity IBS using a chameleon hash function and an EU-GCMA-secure PKS scheme. We also argued, without using random oracles, that the resulting IBS is secure in the full-identity model with only linear degradation incurred. An interesting problem would be to replace the `EU-GCMA` PKS with a more primitive construct. Extending the transformation for Hierarchical IBS could be yet another challenging task.

Acknowledgements. We would like to thank Rishiraj Bhattacharyya for some insightful discussions and Vikas Kumar for his role in the initial phase of the work. We would also like to thank the anonymous reviewers for the constructive comments.

References

1. Boneh, D., Boyen, X.: Efficient Selective-ID Secure Identity-Based Encryption Without Random Oracles. In: Cachin, C., Camenisch, J.L. (eds.) EUROCRYPT 2004. LNCS, vol. 3027, pp. 223–238. Springer, Heidelberg (2004)
2. Boneh, D., Boyen, X.: Short Signatures Without Random Oracles. In: Cachin, C., Camenisch, J.L. (eds.) EUROCRYPT 2004. LNCS, vol. 3027, pp. 56–73. Springer, Heidelberg (2004)
3. Brassard, G., Chaum, D., Crépeau, C.: Minimum disclosure proofs of knowledge. Journal of Computer and System Sciences 37(2), 156–189 (1988)
4. Boneh, D., Franklin, M.: Identity-Based Encryption from the Weil Pairing. In: Kilian, J. (ed.) CRYPTO 2001. LNCS, vol. 2139, pp. 213–229. Springer, Heidelberg (2001)
5. Bellare, M., Namprempre, C., Neven, G.: Security proofs for identity-based identification and signature schemes. In: Cachin, C., Camenisch, J.L. (eds.) EUROCRYPT 2004. LNCS, vol. 3027, pp. 268–286. Springer, Heidelberg (2004)
6. Bellare, M., Rogaway, P.: Random oracles are practical: a paradigm for designing efficient protocols. In: Proceedings of the 1st ACM Conference on Computer and Communications Security, CCS 1993, pp. 62–73. ACM, New York (1993)
7. Cui, Y., Fujisaki, E., Hanaoka, G., Imai, H., Zhang, R.: Formal security treatments for IBE-to-signature transformation: Relations among security notions. IEICE Transactions 92-A(1), 53–66 (2009)
8. Choon, J., Cheon, J.H.: An identity-based signature from gap diffie-hellman groups. In: Desmedt, Y.G. (ed.) PKC 2003. LNCS, vol. 2567, pp. 18–30. Springer, Heidelberg (2002)
9. Canetti, R., Halevi, S., Katz, J.: A forward-secure public-key encryption scheme. In: Biham, E. (ed.) EUROCRYPT 2003. LNCS, vol. 2656, pp. 255–271. Springer, Heidelberg (2003)
10. Chatterjee, S., Sarkar, P.: Generalization of the selective-ID security model for HIBE protocols. In: Yung, M., Dodis, Y., Kiayias, A., Malkin, T. (eds.) PKC 2006. LNCS, vol. 3958, pp. 241–256. Springer, Heidelberg (2006)
11. Galindo, D.: A separation between selective and full-identity security notions for identity-based encryption. In: Gavrilova, M.L., Gervasi, O., Kumar, V., Tan, C.J.K., Taniar, D., Laganá, A., Mun, Y., Choo, H. (eds.) ICCSA 2006. LNCS, vol. 3982, pp. 318–326. Springer, Heidelberg (2006)
12. Galindo, D., Hasuo, I.: Security notions for identity based encryption. Cryptology ePrint Archive, Report 2005/253(2005)

13. Goldwasser, S., Micali, S., Rivest, R.: A digital signature scheme secure against adaptive chosen-message attacks. SIAM Journal on Computing 17(2), 281–308 (1988)
14. Herranz, J.: Deterministic identity-based signatures for partial aggregation. The Computer Journal 49(3), 322–330 (2005)
15. Hess, F.: Efficient identity based signature schemes based on pairings. In: Nyberg, K., Hcys, H.M. (eds.) SAC 2002. LNCS, vol. 2595, pp. 310–324. Springer, Heidelberg (2003)
16. Hohenberger, S., Waters, B.: Short and stateless signatures from the RSA assumption. In: Halevi, S. (ed.) CRYPTO 2009. LNCS, vol. 5677, pp. 654–670. Springer, Heidelberg (2009)
17. Krawczyk, H., Rabin, T.: Chameleon signatures. In: NDSS. The Internet Society (2000)
18. Mohassel, P.: One-time signatures and chameleon hash functions. In: Biryukov, A., Gong, G., Stinson, D.R. (eds.) SAC 2010. LNCS, vol. 6544, pp. 302–319. Springer, Heidelberg (2011)
19. Shamir, A.: Identity-based cryptosystems and signature schemes. In: Blakely, G.R., Chaum, D. (eds.) CRYPTO 1984. LNCS, vol. 196, pp. 47–53. Springer, Heidelberg (1985)
20. Shamir, A., Tauman, Y.: Improved online/Offline signature schemes. In: Kilian, J. (ed.) CRYPTO 2001. LNCS, vol. 2139, pp. 355–367. Springer, Heidelberg (2001)
21. Waters, B.: Efficient identity-based encryption without random oracles. In: Cramer, R. (ed.) EUROCRYPT 2005. LNCS, vol. 3494, pp. 114–127. Springer, Heidelberg (2005)

Author Index